Also available at all good book stores

9781785315466

9781785313929

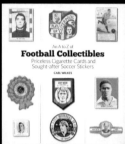

9781785315602

9781909626560

9781909178694

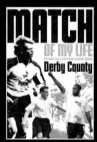

9781908051714

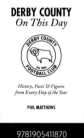

9781905411870

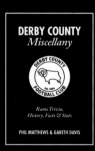

9781908051073

Pride

Pride

The Inside Story of
Derby County

R Y A N   H I L L S

First published by Pitch Publishing, 2020

Pitch Publishing
A2 Yeoman Gate
Yeoman Way
Worthing
Sussex
BN13 3QZ
www.pitchpublishing.co.uk
info@pitchpublishing.co.uk

A CIP catalogue record is available for this book
from the British Library.

ISBN 978 1 78531 727 9

Typesetting and origination by Pitch Publishing

Printed and bound in Great Britain by TJ Books Limited

CONTENTS

FOREWORD BY JAKE BUXTON

I GAVE everything I could for Derby County, right from the minute I stepped in the door at Moor Farm until the minute I left.

It's probably why I built up a connection with all staff members within the club, because I made sure I treated people the same, right from top to bottom. It's a massive factor as to why I got the opportunity to succeed after a tough start.

As I've said on many occasions, I am a slow burner as a player, and it took the best part of three seasons and a special night against local rivals to earn the respect of the fans.

From that day, the connection between myself and the supporters started to grow, and the impact they had on my life and performances was unreal.

I was a six out of ten before supporters warmed to me, and then they just improved. But it's all down to the fact they started to love me.

You started to sing my name. I was living the dream on the pitch and I loved it. I knew that when I got applauded for smashing people and working hard, that the fans were starting to realise what I brought to the team.

At the start I was a non-league player and it was unbelievable to turn it all around and to get the recognition.

Being loved by the supporters of your football club is an unbelievable feeling and one of the best feelings I've had in football.

I will always be grateful for how the Rams fans made me feel. I have memories I will never forget.

INTRODUCTION

I REMEMBER the exact moment the idea for this book came into my head. I was sat in the café at Amazon's Fulfilment Centre in Bardon, just down the road from Coalville, Leicestershire. At the time, my graduate role in communications had come to an end and I needed something to tide me over until January when I'd move into something new.

My destination was the bubble wrap station. Day in, day out, I'd be handed a cart of random products to wrap. CDs, rakes, all sorts of nonsense. Mid-wrapping, I'd begin to consider how this book could look. It began as a potential children's publication (nope, me neither), then the thought of maybe speaking to some players crossed the mind. 'If I could get five or so, that would be great,' I'd think to myself.

I never really anticipated that this would turn into a project spanning three years. But to be frank, I'm glad it did. In that time, I've hopped between jobs, moved to Germany, sat through a worldwide pandemic and experimented with hair dye (not recommended).

It'll come as little surprise that, like you, I'm a Derby County fan. If I wasn't, writing a book about this quite intriguing club would have bordered on torture. My first game was back in 2000, a 2-2 draw against Charlton. Malcolm Christie and Simo Valakari put us 2-0 up, before we threw the three points away. In many ways, it was the preparation for everything that was to come and no doubt will in the future.

Growing up in Leicestershire, there weren't many Derby fans around. So when I would tell my school friends that Izale McLeod was a future England international, the conversations would not take off. I was also too naïve at that young age to realise wearing black and white when walking around Morrisons was a questionable choice. I put it down to fearlessness today.

For some reason, just like you, I adore this club. In the 20 years since I walked in to Pride Park for the first time, there haven't been many reasons to adore them. And yet, I, again like you, keep coming back for more. What is it about them? Because, if we look at the club in this time, there really haven't been many reasons to keep that level of infatuation.

Pride begins where my Derby relationship did. The tales of Wanchope and Stimac, the days when the Bald Eagle would soar. I feel I was sort of cat-fished by this introduction to the soon-to-be Europe-challenging Premier League side. Because, as *Pride* will cover in depth, the darkness begins almost immediately afterwards. The turmoil, the financial crashes, the, well, other crashes. I opted to cover this spell because it's the one that I have grown up with but also because, when taken fully into account, it's crazy.

Producing *Pride* has been an honour. It has been a privilege to be able to tell the story of the club across so many turbulent years, with so many key components. The good times and the bad, all in one place, and all told by those we have watched on in awe at, with the occasional bit of frustration. I hope that through the voices featured, you feel just that little bit closer to the club.

THE BEGINNING

THE BASEBALL Ground. An old, decrepit, wooden stadium. Squeezed between houses, backed on to a railway track. No executive areas to attract major international businesses; facilities that would never pass health and safety tests in the modern era. A shadow of what it once was. A stadium no longer fit for purpose.

The Baseball Ground. The home of Derby County. A place where generations had gathered, where families were united, where grandparents would reminisce with grandchildren. The place where Brian Clough and Peter Taylor did the unthinkable, where Dave Mackay followed on. The beating heart of football in a city dedicated to its club.

They don't make stadiums like the BBG anymore. Primarily because they're not allowed to by law, but more so because the game of football has moved beyond. Gone are the days of it being the sport of the working class, when supporters and players could mix freely and the divide was minimal. Instead it has been replaced by a corporate event, where money drives everything and supporters are an after-thought. Where players don't interact with those in the stands, wearing those same shirts as they do.

The moment the doors closed on the Baseball Ground, football in Derby changed. Twenty-three years have now passed since that final first-team outing against Arsenal in 1997 and the landscape of not only the club but the sport as a whole is in another dimension to what the 18,287 experienced that day.

The Baseball Ground had been witness to Derby's rise through the divisions under Arthur Cox in the 1980s, going from the dreariness of the Third to the glamour of the First in successive seasons.

This culminated with Cox's side finishing fifth in 1988/89, the club's highest position since the glory days of the 1970s.

They were unable to progress further but the successful ousting of Robert Maxwell as chairman after relegation in 1991 lifted the shackles, though Wembley heartache against Leicester in 1994 was the closest they came to a return to the top flight in the next four years.

Enter James Michael Smith – Jim, as he was more commonly known. Or, to be more precise, the Bald Eagle.

When Smith took charge at the Baseball Ground in the summer of 1995, Derby had somewhat begun to stall. Unable to kick on from that day in the capital, a ninth-placed finish spelt the end of Roy McFarland's tenure and Smith, giving up his desk job with the League Managers' Association, returned to the dugout. Chairman and local millionaire Lionel Pickering, having already ploughed his fortune into the club, closed the wallet in favour of blooding youngsters into the first team.

Smith's entry into Derby saw him inherit the likes of Dean Sturridge and Marco Gabbiadini, but it was his summer activity that ultimately brought success. Robin van der Laan, Darryl Powell and Gary Rowett were inspired captures that led the club on the journey to the Premier League for the first time since its inception, especially following the October arrival of Igor Stimac.

It was in February 1996, during a 20-game unbeaten run sparked by the signing of Stimac, that the big news broke. Chief executive Keith Loring announced that the club would be moving for the first time since 1895.

* * *

Today, modern, soulless bowls are commonplace in football. We're somehow at a point where a visit to Turf Moor is almost a welcome treat; a throwback to a different era of the game, with wooden seats, and rickety stairs. In Burnley, they even still have those TVs with the enormous backs; prehistoric. But the Taylor Report, issued after the Hillsborough disaster in 1989, changed the game. No longer could grounds accommodate standing supporters stuck into pens and with crush barriers holding them back. All-seaters, it was clear, had to be the future.

For Derby, too, there was the wooden factor of the stadium to contend with. Following the 1985 fire at Valley Parade, there became an increased worry across British venues of a repeat. The Baseball Ground, largely wooden, was a risk. Factor this in alongside the Taylor Report and the game had to change. Middlesbrough were one of the first clubs to make the switch. Their Ayresome Park home was no longer fit for purpose so Taylor Woodrow Construction began work on the development of the Riverside Stadium, built on the old Middlehaven site overlooking the Tees. The 1995 opening, in which Boro beat Chelsea 2-0, was a success. The eyes of British football fans gazed towards it, a peephole into how their futures would look. Deep inside the Baseball Ground boardrooms, Peter Gadsby was watching on.

Gadsby, a local businessman who had made his money from business and housing developments, sat on the Derby County board. Gadsby's role as associate director led him into the potential development of the football club and avenues for growth.

He said, 'By Christmas time, I saw Middlesbrough's ground on the telly. The story was all about their new stadium, basically an old harbour that had been closed in the north-east. The whole of the football world was starting to talk about new stadia due to the Lord Justice Taylor's report and the demise of traditional grounds due to safety reasons.

'I went up to Boro and I thought it was just fantastic. One of the things about football is, because nobody would support

Middlesbrough from Derby, they were very helpful. In business, people will not be so open. The stadium had been built for approximately £18m by Taylor Woodrow and it was seen as a breakthrough for football and the model held up to be the future of football.'

Middlesbrough were national leaders. While clubs of all statures continued to struggle and look for alternatives following the Taylor Report, they had taken the initiative. For Derby, their initial plan started at home. The Baseball Ground was to be regenerated. Why move from a perfectly good stadium and where would the club get the £18m from to spend on a new home?

Ideas began to grow for the redevelopment of the ground, including the rebuilding of three stands. Gadsby was charged with looking into the plans and, with a wealth of property experience behind him, cast an eye over how it could be done. He set about designing a new stand to replace the ABC and put plans in place for the acquisition of the cottages behind. A capacity of 18,000 would be temporarily reduced to 10,000 during the work on the new stand and the board made the call to redevelop the BBG. Those fanciful plans were soon scrapped.

'At that time there was a thing called City Challenge,' says Gadsby. 'This was a thing by Lord Heseltine, which was designed to regenerate cities with bad sites. Pride Park was then known as Chaddesden Sidings and was full of old coal products, railway machinery and it was a site that needed decontaminating.'

The focused area was a barren, toxic wasteland situated right between Chaddesden and Alvaston. The original home of Derby's railway industry, it had descended into a ground solely for landfill and gas works. It was quite literally a dump. Nothing nearby, nobody nearby. A hole of Derby.

Heseltine's City Challenge was a blessing for the city and for the club. A sum of £30m was given to clear the area in the aim of creating a new hub for Derby. This hub, as Gadsby recalls, would be known as Pride Park: 'My business connected me with the local authorities on a frequent basis. Derby City Council made a bid for the Millennium Dome. I was a board member for the government's regional development programme, so I was told that the shortlist for the Millennium Dome was between Birmingham, Derby and London. Credit to Derby City Council that they were aiming high.

'When I approached them with regards to relocating the Baseball Ground to Pride Park, they were aghast. Football at that time had a reputation of hooliganism and tribal warfare.'

The Dome, a bowl without any real purpose, was never going to be in Derby. In the same way the home of English football would never leave London, there was only ever one destination. Gadsby explained, 'There was a guy called Bob Laxton who was a Labour leader in Derby, very nice guy. I met with the council and they said, "What do you want, Peter?" And I told them I wanted to bring the football club to Pride Park. I said what's happening up in Middlesbrough is changing the world, this is what will happen.'

It was the mid-1990s though and hooliganism was still at the forefront of minds. Football and violence remained intertwined, even if things had settled since the previous decade. It was a bone of contention for the council, wary its £30m handout would become a bloodbath.

'They said, "We want to see businesses, we want vibrancy, we don't want loads of hooligans." But the reason you get hooligans is because you have no facilities. You had one toilet for 2,000 ladies at the Baseball Ground. You couldn't take kids or wives there because there was nowhere to take them to the toilet, there was no corporate stuff, but it was still a great place for all the people who wanted to watch football,' Gadsby continued.

'The Baseball Ground had been condemned because of its wooden stand, the Co-op Stand, and we were going to have the attendance reduced to 14,000. I was challenged by the board to make recommendations for the upgrade. At this point in time, work and design had been committed to pull down the Co-op and build a new stand for between £6m and £8m.

'I went to see Lionel and he said, "You must be mad." I said, 'Lionel, it'll cost £8m to replace the Co-op Stand, a maximum of 20,000 seats, there's all the problems of buying all these cottages, you can't park near the ground, no corporate hospitality, and facilities in the football world have moved on."'

Pickering, another who had grown up with the Baseball Ground an integral part of his own personal development, reacted in the manner thousands more across the city did to the suggestion. 'Ridiculous, you'll get lynched by the Derby people, I've been here for 40 years watching Derby County, you can't do it.'

Pickering would soon be swayed. Accompanying Gadsby on a trip to the Riverside, he was onside when realising the growth that moving would provide the club. 'Taylor Woodrow had a blueprint for stadia and were very keen to reproduce their model. I visited Boro and met Steve Gibson. They spent considerable time showing me around but more importantly passed on from experience many variations that would make it an even better stadium,' said Gadsby.

'First of all, we'd make the press room bigger,' Gadsby was told by Gibson. 'When you arrive in reception it should be grandiose and in the corporate, we have a wall. We should have had glass.'

By this point, a Stimac-inspired Derby rocketed through the league. Sturridge, Paul Simpson, Gabbiadini and van der Laan were rampant. A side set for the top flight needed a stadium to match. Gadsby said, 'Reluctantly, Lionel said "If I am to put money in the board must also financially support me," which we did.

'The council agreed to give us ten weeks to buy the land on Pride Park. At the time it was the regenerated former Chaddesden Sidings of many acres with just grounds around it. They were holding it back for the Millennium Dome. I told them, "You've not got it, it's going to London." They said, "Yeah, but we don't want everybody else to know that, do we?"

'We then gave a brief insight as to the benefits and the stadia improvements including the 22 upgrades, i.e. larger reception, large corporate hospitality rooms that could look out on to the pitch, ample toilets (at the Baseball Ground there was one toilet for every 2,000 ladies), large car parking and more importantly excellent access.'

After Loring's announcement in February 1996, things moved quickly. The blueprint was drawn up, the land was cleared and Taylor Woodrow followed on from their development of the Riverside and began proceedings on a near replica. 'People started to embrace it, companies bought boxes, we did a video thing where you could see where your seat was and it started to take off,' said Gadsby.

'The impact of the stadium was just surreal, steelwork was emerging. At last Lionel was excited and we were on course to sell 20,000 season tickets with a full house of 30,000. Wives and children were attracted to the quality facilities of the new ground.'

The construction was quick and Pickering, never shy to throw money at his club, ordered for the corners to be filled in after initially leaving them open. No expense, nor corner, was spared.

* * *

Promotion to the Premier League was confirmed on one glorious April afternoon at home to Crystal Palace. Robin van der Laan's winner sealed a return to the top flight and opened a pot of financial gold for Pickering to delve into.

The signing of Stimac had proved to be the season's crucial factor. Bar his first game, a 5-1 defeat at Tranmere Rovers, the phenomenal run of form that coincided with the arrival of the Croatian transformed the backline. Such was the long-lasting effort that he had few days go by without a mention of him on any Derby County forum. A quarter of a century after his arrival on British shores, he remains the king. But the signing of Stimac was a catalyst for Smith. A first venture into foreign markets had proved a success and the Yorkshireman's visionary plans for the on-field developments lay firmly across Europe. Come May, the Bald Eagle's transfer plans soared.

The Premier League was no step too far for his young squad. Stimac was in his element, Sturridge too with 14 goals in all competitions. Key additions in the summer of 1996 also helped drive the club forward again. Danish defender Jacob Laursen and Croatian midfielder Aljoša Asanović were signed before Euro '96 in England. Asanović, Stimac's friend and countryman, was one of the tournament's stand-out performers.

Domestic signings, too, showed Smith's canny eye for a transfer. Paul McGrath, in the twilight of his career, put in perhaps the best single season ever seen by a Derby County footballer having signed from Aston Villa in the autumn of 1996. Never training and with legs that barely functioned in the week, the 36-year-old's 24 games were among some of the best defensive performances of the Smith era.

And that's without even mentioning the limby phenomenon from Costa Rica, Paulo Wanchope. Oh Paulo. Has there ever been a more unpredictable footballer? His April 1997 goal at Manchester United is as spectacular as it is bemusing. On his debut, none of the United defenders knew where he was going or where his touch would lead him. In truth, neither did he.

'Wanchope we signed and I don't know where we got him from, but we saw a video and organised a game against a non-league team and the agent said, "He can play in a trial but it has to be under a different name." "Where's he from?" I asked. "Costa Rica."

'So we went to this game and the ball came across, six yards out and he missed a sitter. And another chance. I went, "Bloody hell, Jim." All of a sudden, the keeper kicks it and he leapt, and I remember it to this day, he got unbelievable height, chested it down and volleyed it out wide and then got in the box. Me and Jim looked at each other and went, "Get him off at half-time, get him signed." We took him off, got him signed and the rest is history. Where did he come from? No one knows! Sneaked him in for a trial and you're going, how did we do that?'

They were the words of Steve McClaren. For all the plaudits Smith received over the course of his Derby County spell, he couldn't have done it without his number two. A primarily lower-division footballer who had appeared 25 times in a Derby shirt in the 80s, McClaren first became acquainted with Smith at Oxford, where he would serve drinks after the game to the then U's manager. Not in a barman sense, more as a buttering up process, always looking to discuss a possible route into coaching. It was Smith who made the call to his soon-to-be apprentice when moving to Derby.

'Jim was a larger than life character but he had such a great reputation in football and he was such a football man, a true Yorkshireman down to the bone and just great fun. We developed a great relationship, became very close and were very good together,' McClaren remembers.

It took time, though. McClaren, still new to coaching and with the side struggling in the first half of 1995/96, had to work at the relationship before they could look to the future arrivals. 'The initial first three to six months was a difficult time because Jim had taken over and the squad needed reinventing. The first month or two we stayed in a hotel together and we developed a close relationship, we'd just drive to every game going, so it was really hard work and he worked me hard,' said McClaren.

It was on these hotel nights that Jim would introduce McClaren to one of his true loves. 'We'd chat so much usually over a bottle of red wine. I'd never drunk it before but I discovered it with Jim and it was always Rioja! Oh, he was very honest, very demanding but great company and a great football man,' he said.

The pair achieved greatness. From the early days of McClaren's development, there was little doubt he had an ingenious knack for developing sides. He'd go on to drive the introduction at Derby of ProZone, the player tracking system that in part transformed how clubs look at their players in training and on matchday. The combination of Smith and McClaren was a Clough and Taylor for the modern era, even if McClaren was often left infuriated by the master.

McClaren said, 'His strength was in building his team with the players he signed and he built a great team. They were generally mavericks and foreigners which really helped my coaching in terms of developing myself. I always remember he used to come in and say, "What are we doing today Stevie?" and I had a plan for a training session and he'd say, "Oh rubbish Steve, rubbish." And I didn't have a plan B so I always tell the story that he always taught me to have a plan A, plan B, plan C all the way to Z.'

On the same day as McClaren met Wanchope and Costa Rican midfielder Mauricio Solis for the first time, he was shaking hands with Mart Poom too. Having had issues with a work permit after signing for Smith at Portsmouth, it was a stroke of luck that led him back to the Bald Eagle, the infamous game that never happened between Scotland and Estonia in Tallinn where the two teams turned up at different times and Scotland kicked off against nobody. It was rearranged for February, by which time Smith needed competition for Russell Hoult. 'The February game, Jim asked Alan Hodgkinson [the Scottish team goalkeeping coach] who he knew to have a look at me,' Poom begins.

'That time was much more difficult to get videos for every game, the scouting was much more live. We drew 0-0 and soon after that I heard Derby wanted to sign me. We flew from Cyprus to Monaco, back to Cyprus and then in March I flew from Cyprus to England to have a medical and sign the deal. The day after the game, I think Jim wanted to see if I could still catch a ball so they got me to train on the Baseball Ground with just Igor, Asanović and McClaren. We signed the contract and the deal was done but because Estonia wasn't EU, I had to leave the country again, I couldn't wait for the permit while in the UK. Finally, all the paperwork was done before the window closed at the end of March.'

The victory at Manchester United is best remembered for Wanchope's wizardry and Graham Richards's beautiful piece of commentary, but it also marked the debut of Poom, in front of thousands watching back in his home country as he became the first Estonian to appear in the Premier League.

He continues, 'We had one session at Raynesway and then we had to go away to Manchester. The shirt for me, Puma was the sponsor, the kitman had to get one of Russell's shirts because we didn't have one. He went to the Man United superstore to cover the old name and number and then put POOM 21 on. [Saturday] 5 April 1997, a date I'll never forget. Playing against my hero Peter Schmeichel and United, my favourite team. People in Tallinn were able to watch the game via Finnish TV, who translated that game live. It was big news in Estonia. What better start than to beat Manchester United at Old Trafford?'

Recalling the signing of Poom, McClaren breaks into a grin when remembering a routine he'd have to endure with Smith on a weekly basis, 'Oh, Poomy got constant stick over every goal that went in. It was to such an extent that I used to say to Jim, "Look, let's make a pact that you won't kill him until I see the video and I'll tell you on Monday if it's his fault or not." Every Monday he used to come in and ...'

At this point McClaren adopts one of the finest impressions you can imagine. '"Stevie! Was it his fault?" and I'd say, "No Jim it was so and so" and he'd grumble and get somebody else but when it was Poomy, he used to kill him!'

Derby's return to the big time was an unparalleled success. Comfortably safe in 12th place, the final campaign at the Baseball Ground took in some of the finest days in decades. The win at Old Trafford was joined by home successes over Chelsea and Tottenham, and a run to the FA Cup quarter-final. It was a season that meant more than just results though and after 102 years, the gates closed on first team football at the BBG.

* * *

Barely five miles away, Pride Park was ready to welcome its tenants. Polished, prepared and with the smell of the paint still wafting, it was given the royal seal of approval. Queen Elizabeth II had never, at least knowingly, opened a football stadium. Quite what made her choose to do so in Derby, 126 miles from her Buckingham Palace home, is a mystery. In what would turn out to be a horrendous year for Her Majesty with the death of Princess Diana a month later, it was her arrival in Derby that provided the first opportunity for thousands to get their first experience of the stadium.

For Peter Gadsby, it too was an opportunity to see years of hard work be gazed over by the hardest-to-please eyes. He said, 'John Bather, the Lord Lieutenant at the time, came to see me and said, "The Queen would like to open the stadium." We had wanted a royal and we had gone through his office to see if we could get maybe Prince Charles for the opening. To our pleasant surprise, the Queen agreed.

'She was wonderful but Prince Philip was very prickly! I remember walking out with him into the stadium and he asked, "How much steel has gone in the stadium?" I said I was unsure and he said, "Hmm, I'd have thought you'd have known that. How much are these footballers being paid?" I said, "A lot, sir!"

'So we walked out in front of 30,000 people on a cold July day. The players were lined up across the centre circle and the old boys including Dave Mackay, Reg Harrison, Angus Morrison and Jim Bullions, formed a guard of honour.

'Halfway across the pitch, Lionel, who worshipped the old players, left the Queen to go and shake their hands. The Queen was stood on her own looking around bewildered! The Lord Lieutenant gave me a shove and I had to immediately go and accompany her.

'I arrived at the line of players, led by the captain Igor Stimac, and then Stefano Eranio and Mart Poom. I was then faced with a player who when I looked up at him I didn't recognise.

'The Queen said to me, "You don't know his name do you?" "No ma'am," I replied. It was Mauricio Solis who came with Wanchope from Costa Rica. This amused Her Majesty intensely. Her words were, "How many of these players do you know?"'

The players, too, looking resplendent on the pitch, were given a day to remember. Poom, as he turns away, reveals in the living room he sits in he's staring back at a photo from their meeting that day. He goes on to add that he's met the Queen twice since, which for most would seem like a brag, but not from Poom.

The afternoon acted as a realisation for McClaren though. When he should have been embracing the situation, the dawning of what was to come struck him. 'To put it in easy terms, the Queen would never come and visit us at the BBG. Now she was riding in an open top car with Jim, that's how big it was. But we were frightened to death because the Baseball Ground kind of kept us in the Premier League and all of a sudden, moving to Pride Park with a carpet of a pitch, we'd have to start playing proper football.'

The Baseball Ground's fear factor would be lost. Gone would be its intimidating nature, where the players could feel the breaths of the crowd, sense the almost impending realisation that a stray fan could wander on at any point. It was a cauldron that oozed charisma, where the walls told stories of the club Derby had been and could be again. Sit in the changing rooms and the noise from above was unavoidable. To ease them in, the club needed to find something new to provide the momentum on the field, a new reason for fans to generate the excitement that came so naturally in the Pop Side.

'Milan to Derby? Now that was a big change!' Stefano Eranio was a giant of European football, having earned three Serie A titles, three Italian Super Cups, one Champions League and played in two other losing finals. He'd appeared 20 times in one of the finest Italian sides ever forged and had shared changing rooms with George Weah, Paolo Maldini and Marco van Basten. On paper, he was the biggest signing in the history of Derby County, and he arrived for nothing.

'In that period I was in the national team and I had many possibilities to become a player-manager. Porto wanted me to play there, Munich too. But my dream was to join a team in England because I used to watch the games and the atmosphere was brilliant. I always believed that the real football was there and for that reason

I had the possibility to speak with a very big friend of Jim Smith's. Jim had his Italian friend too who he spoke with about which players he'd like to take and he decided to watch one game in Milan.

'When Jim came to Italy, Milan played Udinese. He came and in that game I played right-back and we won 1-0, I was the best player on the field. In two days, he came back again to England, called me and said, "Stefano please, I'd like to come to Milan and sign you for Derby." He came and then we went along to sign the contract.'

Eranio was an enormous capture as a footballer, but Smith and McClaren both knew what would really be setting them apart from others was the Italian's footballing mindset. A brain elevated beyond what many British players possessed, his ability to see the game in slow motion took Smith's side from a steady Premier League side to a force to be reckoned with.

Beyond that majestic mind was a work ethic though, one unseen at Ramarena in the past, as McClaren recalls, 'I remember Eranio's first training session coming from Milan and it was incredible. He did everything perfectly, just spot on. He'd be passing, every pass and every run. I stopped and I just said, "Have a look at that. That's what being professional is all about. He's there early, warms up properly and is ready to train, trains perfectly and stays afterwards to do extra. That is it boys! And he's got European Cup medals!"'

That ethic was evident from day one. Upon his arrival in the East Midlands, Eranio met Jon Davidson. A former Derby trainee who represented the first team, Davidson had grown back into the club under Smith. Now working directly with club legend Gordon Guthrie, Davidson was still young enough to get involved in sessions from time to time.

He said, 'I remember Jim nearly gave me the sack one day for tipping Mikkel Beck's shot on to the bar and he went mad at me for saving it. But there was another one with Stefano. We were in this practice match and he's taking me on one-on-one, so I've come flying out and saved it but just caught him. He's gone rolling over and I'm whispering, "Stef, get up. Please get up, you're going to get me a bollocking here!"' The bollocking was avoided, and Davidson is still the glue holding the changing room together to this very day.

Immediately, Smith and McClaren got to work on plucking some of that brilliance from the brain of the Italian – starting with his contact book. 'Jim told me, "Stefano, our team is not big enough. We came up last year but we'd like to build a good team. If you come you can help us to sign different players." So, when I moved, the manager asked if I knew anyone who could play as striker and who would score a few goals. I called Baiano!' Eranio said.

Francesco Baiano was the latest in a long, beautiful list of imports who would transform the face of the club. McClaren, following one of Baiano's first practice sessions, reminisces on picking up the phone to Smith and simply saying, 'Wow. He is a player.' In his first eight games, he found the net eight times.

It was a time where Derby could attract almost anyone. Smith wrote in his autobiography about being close to enticing Emmanuel Petit to Derby, but it was another ponytail that really would have astounded.

Eranio's contact book stretched to one of the best players on the planet, Roberto Baggio. Smith flew to Milan to discuss a deal, describing the likelihood as '50/50'. Terms were agreed before a last-second intervention from Baggio's agent led to the move collapsing. Ultimately it was Baiano who got the call.

* * *

Those eight games saw Baiano kick off not only his Derby career but the life of the club at Pride Park Stadium. After years of preparation and a visit from Her Majesty herself, it was an August night that was to provide the first taste of competitive football at the new home. At the time, it was a sparsely populated Pride Park from the outside. Absent were the businesses and the buildings, the Derby Arena, the pubs and even the Wyvern. It was simply a stadium.

'If you go there now you've got Frankie and Benny's, Harvester, Merlin, Subway,' recalls journalist and supporter Nick Britten. 'But you had to go to the pubs in town beforehand if you wanted a drink or something to eat. But if you walked from town and walked from the flyover to Pride Park, as you walked up the roof would come into view and as you got to the top, you just saw this shiny cathedral of football which was surrounded by nothing, it was absolutely fantastic.'

That was the view that 24,000 had on their maiden voyage. Bar a pre-season friendly against Sampdoria, this was the first taste of football at the stadium largely expected to guide the club into a new, exciting era. Gadsby recalls seeing a mother and son walking towards the Rams' new home, the thought of 'that wouldn't have happened at the Baseball Ground' running through his head. Neither would what happened next though, an omen as to what life would feel like over many of the next 22 years.

'I was working at the *Daily Record* and travelled down and of course the fucking lights went out and it was a nightmare. Everybody could see the floodlights of the Baseball Ground from the stadium and you just looked longingly at them,' Britten remembers.

Fifty-six minutes into what should have been a landmark evening, the floodlights failed. More than half an hour of darkness followed, a boardroom in despair and a group of men frantically running around with pliers hoping to find the answer. Gadsby, welcoming a raft of new sponsors to the new stadium, was in among it all.

'The first proper game of the season was a nightmare. We were 2-1 up against Wimbledon under the lights with a full house. We were playing well and at half-time, the lights went out. Minutes ticked by and Jim was going mad shouting to me "this bloody club, get the bloody lights on".

'I went in to the Wimbledon dressing room and Joe Kinnear faced me. I explained the problem, that the surge at half-time had created a circuit break, and we anticipated the lights coming back on in a few minutes so please could they be ready to go out to play again. Kinnear said, "Is that it? You can fuck off." They had already changed.

Wimbledon forced the hand of referee Uriah Rennie, on his first night officiating in the division, and the match was abandoned. 'The mistake we made was not testing it for a half-time. The peak time at Christmas is 3.10pm when the Queen comes on and everybody puts a cup of tea on. All the stations have a surge. But we hadn't tested for half-time, which is the same,' said Gadsby. It was a shambolic beginning, albeit one never repeated from that day on.

Ashley Ward was the first man to score in a Derby shirt at Pride Park, before the lights went out, but it's Eranio who takes the credit after striking against Barnsley. 'Baiano shot the penalty but he made a mistake in his step or someone moved before he touched the ball, so I took the ball and I scored instead. So I am the first scorer. Nobody can ever cancel that out now, I will always be the first scorer there!' Eranio smiles.

For two years, Pride Park was a haven. The atmosphere of the Baseball Ground may have been sacrificed but it mattered little on the field when Eranio, Wanchope and Baiano were on top form. It took 12 games to be beaten on new home soil, in that time dispatching champions-elect Arsenal 3-0 on one of the great days. By the end of their first year in DE24, Derby had risen to the brink of a return to European football. Just two points away from the UEFA Cup, Smith and McClaren had transformed the club and they had the facilities to match off it. In many ways, it was a brand new Derby County.

The Italian additions had the desired effect. Baiano's 13 goals saw him crowned player of the season, Eranio's impact as powerfully felt. But it was the old guard of international additions who had started the movement and laid the foundations for a universal football club.

One of those, Poom, remembers a changing room on the turn: 'When I signed, Eranio and Baiano came a bit later but it was a multicultural club. It was full of characters and interesting with these different nationalities. I knew a little bit about British dressing room banter from my time with Portsmouth. When I was young and I signed for them, I was taken aback by the football language and the English humour but Derby, I knew what to expect. We had a great team spirit and Jim's strengths were that he had a good scouting network where he knew a lot of people in football. He knew all the managers, players, coaches, across Europe.'

For Eranio too, it was people like Poom and Stimac who allowed him and Baiano to bed in. 'It was great to have people from all over the world,' begins Eranio. 'Stimac helped me because he knew the Italian language, he would speak to me if the boss or a team-mate had something important to know, I would call him and say, "Stimac, please come here and help me" because I learned some phrases and it was not easy for me to make questions because I didn't know words. I'd point at the object or whatever and ask how you say it in English and he'd just help me.'

And McClaren? A man who went on to redefine his management after failure in the England role over a decade later, the chance to work with minds established far from the British Isles saw his methods and thinking grow. He says, 'I was always looking at new ideas, thinking of new sessions. You're eager to find out what's out there, what's new and what's coming, and so we used to do all sorts. But I think the key thing was relationships with players. In terms of where the game was going, it was going more foreign so therefore I knew that foreign players were coming, and we needed to adjust. I used to say, "Look Jim, foreign players, they don't like this. They don't like staying over at games" etc., but it was an "Oh they're in England, they adapt to us" and I understood but we also needed to adapt to them. That's what people like Eranio brought. They weren't just foreign players, they were characters.'

Beyond being good for McClaren, it was the same for the youngsters emerging too. While Eranio and Poom had little idea just who Derby were when first presented with the name of the club, Chris Riggott certainly did. His childhood Saturday afternoons were spent standing on a milk crate at the BBG and Derby County was firmly running through the Riggott blood. To have the chance to represent the club, and with some of the finest minds in European football, was an opportunity he could barely believe.

'I remember one day when I was a young pro, Steve Round told me to come and do some bits after training where I'd be doing some one v ones. I looked up and it was against Wanchope,' laughs Riggott. 'He didn't know what was going to happen so there's no chance that I would! But that type of thing was surreal for me, especially as a fan. I'd be training with Wanchope and Sturridge and Baiano. Not just football stuff, you learn from people like Eranio. He is a fantastic man in how he conducts himself with everybody. He had this amazing career but was the most humble of men. These are important lessons for a young lad when you're watching these guys and how they interact and how they handle themselves.'

The Riggott family would have been part of that outpouring of sorrow upon leaving the Baseball Ground, but they would have been heartened to know there was still one key remnant of the old club. Tradition remained on a daily basis in the form of a grassy knoll beside Raynesway. Like the Baseball Ground had been, Ramarena was no longer fit for the purpose of a Premier League football club. Situated by a main road and adjacent to the Rolls-Royce factory, it provided easy access to anyone who fancied popping to watch training for the day and had barely enough room to run a practice match. It was a far cry from the state-of-the-art facilities Eranio and Baiano had been shown at the stadium, perhaps hidden away for good reason.

'The training ground today? Yeah, I'm very jealous!' Poom laughs. He wasn't used to quite the luxury Eranio may have been, but even he found Ramarena to be a culture shock. 'I came from Estonia so Raynesway was still okay, I was just grateful to be on grass. We had one and a half pitches here, we had this little canteen and two small dressing rooms, a boot room. It would get very muddy during winter. I remember we had a little corner for goalkeepers behind this building where we worked, then we had a gym where it was freezing cold.

'We'd have the canteen where it was always chicken and beans. We had this gym which had a little indoor hall so you could play a bit of basketball, which Wanchope was good at. Next it was a small weights room downstairs and then a little fitness room with boxing bags. I used to go there before training and do my exercises and a bit of boxing to try and get more aggressive. Jim was very demanding of his goalkeeper dominating the box, getting every ball and it was my strength. I remember I would run against the boxing bags and then jump against the wall.'

One man who regularly made the drive down from his university home of Sheffield was Ross Fletcher. Already aware his decision to study advanced econometrics was a poor choice, he soon found himself spending more time standing around in Ramarena than in lectures. 'You had one and a half muddy fields with a ramshackle office area, then the little five on five bowling green for short-sided games which Jim would get involved in and that was about it,' he looks back.

It was here that Fletcher would wait, patiently, in anticipation of capturing a few soundbites for BBC Radio Derby. 'Then you had the off room where Steve McClaren built up the ProZone suite where they had the comfy chairs but that was about it, nothing like the palatial surroundings of Moor Farm and the multiple fields of different sizes and the sport science set-up. It really was the bare bones but it had a genial charm about it.'

Look at greying images from the time and describing Ramarena as 'nothing special' is putting it lightly. To the more recent mind, it was simply a target for arsonists and travellers. But within, particularly the work that McClaren was doing, was slowly beginning to change the face of the game. Analysis was to grow in importance thanks to McClaren, along with new ideas in terms of treating the body in the right way in between matches became the focus.

McClaren was at the forefront of these ideas, 'Jim was 58 when he got the job. Many called him an old dinosaur but we created at Derby, we were way ahead of our time in terms of technology, we brought a fitness coach in which nobody had done before, a sports psychologist in. We helped develop ProZone, no one was doing that. We had a meeting room with massage chairs, we'd do yoga, he was up for anything. That is great for me because it threw me lots of ideas and I got my reputation from it. I have to thank Jim because he allowed me to bring these ideas in and he'd say yes. We were so forward-thinking.'

The methods only improved the club's on-field fortunes, and second season syndrome at Pride Park (which had by now had its capacity increased) never materialised. An eighth-place finish only brought the club closer to European football, but again they fell agonisingly short. Never, at least by the time of writing, would the club get close to it in the following years.

It wasn't for the want of trying, as Lionel Pickering continued to plough his fortune into the club. Seth Johnson arrived in the summer of 1999; powerful Belgian striker Branko Strupar in the following December.

Promising young forward Lee Morris came in October 1999 on a club record deal. He recalls, 'It was Derby and Arsenal who were both in for me and I believe Derby outbid Arsenal. I got a phone call on the Sunday afternoon from our manager and he just said, "You're going to Derby tomorrow." There wasn't anything specific in terms of Europe, but it felt like a club on the up. Pride Park was fantastic at the time compared to a lot of the stadiums around and they were established. They were going in the right direction, it just felt like a nice, stable club to go to.'

All were strong signings, particularly when following on from individuals such as Horacio Carbonari a year earlier. The issue was the other way though. By now, Derby were a known force and those with wider wallets began to circulate around key assets. Chris Powell departed for Charlton Athletic in the summer of 1998, followed by Christian Dailly and Lee Carsley to Blackburn Rovers a few months later. By the summer of 1999, Igor had left his kingdom for Upton Park, following Paulo Wanchope to the capital. The tide had begun to turn. Whether driven by potential financial worries or ambition, the loss of the latter two can be traced back to McClaren's own departure.

The tactical side of the management duo, he had by now become the most talked about coach in the country, arguably Europe too. Plucked from obscurity by Smith, his nous was outgrowing the club and come February 1999 he linked up with one of Smith's closest friends, Alex Ferguson. He remembers, 'I think it was a logical next step. We came to a stage where I was thinking maybe if Jim retires, but he would have worked and worked and he loved football, so that move was just a logical next step. I had no hesitation and Jim just said he'd drive me there himself because it was such a great opportunity. He knew it would happen one day, but the grounding with Jim in terms of dealing with the manager, the demand and the honesty, was vital.

'Jim had a hairdryer and I saw more from him than with Sir Alex, we had some right ones in the dressing room. But it was a great grounding with foreign players and big characters. I remember asking Sir Alex what he wanted me to do and he'd say, "What would you do at Derby? Whatever you did there, that's why you're here so go out and do it" and that was it. They were the words, no advice, just get on with it and do your job.'

The loss of McClaren put Derby back on a downward curve and Pickering sensed it. Gadsby recalls the words of the chairman in response to the approach, 'Alex Ferguson came calling for him. And Lionel said to me, "Steve's your mate, isn't he? Tell him he can't go; we can't lose him. Just tell him he has to come back, Jim and him are a team."

'I rang Steve and asked him where he was and he said he was in Stockport on his way to United.

'I said, "Well Lionel wants you to come back. Will you please consider it?" "Yeah, I will Peter, but United are currently top of the league, in the semi-finals of the European Cup and in the quarter-finals of the FA Cup. And I'm on £38,000 here and they're starting me on £180,000." So I asked him to think about it.'

Almost immediately, with McClaren gone, Smith suffered. His invincibility cloak had been torn away and by the end of 1999, with a side a shadow of the one he had at his disposal in his previous two seasons, talk of Europe was silenced. Come the millennium celebrations, Smith's Derby were in the thick of the relegation battle. The city was about to experience its own Y2K problem.

WEST BEFORE SOUTH

THERE'S A divide between football fans and the rest of the world. The minutes after each new year are filled with excitement and a wealth of opportunities about what could come over the next 365 days. Families embrace, text messages struggle to get through the system and the same vow of never again enduring the Hootenanny is agreed upon. But for football fans, it's a different mindset.

Where will your club go? Is this the year we finally kick on? Particularly today, it's more about checking your club's Twitter feed in case they've got themselves in before the crowd on signings. Then there's the realisation that you're hours away from another match, as long as the hangover isn't too debilitating.

When the millennium ticked into place, Derby supporters had one thing on their minds. How are we going to survive this? The late 1990s offered so much, with very real ambitions of Europe and a return to the upper echelons of the English game. But everyone involved with the club knew that the next five months would go a long way in determining the immediate future of Derby County.

Heading into 2000, Poom was entering a different changing room. The bigger personalities had been moved on, leaving only the scraps of success. He said, 'I think when Steve McClaren left for United it started. He was a great coach; he took training and was a modern coach which helped Jim a lot. Then Eric Steele left a year later and some players too. Igor and Wanchope left, Sturridge was sold, Asanović too. But when Steve left, we didn't manage to replace some key players. Football is a cruel business and a club like Derby, you can't stand still because you end up going backwards. Some of the key coaching staff and players left and we didn't have the same quality from there.'

It wasn't for the want of trying for Smith. Still actively looking to replace those who had moved on, his attentions remained on foreign fields and at the end of the decade Branko Strupar landed in Derby.

He was no Wanchope in terms of his style but like the Costa Rican, it didn't take long for him to have an impact, the Belgian striker kicking off 2000 with a double against Watford to secure a fifth win of the campaign.

Strupar hadn't been the first forward to be added, however. Nine months previously, Mikkel Beck was expected to be the latest success after an impressive run at Middlesbrough. Instead, he wrote himself into folklore as potentially the worst player to wear a Derby shirt. And considering much of what is to come, that's quite the claim. Then there was Esteban Fuertes.

Personally, I'm not sure quite how lax the UK's border force was in the 1990s. My first journey outside of England was to Disneyland Paris and despite sporting a truly awful Winnie the Pooh hat, I wasn't quizzed. Then again, I was five. But the tale of Esteban Fuertes hints that it was a little less restrictive than it is over 20 years later.

Three months it took to complete the Argentine's capture. That's three months that Smith spent chasing the then Colon de Santa Fe striker and having to spend £2.3m on the unknown forward only for it to be a bum deal. A winner against Everton was a strong start; being stopped at the borders and being proven to have a forged Italian passport, not so.

In his autobiography *It's Only a Game*, Smith wrote, 'The immigration officials chose to scrutinise every detail of every passport, even down to using infra-red. It seemed clear to us that somebody knew about the fake passport and had tipped off the authorities.'

Fuertes was never to be seen again in British football. It's a saga befitting of Derby County though and considering all that will come from this moment on, it fits in quite nicely. But Strupar was an able replacement. With Dean Sturridge still leading the line, his capture led to a return to form after a shoddy first four months.

The first seven games of 2000 only resulted in one loss, 2-1 at an Everton side who hadn't been beaten at Goodison Park yet that season. As the experienced front duo struck up an early understanding, they were able to mentor a rising talent plucked from Nuneaton Borough. Sporting a Beppe di Marco-inspired goatee, Malcolm Christie didn't arrive with any media attention. He wasn't discovered in South America and he wasn't on a level that would help to attract international stars. But on a budget, he was a revelation.

Christie was a supermarket shelf stacker around his Saturday afternoons with Nuneaton. In recent years, he has even spoken about playing for his brother's work team before joining Derby. So when he took to the Premier League as easily as he did to the frozen aisles, Smith knew he'd struck gold.

Christie's first goals came during this seven-match spell, a timely announcement considering that by the end of it, the Rams were still only two points above third-bottom Bradford. He scored twice on his first start in a 4-1 win at Middlesbrough, added another in a draw at Sunderland, and was one of four scorers at home to Wimbledon. After that initial burst, a dry spell dropped Derby back into a danger zone they had yet to truly break free from.

A run of three defeats were only a blessing as Bradford emulated that form and with a seven-point gap over Sheffield Wednesday in 19th, it looked like it would be a battle between the Rams and the Bantams. But aided by a 3-0 win over Leicester, Smith's men had opened a six-point gap between the sides prior to a meeting at

Valley Parade on the 34th afternoon of the season. Craig Burley's brace from the penalty spot (he also missed a third penalty late on) was enough to as good as seal safety and left Bradford and Wednesday preparing for life in the Football League.

A goalless draw at home to Newcastle in the penultimate game was enough to confirm survival, although the final table did show that the gap had reduced to a single point. Despite staying up, it felt a lucky escape. The sides in the bottom five of the division were poor by Premier League standards and to have narrowly escaped teams like Bradford and Sheffield Wednesday was a cause for concern.

The signing of Burley in December 1999 helped enormously but having come from a Celtic side who quashed Rangers' hopes of ten Scottish titles in a row, it was a new world.

Burley recalls, 'Coming to Derby was a sharp contrast and I could see why they were second bottom. The squad was diminished, it lacked quality and it was tough. Every week we were scrapping for survival and that's tough for a manager. But working with Jim was great because he brought me in to do a job and for two years, I did that and we stayed up. And we really should never have stayed up, honestly, we were cracking at the seams. How we stayed up in 1999/00 and beyond is a bit of a mystery. There was always the hope that Jim was going to go on the spend again and we were going to get some money and help the squad but it didn't really happen.'

* * *

Who was Jim Smith's ultimate capture? For a club like Derby to sign Asanović and Eranio, they are definite contenders. Stimac too came out of nowhere, Wanchope was a player like no other. But when Taribo West rocked up at Pride Park, he made the rest look routine. West was an enigma. He'd played for both Milan sides, French outfit Auxerre and a range of Nigerian clubs. Arriving with World Cup experience and an army of *Championship Manager* fans, quite how Smith managed to cope with him is indeterminable.

Throughout the 18-month interviewing stage for this book, West appeared at every turn, which is more than can be said for his Derby career. Everyone who shared a changing room with him had a story about the man with the best hair in football. Almost all stories revolved around the word of God. That and his tendency to disappear. Chris Riggott and Lee Morris begin.

Riggott says, 'I had never seen someone quite as outlandish as Taribo, very extroverted. He was one of them signings that came out of nowhere and Jim handled him differently. It's so funny thinking about him. I remember him saying a prayer, Arsenal I think it was. Jim left the team talk to him and he got us in a big circle, interlinked with arms around each other and he was giving it the "Our Father".

'He started preaching at us and I remember Seth Johnson and Rory Delap just trying their best not to laugh. Anyway, 90 seconds into the game the ball goes into the channel and Taribo tries to shepherd it out of play, someone bumped him over the advertising hoardings, he fell into the ditch and the guy squared it and scored. Jim said, "That's the last time I let Taribo take the pre-match prayer."

'We had West Ham away where he just didn't turn up. He showed up just before kick-off and the club got him some random gear. He had black slip-on leather shoes with a tracksuit, it was ridiculous. But he had just gone AWOL. He would show up sometimes, then he wouldn't. He'd have five or six Bibles stacked up and he'd be on his phone, back when not everybody did the whole phone thing, it was still quite new. But he'd be on the phone preaching to his church in Milan.

'On the way to big games, Jim would walk down and say, "Taribo come on, it's time to focus" and he'd be there preaching the word of God, not even in English, but he was so passionate. It had been drilled into professionalism in the game but here was Taribo, totally off the cuff and off his rocker.'

Morris adds, 'I remember being at Fulham and he always used to call Jim Smith "Jimsmith". He never said gaffer or boss or anything like the rest of us did. He tried getting the team pumped up before Fulham away and said, "Right, we're going to say a prayer." So, he got everybody in a circle and everyone was giggling, but he got a true big prayer going on. Charlton away, nobody knew where he was, and he just didn't show up. He was a true character.'

Burley builds on that night at The Valley, 'I remember being at Charlton on a Tuesday night and Jim was delaying putting the teamsheet out because we were still waiting on Taribo coming back from Milan. I said to him, "Jim, he ain't coming, I'm telling you now" and he didn't come. That's where we were, there was a little bit of desperation.'

Even for Eranio, with all his years at the top of the game, West was a rare beast, 'The bus was waiting for Manchester and everybody was in there, but nobody knew where he was. We called Taribo, we called the hotel because he was in the Mickleover hotel, nobody knew where. And he had just left for good. I saw him five years later in Milan, that was the first time since that day. He was a great player for us, could help the team but he just left with four games before the end of the season. In Milan, I asked him why he left, and he didn't tell me why. "No Stefano, it's too late now!" Incredible.'

It wasn't only Derby who experienced the full extent of West's character. Javier Zanetti spoke of similar when the Nigerian disappeared for a month at Inter Milan, opting for a vacation without informing his club after getting married. 'He invited us to his house because it was his birthday,' Zanetti said. 'He was praying for three hours. We left without eating anything.'

Smith spoke at the end of the campaign about international commitments that meant West wouldn't return, presumably alluding to his adoring army of churchgoers back in Nigeria, for whom he was their pastor. West has also spoken in the years since about practising a form of witchcraft. Naturally, he arrived back in England four years later at Plymouth Argyle. His last known sighting came back in Lagos, where he is a full-time pastor.

But West was good when he did turn up. Really good in fact. Debuting in November 2000 with the club still winless, he entered a frail back four that had shipped 28 goals in their first 13 games. Smith immediately went West, his debut at home to Bradford City coinciding with the first three points of the campaign in a 2-0 win. It was this – an extremely late wake-up call – that sparked the club back into life.

West was one of seven signings in the early months of the campaign. Joining young talent like Danny Higginbotham and Youl Mawene, his experience shone in a defence lacking in it, aside from Horacio Carbonari.

Almost coinciding with West's arrival was that of a Derby County legend, a defensive guru. Without McClaren, Smith had a slot available as his assistant. For it, he turned to Colin Todd. Who better for the role than a man synonymous with the greatest backline in the club's history? 'Jim knew me but he knew what my capabilities were. Steve Round was still there but he wanted a bit more experience. I got the phone call and he just tried to suss out if I was interested. Even though I was a manager at Swindon, I decided to go back to Derby,' Todd said.

Todd's spell on gardening leave gave him time to look into the squad he would encounter and joined with Steve Round in the position of supporting Smith. They would never be able to build a relationship like McClaren would but the addition of Todd worked. It was he rather than West who received the plaudits, although Morris only had praise for the role of West in tying things up at the back, 'As soon as Taribo came in we had pace, power, aggression. For that few months he never got the credit he deserved, but he solved all our problems and was so good.'

As both arrived and victory was finally secured against Bradford, Smith was able to routinely send a side out he could trust to keep things tight. In the next nine games, the side conceded eight times; seven of those came against Manchester United and Chelsea. And anchored by a backline centred around West, Riggott and Carbonari, they picked up 16 points to elevate them away from immediate danger.

* * *

Come mid-March, a finishing location of mid-table looked the likely destination. It was at this stage that Smith could have been excused for contemplating a new era of excitement.

Eranio and Poom aside, he no longer had the European influences to guide his club back towards the top half. What he did have was an exciting crop of young talent progressing through the ranks. Riggott and Christie were the most notable. Christie's goals were pivotal and talk began of a potential move to Manchester United, but the lanky frame of Riggott was arguably more important to Rams supporters. A man who grew up with the club ingrained into his being, to see him develop over the course of his first full season as a senior professional was cause for pride and optimism.

Riggott says, 'Steve Round said, "Look, the gaffer just needs to know that he can trust you as a centre-back. It's all about trust. Can he trust you every game?" and that stuck with me. I felt like he did. I never had a conversation longer than a minute with Jim, we wouldn't go through tactical stuff and he wouldn't ask me about my family life, nothing. But he had a great way of caring and showing he cared and believed in you. But you wouldn't cross him. Coming through the system I'd see the manager's office and think, "Wow, I wonder what it's like to go in there?" Years later you end up sitting in there.

'He got the balance right between getting players to be at their best and being hard. That's what management is. He knew what made each player tick. Jim's passing brought a lot of memories back for me, things like on a Friday when we'd go to the BBG to do the shape and he'd just change it at the last minute. He'd get someone out of the bomb squad as he used to call it, the shadow team, and he'd just change the team. You could see Steve Round just sigh. But he was so genuine, I don't think anybody ever had a bad word to say about him.'

Riggott's words are true. Of those interviewed, there were many references to Jim as a person, his temper and his nature, but never a word said with negative connotations. Burley remembers he could be a little intimidating though, 'As a senior player, I could take all of the nonsense from Jim and the grizzly old comments. But some of the young boys were absolutely petrified of him. Training would go great and Malcolm Crosby at the time was coach with Billy McEwan, great guys. The boys would be out there and Jim would be in his office looking out.

'Jim would be looking at training from his office, putting bets on for Kempton and ringing other managers to try and do deals. Jim would come out, the knees would be knocking together with his shorts down at his knees, he'd have a cap on with a big old belly. Out he comes and I'd be like, "Oh, here he comes." We'd be doing a crossing drill and it would go great, then Jim would come out and a couple of crosses would get shanked over the bar and he would go bananas. The young boys used to literally go to tatters every time he'd come out. But some young boys were a little frightened of him at times.'

From speaking with Burley, one thing was clear; he adored Jim Smith, 'I wanted to work for a no-nonsense manager again. I knew I'd get that in Jim. I knew of his reputation which was that he'll tell it as it is, he's straight talking, no bullshit and you could have a fall-out with him on Saturday and by Monday it was forgotten again. That was the main draw for me.'

Signed in December 1999 with the club struggling at the foot of the table, Burley's £3m capture was done with the intention of adding fight to a side increasingly lacking in it, 'One of the reasons he brought me in was to get goals from the midfield but also to rile up the dressing room a bit. He got a bit fed up of screaming the same things week after week and so even though Darryl was the skipper and did a very good job, I would go around the dressing room after a game and say a few home truths. Jim liked that because if you're hearing it from the same person all the time, it goes in one ear and out the other.

'I remember I'd been there for two games before this. I was in the dressing room five minutes before kick-off and I went for a quick call of nature. In pops Jim and he just said, "Craig, I brought you here to score goals. You've not even had a shot yet" and I said, "Jim, I've only just got here" but that was him. He'd say those kinds of things to people but that's the way it goes.'

Back to the make-up of the side and as solidity in the backline grew, it began to be replicated throughout the team. Aside from the maverick Georgi Kinkladze, there was little else in the way of invention. Forced to learn from his losses, Smith's ideology changed from the excitement of Asanović and Baiano to the endeavour of Burley and the rapidly improving Seth Johnson. Eranio still remained but a more industrial build was in order.

For as much as the side began to thrive mid-season, they were never entirely free of relegation concerns. That's why a late run that brought just three points from six games put them back on the brink. Victory against Leicester amid this helped but it never looked like being enough when considering the final two games.

Manchester United away would be the first. Sir Alex Ferguson's men had already sealed the title and having lost only three times all season (at Arsenal and home and away to Liverpool), it looked almost a write-off. The second would be the visit of George Burley's Ipswich Town, themselves impressively overachieving by sealing a UEFA Cup place. Heading into these with a four-point gap over Manchester City, who themselves had two wins in their last three, Derby's Premier League survival was firmly in the balance.

Sometimes though, the footballing gods can shine on you. For any other manager in the division, a journey to Old Trafford was a daunting occasion. Smith and Ferguson, however, were old friends and the finest wine connoisseurs in the British game. They also shared the common bond of Steve McClaren.

To the outside, it would be easy to suggest that Ferguson did Smith a favour with his selection. Where many expected Ryan Giggs and Jaap Stam, United lined up with the likes of Luke

Chadwick and Ronnie Wallwork. Riggott remembers 'one or two stories about them helping Jim out a bit, but who knows'.

Smith too opted to freshen things up. Youl Mawene was one of the surprise names to be handed an outing at Old Trafford, helped in part by a non-appearance by West. The young Frenchman recalls, 'I had totally forgotten about that Man United game, but Jim got his plan spot on. He said, "Kids, you will never have a better opportunity to come to Old Trafford and win in your lifetime." They'd already won the league, you'd expect them to be on a high but possibly to be a little bit on the wind down, so "guys, please, respect the plan".'

Mawene was placed on the right-hand side of a 3-5-2 formation. Riggott, Carbonari and Danny Higginbotham formed the three, with Paul Boertien on the left. Eranio, Delap and Kinkladze through the middle, with Christie, without a Premier League goal in five months. Beside him came a surprise, Lee Morris.

Morris said, 'I didn't feel much pressure, just frustration. I missed the whole first season, came back the next season and felt in a position to start playing games, but always felt I was trying to get it and never had total confidence.' Morris had yet to score in a Derby shirt, the £3m signing spending much of his career so far in the treatment room. Even when he was fit, he was rarely looked towards. He remembers, 'What's really hard is when you're on the outside and you don't feel you've got the belief of the manager or the staff. I remember scoring a hat-trick in a reserve game at the BBG against Arsenal under Colin Todd, and I wasn't even in the squad for the Saturday. This was a time when Malcolm couldn't buy a goal in the first team, I just couldn't understand. I felt I'd never get given a go, so what can you do?'

He was given his chance on the biggest afternoon of all though, even if he didn't expect it, 'Darryl Powell got injured in the last kick of practice before the game and I didn't know he had been ruled out. The team was getting named at Old Trafford and there was a squad of 17 travelling. I sat down in the dressing room and only looked at the board to see if I was on the bench or not and I wasn't, so I was all pissed off. I remember going into the baths area to sulk. Jim Smith comes in afterwards and starts telling me I need to get back when the wingers are going forward, and I thought, "What the fuck's he talking about?" Then I realised I was starting.'

Morris and Mawene rose to the occasion. Christie's first-half goal, a delightfully struck left-foot finish on the turn, provided a lead at the break. He should have doubled it midway through the second half, failing to turn Morris's square ball in from six yards. As for Mawene, he was on hand to clear Giggs's effort off the line as United grew in the final stages. Mawene continues, 'It was a masterclass with a tight defence, Stefano and Kinkladze holding the ball for us behind Malcolm that was stretching their defence up front. I remember when the goal went in and at the end, you can't describe that feeling. I never won promotions or titles but on that day when we went to thank the fans in the corner of Old Trafford, and we knew we made it together and stayed, this was a very special moment.'

With safety secured, all that was left was to say farewell to a great on the final day. Besides Poom, Eranio was the last of the old guard, the only face remaining from Smith's golden years. 'It was an incredible moment when I left,' the Italian reminisces. 'The farewell I had against Ipswich I had never had before. I would have liked to have had something after my career because my aim was to try and do something to continue for Derby.'

Although he would return temporarily the next season but didn't play through injury, his daughter's health meant the eyes of his family were on a permanent settlement in Italy. He continued, 'When something happens to your family, it was difficult. Stephanie moved to stay in a hospital in Birmingham and it was difficult speaking with doctors because she had 20 stitches in the face and it was difficult to understand. My wife decided we had to come back to Milan because it was so sad. It was hard for us to continue because we suffered so much and although the people had been very, very good for us we had to do the better thing for our daughter.

'I left Derby when I still could have done two more seasons because he asked me to sign a new contract, but the family came first for me and when my wife said it was maybe time to go back, we did. But if it didn't happen, maybe I could have become a coach with Derby. Or even the manager.'

For the second season in succession, Smith had survived with a shell of the squad he had originally built. Colin Todd, forced into the stands at Old Trafford after a ban, was party to the celebrations that night. He knew though that they were lucky to be opening the red wine for positive reasons.

'To stay in the Premier League was a big occasion so the celebration was big and Jim liked a drink anyway so there was plenty of that flowing. You don't like to have to come to the final day to survive but survival is what a lot of clubs look for anyway. Derby should have been better than that because they had good players,' he looks back.

In the back of his and Smith's minds was worry. They knew Eranio was heading back to Italy, there was no hiding the dwindling fortune of Pickering and the unavoidable truth was that safety at Old Trafford was only a temporary delay.

THE DROP

IT ALL started so promisingly. The three years of pushing Europe, the legion of foreign imports who would transform the outlook of both the club and the city. McClaren and Smith, Derby's best double act since Clough and Taylor. Yes, things had deteriorated but there were still reasons to remain excited for the future of the club. Still a Premier League outfit after gallant fights amid the threat of relegation, still with the talismanic inspiration of Smith at the helm and come the summer of 2001, a strong core remained.

There were losses, there always are. Wanchope and Stimac were already long gone and come July, Rory Delap had departed for Southampton. Still though, with an experienced squad ably levelled out by promising youngsters Christie and Riggott, in addition to the excitement of Kinkladze, optimism still lingered. And then the White Feather landed.

'I remember Eric Steele asking me in pre-season what number I wanted, because Ravanelli was to be 11. So that wasn't off to a great start,' Lee Morris, still the record signing at the club at this time, recalls. He was always set to be de-numbered from the moment Ravanelli was first rumoured to be joining.

Another of those international stars that Smith and Pickering so savoured bringing to the club, the Ravanelli rumours were different to those of Eranio or Wanchope. For a start, he was older

47

than any other recent signing Smith had made. At 32, his best days were firmly behind him and although he'd had success with Middlesbrough five years earlier, he did so in the peak of his career. His singular season was during a time that he was a regular in the Italian squad after four years of profitable displays with Juventus. He contributed 16 goals in an ultimately losing battle against the drop.

But it was a different Ravanelli who would first hold talks with Peter Gadsby. He'd scored ten goals in his past two seasons with Marseille and Lazio and his days with the Azzurri were over. The white hair remained, the customary shirt over the head too, but the ageing frame was different to the one Bryan Robson added in 1996. The hope though was that with Christie, Morris and Deon Burton still young, the addition of the Italian would not only grow the club again but progress those youngsters who could learn from him.

Ravanelli's capture, confirmed on 27 July 2001, was a free transfer. Truth be told, his later Lazio days hadn't been kind to him and although he'd just picked up a Serie A medal, his two goals came after being outshone by a young Hernan Crespo. From the best in Italy to a struggling English side, there had to be enough of an incentive for Ravanelli to return to England for a battle.

'Ravanelli, Keith Loring [CEO] and I met at Breadsall Priory,' begins Peter Gadsby, by then the club's vice-chairman. 'We had a meal at about 8pm with Ravanelli and his agent [former QPR chairman Gianni Paladini]. Jim desperately wanted to sign him and so Lionel told me to go and sign him. He wanted £40,000 a week or something silly.'

By this point in the English game, the meteoric rise of the average footballer wage was still in its formative years, so such a demand was out of place in the game, particularly for a struggling side. According to statistics from internal PFA union files, the average Premier League footballer took home £556,932 per year. Ravanelli, who it was later confirmed collected £38,000 per week, was light years ahead of his team-mates when it came to his demands.

Gadsby continued, 'He wanted two years but we were only offering one. Keith and I agreed on that. I said to Paladini, "We will only give you one year because we don't have a budget for more than one."

'Ravanelli and Paladini only spoke in Italian and Paladini translated to us. Ravanelli expressed his love for the club in Italian and that he'd like two years because he felt that he would be happy in Derby. Paladini said, "You insult him because he wants two years and he is going to be a big success."

'We stayed firm on one year and the negotiations continued including travel, accommodation, and a BMW. Immediately Ravanelli piped up. "Mercedes please." I just looked at him and said, "Your English isn't bad then?" He grinned.

'It turned out that after our meeting, Ravanelli and Paladini and Keith had gone to the Yew Tree pub, where they met Lionel and Jim also popped in as he lived local. They all left at two o'clock in the morning, drunk as wotsits and Lionel had agreed a two-year deal.'

The gradual decline of the club had started long before Ravanelli's arrival, but the second burst of Premier League life that was meant to be injected into the squad never materialised. Pickering's millions were disappearing, all pumped into the club over the previous decade. While Ravanelli was another show of intent, he was backed by no other additions in the summer months.

It would prove a source of frustration for the Italian, remembers Craig Burley. 'He got frustrated and I could see it. It's an eye-opener when you come from certain places to a club that was struggling and the squad is down. Frustration would get the better of him but I can have nothing but praise for his attitude.'

Pickering couldn't afford anybody else. Delap had departed, Eranio would too after originally agreeing to return for a year. The midfield was sparse and weaker than it had ever been under the Bald Eagle, with youngsters like Adam Bolder and Paul Boertien left to fill the voids.

Another youngster who had already nailed down a first team spot was Chris Riggott. The reigning player of the year having emerged from the shadow of Igor Stimac, he was mature beyond his years at 20. That maturity allowed him to recognise where the shortcomings were though. He says, 'I remember we lost some of our best players, no doubt, so it was the next phase when Ravanelli came in. If you look at it, the reality is things started to slide when Stevie Mac left. It's not a coincidence that when he left, performances dipped.

'I wasn't part of the team that you would class as being the best team Derby had in those years, there's no argument from me about that. Two years prior Jim had his best team and if I was a couple of years older, I probably wouldn't have ever played. If you think about how good the centre-backs were, you wouldn't knock them out of the team. But the timing was right for me to play then. The team wasn't as good but it gave me and other young players the opportunity to play, so I was just happy to be playing and fighting to win games for Derby.'

Come the beginning of the season, a largely unchanged Derby squad to the one that finished the previous season made a dream outing. It took just 45 minutes before Ravanelli's shirt was being tucked over his head, a beautifully struck free kick followed by a Christie winner on the hour. The media fawned, *The Guardian*'s report stating, 'The Premier League is not a tough nut to crack. Simply throw some money at a proven top-flight goalscorer and watch the points pile up.' Derby had thrown money, but the points wouldn't come.

Defeat, two draws, three defeats. The previous season had started woefully, and things took a turn for the worse after the opening day this time around. Ravanelli had scored four, Burton and Christie one each. Nobody else had even come close and with five points on the board, it was once again time for a good old stare into the abyss. Defeats at Ipswich and Leeds, tunnel-shaking brawls at home to Leicester after Robbie Savage's last-minute penalty win. At least that day provided some emotion, with the Welshman hunted off the field by Craig Burley as police struggled to maintain order on the field.

'I don't hold grudges but Robbie was just annoying me as he did a lot of people and it all spilled over,' admits Burley. 'I remember grabbing him and at the final whistle, there was a bit of hustle and bustle in the tunnel. That was until Ade Akinbiyi took his top off and then there was a run for the hills because he got aggressive and he was huge. Jim said, "If we had as much fight on the field as we did in the tunnel we might have done better."'

Many would attribute that defeat as the beginning of the end for Smith, but it was just another jot in place on the road back to McClaren's departure. The addition of Colin Todd the following season helped to shore things up defensively but without McClaren at his side, Smith was weakened.

Youl Mawene, added to the side after McClaren had left for Old Trafford, never got to experience his methods but knew the rest of the squad felt things change for the worse at the Ramarena, 'I heard all the players mentioning that the departure of Steve was probably the big loss because in terms of first team coaching, the game was changing and you had to be more scientific and meticulous. Steve going to United was a massive loss when you look at where Derby came from, the BBG and promotion, all the way to near European level. Losing someone of his stature, he would always be tough to replace.'

McClaren had gone from strength to strength since his departure. He had three Premier League medals, one FA Cup and a Champions League on his CV. Smith's Derby had in the same time struggled to successive relegation battles and were already paving the way for a third.

Reluctantly, Pickering and the board were forced to act, making the most difficult decision of their ownership. The man who had delivered more than any supporter could ask for was dismissed. Well, he was more shunted at first. Offered the role of director of football, Smith was aghast. Instead of moving upstairs, he simply told them to, as imaginable when listening back to Smith, shove their job. 'I appreciated the chairman offering me the position but felt I had more to offer the club,' he told the media. 'I will always appreciate Derby County and their magnificent fans for everything they have done for me and my family.'

The loss of Smith was anticipated but never truly expected. Jim was Derby County not only to supporters and the watching world, but also to his squad, particularly youngsters like Lee Grant, who recalls, 'I remember sitting at home and hearing the news that Jim was no longer the manager and I was really shocked by it. Because of his character and his nature, he felt like part of the fabric of the football club, because of the way he was treated and adored, it felt like Jim Smith was Derby County and that was how it would always be.

'So when that changed, it was a real big eye-opener. A lot of senior players said it was normal and that it always happens but I had never experienced it. From that point it felt like BANG BANG BANG and it was happening constantly, so it was quite hard to adjust and figure out where you stood in all of it. I remember feeling uneasy about my position all the time in terms of where I fit in.'

Burley had by now been handed the captain's armband by Smith and built up a harmony with the manager, 'It was tough on Jim because the trapdoor was eventually going to open and he was going to get the sack. I knew when I went in there that the squad was threadbare and it was a minor miracle we stayed up for the time we did. But ultimately, we signed players who weren't strong enough. And it's no fun looking at the fixtures every week and saying, "Oh my God, we've got Arsenal. And then Liverpool." That's where we were.

'But I loved Jim. Nobody compares to him. I'd have run through a wall for Jim and I loved him. Even when he was calling me all the Fs and the Cs. He said in an interview once, which Eric Steele told me, he said, "Pound for pound, Craig is the best signing I've made in a long time." Not the best player but value for money. And then on the Monday, he came up and said, "Craig, did you see that interview? I was lying, you are the fucking worst!" But that was Jim.

'What I would have loved to have happened was to play for Jim for a few more years and Derby were successful in terms of staying up and pushing on again to where he had them before. But to play for a guy who was no-nonsense with no politics. Maybe Jim was getting old but it just didn't work after him.

'Sometimes I wonder if I made the right decision but I look at it as a privilege to work with somebody like that. He's got such a great reputation in the game and he was great. I remember he called us "moral cowards" one Monday. "You're all moral cowards," he said. "Oh, piss off, Jim." He could stand and shout at me but I'd still give him a hug afterwards.'

The man who provided the city with a new stadium, the most exciting players ever to wear black and white and the greatest seasons in recent history, was gone.

* * *

'Colin Todd was my dad's hero. I could never get anywhere near his level and I was almost in awe of him because I knew all about his background and history with the club.'

Chris Riggott's words can be echoed by any number of supporters or academy players at the club around this time. One of the greatest English defenders to play the game, Todd's name is synonymous with the success of the 1970s. Historian Andy Ellis was treated to a defensive masterclass on a weekly basis. 'As a player, he was unbelievable. He wasn't tall but he was superbly powerful and very, very quick. You'd come up against Kevin Keegan and they wouldn't get a kick. He'd tackle so cleanly and come out with the ball from it and then be able to pass it as well. There's nothing comparable today to what he was like.'

Now, it was his time. Someone had to have the unenviable task of following Smith and as it turned out, it was the assistant who made the step up. 'I got a call from Jim to say that he was leaving the club and I was taking over as manager,' Todd says. He had pedigree, having taken Bolton into the Premier League a year after Smith had guided Derby there, but departed early into the following campaign. Still, this was Derby, not Bolton. If anybody could transform the club to what they had been, it would be somebody who had been there during the very greatest days, right?

The fairy tale was over before it even began. First came defeat at Tottenham, followed by two draws and a 5-1 hammering at Middlesbrough. Derby were struggling badly and although Ravanelli struck in all four of those matches, the well of quality around him was running dry. Matters would only get worse as Pickering, by now aware of the potential financial catastrophe that could come within the next few months, sold Seth Johnson to Leeds for a record £7m. The switch, much discussed in later years having come at the height of Peter Ridsdale's debt-ridden tenure, was a major loss. Johnson, Delap and Eranio were effectively the midfield and now all were gone. Injuries to the likes of Mart Poom and Horacio Carbonari didn't help.

To counter these losses, Todd went on the offensive in order to try and mould his own side. These being days before the invention of the transfer window, he went with Smith's tried and tested model of focusing on talent from overseas first. Pierre Ducrocq and Luciano Zavagno arrived on 16 October from France, Benito Carbone next on a loan spell from Bradford. He combined nicely with Ravanelli (aided by the fact they resided together), the Italian duo achieving some success.

Then there was Francois Grenet, from Bordeaux for £2.2m. His signing sparked Todd to tell the media, 'The only reason he is not part of the senior French squad is the fact that Lilian Thuram is in that position.' Grenet would never play for France and come January, *The Guardian*'s Martin Smith wrote, 'For a defender, Grenet is not very good when players run at him. Like [Bristol Rovers' Nathan] Ellington, [Aston Villa's Lee] Hendrie had Grenet turning so much he looked like a French plait.'

There were rays of hope for Todd, his first win coming in the game after that November defeat at Middlesbrough, but they were too rare. Youl Mawene, who scored a bizarre winner against Southampton to get Todd off the mark, remembers how the loss of Smith changed the mentality of many of the squad, 'We were a family for a year and so with a family, if you make mistakes you take a slap and you learn your lesson and then you try and be better. But when the leadership changed, people looked after themselves instead of the group. People look after their contracts, they stop taking responsibility on the pitch to get on the ball, to do the extra bits and they would just say, "You know what, I'm just going to look after myself for this one."'

Without pushing into exactly who Mawene is referring to (Lee Morris also said something similar), Todd knows who he accounts it to, 'I was only there for three months and it was very difficult. When I say it was very difficult, I mean we had Ravanelli, someone who wasn't good in the dressing room and caused problems. I couldn't trust Fabrizio and I think the players lost trust in him as well because they felt, and this isn't my thoughts, but they felt he wasn't giving enough in terms of desire. He was a difficult man and even the supporters went against him at the finish.'

The two would never see eye to eye and it's ultimately this relationship that Todd attributes to his dismissal in January, after four wins in 15 games left the side rooted in the bottom three. 'I remember we went to Newcastle when Bobby Robson was manager and he said to us, "If you continue to play like that you won't be in a relegation battle." We missed a penalty and lost 1-0, then lost to Liverpool after another penalty that Ravanelli missed. Things were difficult but there were still signs that things could happen but we just never had the opportunity to see it out.'

As Todd looks back with the blame on the doorstep of Ravanelli, it becomes easy to use the Italian as a scapegoat for the problems Derby encountered over this and the following season. The wages signed off by Pickering would have been enough to sign five other first-team players and with the benefit of hindsight, the costs were the worst money the club have ever spent. But for all his quirks, Ravanelli was a man who cared, his pride dented.

Speaking with RamsTV, Danny Higginbotham remembers the Italian's reaction after the Liverpool penalty miss, 'Rav was in the changing room crying his eyes out. This was an unbelievable professional who was so emotional that he was crying his eyes out. I went to see him and said, "Are you okay?" and he just said, "No. I've let everybody down and I feel ashamed." That was a measure of how he took everything on his shoulders.'

The longer the campaign went on, the more the Italian became a scapegoat. Finding the net less frequently and picking up an array of injuries, his signature quickly went wrong. But as Burley remembers, the targeting of anger towards Ravanelli was misplaced: 'He is one of the greatest professionals that I have ever seen. I've seen the Italian boys like Zola, Vialli and Di Matteo at Chelsea and they're in the gym before training, in the gym after training. Rav was an absolute consummate professional. I've never seen anyone train like him. It was seven days a week.

'I get annoyed when I hear people say that when people like him were over here, they were just greedy money-grabbers. That angers me because he never had a day off. He was in David Lloyd in Derby on a Sunday. When Jim signed him, we didn't have a good enough team to give him what he needed to do the job. Him and I were just *persona non grata* really but I still speak to Rav now. He played up front with Vialli in that great Juventus side and there's a podcast out there where Vialli talks about how they were all desperate to beat each other to be first into the gym. That's how competitive that team was and he was of that mould. The guy worked his socks off every day.'

'When I got the sack,' Todd continues, 'I knew there was something happening and I smelt a rat. I was sitting at home, and we had Villa on the Saturday, but we weren't travelling until the morning of the game. Anyway, my phone went and it was my PA who said, "Have you heard about Ravanelli? He's not coming back until Monday." And I said, "Well I find that strange because he doesn't normally." I sat down and just said to my wife that there was something not right going on. What I did was give the players Monday off regardless of the result and we were sitting watching *Match of the Day*, it finished and then they did the little clips of the Sunday papers. And it said, "TODD TO BE SACKED". So yeah, I was right that something was happening.

'Anyway, I phoned the club secretary and he said he knew nothing about it. I eventually got through to Keith Loring who said it was all speculation. On that Sunday morning it was in all the papers and I couldn't get any answers on what was happening. But what I thought was happening, because Ravanelli didn't tell me he was back until Monday, I scuppered them because whatever they had planned on the Monday, which I'm convinced was to appoint Ravanelli as manager, because there was a lot of talk of it, I stopped it. I got a call on Monday from Loring and I got the sack over the phone. It can't be proved that Ravanelli was going to be appointed but it pointed in that direction because of the events that had taken place. I think I was right when I sussed out what was happening. It was unprofessional being treated like that and it hurt a lot.'

It's a point Loring and Pickering were quick to dismiss at the time, with the chairman telling the press, 'I want to make it absolutely clear no conversations have taken place with Fabrizio Ravanelli concerning a managerial or coaching position.' But there was no denying the conclusion that Ravanelli's presence and aura had been a factor in the decision to remove Todd. Not only had he been touted for the managerial role, his form on the pitch had deserted him.

As it happened, the next manager wasn't the White Feather. It was probably a blessing, considering his first conversation with Derby hierarchy led to him feigning ignorance when presented with the English language. It wasn't an opportunity that he denied in the press when put to him, but ultimately it was another familiar name who, five days after leaving Aston Villa to 'take a break from management', became the third permanent Derby manager in four months.

* * *

As a player, Todd was almost untouchable at the elite end. The newly appointed John Gregory wasn't far behind him. A midfielder with 103 appearances under the great Arthur Cox, his three years at the Baseball Ground saw the side rise from the doom of the Third Division back to the top. Todd may have won the league twice in his playing days, but Gregory was almost as fondly remembered for dragging the side through the divisions, starring alongside the likes of Bobby Davison and Phil Gee.

As a manager, he was a huge coup for the club. He'd taken Aston Villa into the UEFA Cup and reached an FA Cup final, while even having them top of the league midway through 1998/99 before a slump. Todd had come from within and struggled to motivate a side used to his methods on a daily basis, but Gregory came in on a clean slate.

'The day John Gregory came in, the whole club atmosphere changed and it needed to,' said Lee Morris, frozen out so often by Smith and Todd and hit by a barrage of injuries, who relished the opportunity of new eyes on the training ground. It was Morris who, when presented with a rare chance in Gregory's first match at home to Tottenham, took the bait. His first Derby goal, more than two years after signing against Tottenham, felt a major turning point for the club and for the season.

It should have been for Morris too, a youngster whose quality was evident to Gregory. Early on, there were hints at what the club could look like given time, and Morris saw a side to the manager the media didn't tend to portray, 'I felt if he'd have come along a couple of months earlier, we might have got out of it. John had belief in me. I'd been out in the wilderness but it was just little things that showed he was a top bloke. He sent my parents some flowers after

I scored my first goal just to say congratulations to them. I hadn't felt part of the team and suddenly, someone believed in me and I started scoring.

'I remember speaking to Chris Riggott a few years after about the experiences and the practices. We did all these drills at the BBG in his first week about desire, determination, aggression. He did this one where we had 22 attackers against our back four and we still couldn't score. It was brilliant from the off and as soon as he came in, we felt he was a big influence and he had an impact.'

Riggott adds further to the early days under Gregory, 'I remember his first day we jogged out at the Baseball Ground for our first training session and John was a real breath of fresh air. He was very energetic, upbeat, positive and I felt he was a real coup for the club. He'd been successful at Villa and he had them top of the league for 20-odd games and they were absolutely flying. To get him at the time, I felt like it was a good statement. It was very positive to begin with, and without being disrespectful it was nice to have someone who wasn't such an older guy.'

Age can have its benefits though, and that's what Gregory looked towards. Two experienced heads from under the Angel of the North journeyed south. First came Warren Barton, the blond bombshell of a defender who had formed part of Wimbledon's 'Crazy Gang' and Newcastle's resurgence under Bobby Robson.

'I was in my last five months at Newcastle under Sir Bobby Robson when I got a phone call to see if I was interested,' said Barton. Now residing in California as a pundit for Fox Sports, he came with a wealth of experience, from over 400 career appearances. 'Newcastle wanted to look at getting me into coaching but I still felt I could play, I was only 32 and I was very interested because I knew Derby was a great club with a great fanbase, great people and it was a no-brainer to have a conversation. I put the phone down from Bobby and then got a phone call from Keith Loring and John and within 20 minutes, it was all done.'

Following Barton was his then Newcastle colleague, Rob Lee. A 21-time England international who had just turned 36, his signature represented a short-term goal of safety as opposed to any planning for years in advance. Lee said, 'Derby were towards the bottom so I wasn't over keen to do it if I'm being honest. It wasn't until I spoke to John, he's the one that persuaded me. I went because I liked him. He said there would be a few more players coming in. I think Peter Gadsby was going to take over from Lionel Pickering too, so he said he'd have a few more players.'

That was the rumour at least. Had Gadsby been given the keys to the ground, much of what follows could have been very different. Gregory, appointed in part with the idea of a takeover, was under the impression he would have new ownership and more money to play with. 'When I arrived,' Lee continues, 'I was speaking to Gregs [John Gregory] and he was telling me that he'd be getting people in to help. He mentioned Jason Wilcox and Tim Flowers and a few other senior players. I'd been there about a week when he pulled me and said, "No one else is coming, Peter Gadsby couldn't get the club because Lionel wouldn't sell it to him."

'He was bashing his head against a brick wall because he had the financial problems of the club, the fact that Lionel Pickering didn't really want him there because he wasn't his guy. Once Gadsby couldn't get it, that was the start of the end.'

The doom and gloom would follow, but there was still that early hope. Barton, who himself had been influential in the capture of Lee, quickly took on the armband, and remembers, 'There was the feel-good factor from John getting the job and the likes of Fabrizio Ravanelli, Craig Burley, Mart Poom, good players and leaders at the club. John told me he needed someone to lead the team and be vocal and he knew I'd been a captain at every club I'd been to and been that kind of professional. I'm a positive person and I went in there from playing non-league to Champions League. The people around the club, Davo [Jon Davidson] the kitman, the canteen staff, they were just great people. We got to work straight away.'

Survival started to become more of a possibility as the Saturdays passed and Gregory's first away outing only raised levels of hope. The 3-0 victory over Leicester, ultimately relegated themselves under a cloud of financial problems, saw Morris strike again, with Branko Strupar and Georgi Kinkladze netting too. Then came the infamous visit of Manchester United to Pride Park.

It's a day that Gregory must curse, although not as much as Malcolm Christie. A full strength, table-topping United escaped with a point, Christie being denied a last-minute hat-trick and winner after being adjudged to have kicked the ball from the clutches of Fabien Barthez. It was a bitter blow and although followed soon after by victory at Bolton, was a turning moment, as Barton remembers, 'If only we had VAR then. That was a killer blow because even Sir Alex said we deserved to win. We played with energy, belief and we pushed them all the way. Malcolm got his goal and unfortunately, we didn't get the rub of the green and then you start to think, "Is it going against us here?" If you took a step back and said you'll draw with United who probably went on and won the league that season, you'd have taken that. But in the circumstances, it was a kick in the teeth because of the effort.'

A 3-1 March victory at Bolton was the peak of the resurgence. Gregory's new manager bounce had lifted the Rams to within two points of safety and with a cluster of sides within two to three points of one another, hope was on the horizon.

But, as experienced many more times within the following 18 years of Derby's tenancy at Pride Park, it's that hope that kills. With eight games to battle and two points to make up on those above came capitulation. Gregory's powers lost their effect and just a solitary point was picked up. A 4-3 defeat against struggling Everton started the rot, with a 1-0 loss at Middlesbrough proving to be the pivotal afternoon. Defeat at Southampton followed, with a particularly dismal afternoon at home to Newcastle leaving just the final nail to be hammered in. Despite a 2-0 lead through Morris and Christie, Robson's visitors snatched victory with a late Lomana Lua Lua strike. The afternoon was too much for many, including Gregory himself, whose fury left him as purple as his matchday attire as he was sent to the stands. One week later, with defeat at Anfield, the Premier League stay was over.

It was in the Anfield changing room that Lee began to see the troubles the club would face, 'We had a lot of foreign players who … let's just say they weren't playing to the best of their abilities. That's a nice way of putting it. That's the problem that John had, he could see the players on big, big money who weren't performing well and weren't that bothered, just picking up their money. I saw a lot of that around the club. I didn't notice them until the last game of the season. We'd been relegated and we had one half of the dressing room in tears – I hated it. The other half were smiling and joking around. I think afterwards, Gregs tried to get rid of them. He told them to find other clubs and we would go back up.'

Gregory, who by now had nothing to lose after failing to take the club out of the hole they were in, let his feelings be known to the media. 'I've got no time for part-time players and there have been problems this season within the club,' he said. 'On the football side it's been very unprofessional, but we have slowly changed things over the last ten to 12 games and I hope at the start of next season we will be better geared up. It all needs an overhaul.'

It could have been a much different situation. Since signing, Lee had lost only twice by more than one goal, despite coming up against every major player in the division. He said, 'I look back at the games we had and we could have easily stayed up. We were up against Man United, they got back to 2-2 with a dodgy goal. We played on the Sunday and went straight down to London to play Arsenal on the Tuesday night on TV, got narrowly beat 1-0. We were 2-0 up against Newcastle, lost 3-2. There were so many games where I look back and we could have got out of that. You look back now and we weren't that bad. For a team who was second-bottom, normally you get trounced a couple of times, but we didn't. We were always in the games.'

With mounting debts in excess of £20m, the likelihood that Gregory would be financially capable of completing that overhaul was slim, and barely had the R been placed next to Derby's name on the *Match of the Day* table than the situation worsened further.

Within two days of relegation on Merseyside, Derby's PFA Community Board representative Barton was forced into discussions about job losses. Pickering, committed to paying the likes of Ravanelli astronomical fees for at least another 66 weeks, was running out of money, as Barton was finding out all too late.

He remembers, 'We had a meeting on the Monday or the Tuesday that I got called in for just to let people know that in the next few weeks and even days actually, that there would be people losing their jobs. People who had worked for that club for over a decade were going to lose their jobs, people in offices would have their computers taken away because we couldn't afford to pay finance on them, that's how dire it was.'

Canteen staff, media personnel, those who had the behind-the-scenes tasks of bringing Pride Park to life on a Saturday afternoon were the first to be culled. Barton continues, 'We had players that were on phenomenal amounts of money and weren't in a situation where percentages would drop on salaries and would find it hard to move on. We had the parachute money but what really hit me was people losing their jobs. The big alarms were losing people in the offices and going to see these people who were in tears because you know, it's their club and it's a great town of great people. But people were becoming not only unemployed but unemployed in the job that they loved, which is very rare. It's rare to work in a place where you really enjoy it.'

Those roles were the easier to cancel, but the money they would be taking out of the club wouldn't even register when compared to those wearing the shirt. As in recent years with the Covid-19 outbreak, lower-paid staff on less secure contracts are always the first to be disposed of from the wage bill.

Barton remembers the situation he was faced with, 'I had to speak to the PFA about players' wages being deducted, salaries being deferred, in some of the cases players who had a good career would defer their wages for six months so players on lower wages could get their money. Young players like Chris Riggott and Danny Higginbotham who were living month to month, they had cars and it was a wake-up call for them. I remember sitting there with Danny and Chris and Malcolm who were linked to be moved away to other clubs, but they didn't know what would happen. I was having to sit there and say to these young players that at that moment, they might have to lose 50 per cent but would get it back and you could see faces drop because it was happening in such a short space of time.'

With no money, no knowledge of who would be in the squad come the first game of the season and Gregory's initial fire extinguished, no signs pointed towards a temporary stay back in the Football League.

HURLY BURLEY

RELEGATION TO the second tier provided new opportunities for the football club. Having barely been able to keep their head above water from the moment Steve McClaren left, the final confirmation of the drop was in many ways a blessing. Unless you're one of the elite sides, a Premier League dream has to come to an end at some point and Derby's six-year spell was just enough time to make their mark.

Three consecutive relegation battles did little to drive the club forward and with funds drying up and the elite signings made by Jim Smith in the past, the option to rebuild a division below should have been a welcome one. As it turns out, it would be only the first step back to a greatness that is still yet to be achieved.

In John Gregory, Derby at least had a manager capable of taking them back there. His signings offered a smidge of comfort that the stay would be short. With Rob Lee and Warren Barton, he'd surrounded himself with two generals who still had the hunger of life at a higher division. On the experience level, his squad still had it in abundance. Fabrizio Ravanelli remained (on £38,000 per week, without a pay cut, as Lionel Pickering stared into financial doom). So did Georgi Kinkladze, Craig Burley, Mart Poom, Horacio Carbonari and Branko Strupar. Derby had probably the biggest wage bill in the Football League, combined with the highest-paid manager. It looked like cuts would need to be made to stay afloat.

In actuality, Gregory lost nobody, looking to increase the squad rather than reduce it. Ravanelli told Gregory and the press he wouldn't be leaving, adamant he wanted to take Derby back to the top flight. It looked like the striking department would get even better too, as Nigerian hitman Yakubu prepared to sign. After he trained with the club for six weeks and scored in three behind-closed-door outings, Derby failed to secure a work permit for him. He went on to score against the Rams twice that season with Portsmouth, amassing cumulative transfer fees of over £25m in his career.

Even prized possessions like Malcolm Christie were still there on an opening day that would not hint at the commotion that was to come as Derby eased past newly promoted Reading. Christie, Ravanelli and Lee all scored, in an XI that still had seven of the individuals who had drawn at Sunderland in their final Premier League fixture.

'Derby showed why they are tipped to make a quick return to the Premier League as three of their stars scored to see off Reading,' read the *BBC Sport* report. It was as good as things would get, a false indicator of the season ahead.

Next up, Derby went to Gillingham and lost. And then Wolves put four past them at home. Defeats came at Rotherham and Leicester. The latter result brought more unwanted headlines for the club, with BBC Radio Derby commentator Graham Richards facing a barrage of complaints after stating that Leicester's Brian Deane 'collapsed like the World Trade Center'.

Burnley and Preston came to Pride Park and both took all three points. It was a shambolic beginning that left the side in the wrong half of the table after ten games and with the third worst defensive record in the division. The worry was that this was still the same make-up of the side relegated. Gregory's starting XI against Preston had five full internationals and they were still being eased past on home soil. Already, supporters had reached their limit.

But they were watching a group of players who had almost reached their own limit with the club. The final weeks of the 2001/02 campaign had seen Derby's finances come to a crash, players forced to defer wages and members of staff handed their P45. One of those was Lee Grant, at the time the third-choice goalkeeper who was about to be sped into first team proceedings. He recalls, 'There were all sorts of things going on in terms of the finances at the football club. I remember once being asked to defer wages at one stage when we were down at Ramarena. I remember the uproar because we'd just been relegated, and people's wages had been cut. It was a difficult time as a young player, you put your tin hat on and hope for the best while the older guys fight for it. You don't really have a clue what's going on because as a young lad, you're focused on "am I going to be playing on Saturday?" and that's the extent of where I was at as a young player. It was quite terrible for a large period.'

Grant would soon be playing because Mart Poom was to be sold. He had to be; such was the dire situation in the bank accounts of the club. The Estonian looks back, 'I think salaries were paid later. But we knew about the problems, players were sold. I was linked with different clubs and there were offers, even from Man United but the club didn't want to sell me, Everton too. We knew about the problem but then when we were relegated, there were offers but some other clubs want to get players cheap and Derby didn't accept it. The plan was to keep our best players and to try and go straight back up but when the season started in the First Division, the situation was worse than we expected. The financial problems kicked in quickly and they had to have a quick sale of players. But they were difficult times then.'

Poom would be loaned out to Sunderland before his switch became permanent. Then Brian O'Neil was sent on his way too. Derby were in disarray, but the situation was to become far worse.

* * *

As with 71 other Football League clubs, an organisation out of their control plunged Derby further into the financial mire. ITV Digital was supposed to be the future of sports broadcasting in the UK, with 88 live Football League games dedicated to its new ITV Sport channel. Clubs were promised money but it soon became clear that wasn't there. Having suffered relegation, Derby dropped into a division starved of any television money.

Bitter at losing access, Sky TV refused to host the channel. With under one million subscribers compared to Sky's five million, the new hope of British football was dying within its first months and with that came the prospect of clubs up and down the country following. Their £105m deal with the Football League was a bill that couldn't be paid and with that money set to trickle down the division, clubs who had already pledged funds behind signings under the assumption the agreement would cover it were left heavily out of pocket.

Derby were one of those and Lionel Pickering had to strip the assets. He'd already managed to get some of the highest earners off the wage bill, with Poom moving to Sunderland temporarily and a settlement arranged for Carbonari's return to Rosario after a loan at Coventry. As it became clearer that an automatic bounce back to the top flight wasn't on the cards, he was left with no other option than to rid the club of talent in the pursuit of financial respite.

By January 2003 the relationship between Pickering and Gregory was on the downward slide. Gregory had failed to keep the club afloat, Pickering had failed to financially back the manager. 'I gambled that if we kept our young stars and achieved promotion our financial problems would be over,' Pickering said at the time. 'But it was a gamble I lost.'

He'd gambled on survival. Then he'd gambled on a return. His luck was up though and again he was faced with the prospect of freezing wages. Gregory himself agreed to defer his, players again forced to follow suit. 'I took a little bit of bad advice at the time,' Higginbotham told Colin Gibson when speaking with RamsTV.

'Someone said I should hand my notice in. I would never forget that I handed it in and Craig or Brian O'Neil, they turned around and went, "What have you done? Do you know how badly you're going to come out of this?" I didn't think I'd be free to leave in two weeks; my biggest thing was I wasn't getting paid. I was seen, myself, Chris [Riggott], Malcolm [Christie], we were players that could bring money into the football club. I just thought that if I hand my notice in, they're going to pay me because they're not going to want to lose one of the few assets at the club. Lo and behold, everybody was paid.'

It's no surprise that the issues caused unrest. Youl Mawene was one of those who was told by Gregory he could leave but having packed up everything to come to Derby and work for Jim Smith, he wanted to stay at a place he considered home. 'I remember Danny refusing to take a delayed payment, Craig Burley and Brian O'Neil had problems with it too,' he recalls. 'They didn't feel that Warren was on the players' side and that's what happens. I mentioned how everything changes and from the family working for each other, it becomes the group of people where you're thinking, "Am I going to be represented properly?" Brian was ready to fight for the players and say, "Look lads, we need to be together. If none of us accept it's better because if someone does, it weakens our hand."'

Mawene, one of the younger and therefore lower-paid players, experienced one side of the financial strain. Burley's was a different matter, for his payments were halted more regularly than anyone else experienced. 'After one of the games I came in and someone said, "Craig, man of the match today" and I said, "Not bad for somebody who's not getting paid." That jolted one or two into seeing how messy the situation was,' the Scot admits.

The bold step worked for Higginbotham. Gregory fought to keep him but was powerless once a £1.5m bid from Southampton had been accepted. The defender would link up with Rory Delap, another man sold earlier to try and accumulate funds in the earlier stretches of the cost-cutting. Like Poom, the switch was only temporary to begin with but was always set to become permanent.

Riggott and Christie would join him on the move, opting for the other end of England.

Riggott looks back, 'I remember when me and Malcolm left for Middlesbrough, John was difficult. He wouldn't let us get our boots and pick up our stuff to leave because he wanted to block the transfer. The club had told us we had to go for the money, he was annoyed that the club was selling players from underneath him and he had no control. So, we couldn't physically get our stuff to drive up to Boro. That was strange.'

The duo would leave for a combined fee of £3m, with the potential to rise to £5m. For two England Under-21 internationals, it was a feeble amount. But such was the dire straits of the club, any money was simply a bonus. Riggott continues, 'Career-wise that was a good move for us, Boro were doing well, [Steve] McClaren was there who I knew with Steve Round. In fact, Steve was the reason for me going there. It was a good deal for Derby at the time but I didn't have any choice, it was just "you're going". It was extremely quick. With deadline day, I didn't have any conversations with an agent or anybody about moving, it was just out the blue. Now, I've put two and two together and realised they were after Malcolm and bolted me on at the last second, that's my guess, for some cover for [Ugo] Ehiogu and [Gareth] Southgate. Maybe they were after Malcolm and Derby probably said "for a bit more money, here's Chris as well". That's my guess of how it went down.'

The January sales, part of the first transfer window in British football, did the job of raising funds albeit only the start of what was required from Pickering's perspective. With Christie, Riggott, Higginbotham and Poom all sold, just over £5m had been put back into the club. Francois Grenet and Bjorn Otto Bragstad went too. With the side heading into February in 14th – although part of a congested mid-table that had them only four points short of the top six – these sales abandoned any hopes of the top flight. Carnage would follow.

* * *

'We didn't know the ins and outs. Me and Rob were driving in every morning wondering what would be happening today. It was a soap opera,' remembers club captain Warren Barton.

'It was one thing after the other, after the other and it was a new experience for me. I'd never been in a football club that had been deteriorating so quickly inside like that. Not the stadium, not the fans but the inside of the club. I'm talking about how it was deteriorating so quickly with people leaving, people getting the sack, this and that going on. It was so many aspects of what was going on.'

Barton had seen most of what there is to see in the game. Having progressed through non-league with Maidstone, an introduction to league football with Wimbledon's Crazy Gang leaves a thousand stories to be told. Two hundred games later he left for Newcastle, playing almost as many games and playing under Sir Bobby Robson on European weeknights. When all of the hysteria of his career should focus around these two intriguing clubs, the real circus was firmly in the goings-on in his final few months at Derby.

'From my point of view, what we should have done is take a leaf out of Leicester's book,' he said. Leicester, the only side in the division worse than Derby the year before, returned immediately, second behind champions Portsmouth. Like Derby, they kept their squad. Unlike Derby, they used them all.

Barton continued, 'Because of the situation financially, the club said to five of the senior players "go and find yourself a club next season because you're not going to play", which wasn't the right thing to do. Because they were on big money, nobody was going to take them because of what they were on.

'So instead, and I've spoken to John afterwards about this, we should have come back as a group, all of us, instead of isolating five or six people, we should have come back and said, "We're going to make it work." I was a senior player and friends with them and for them to be told to go, they're not welcome and won't be playing, with all due respect I might have done the same. There was a real bad vibe around the place and I'm walking in and seeing Craig Burley and seeing Fabrizio, he was a bit different. But I got on well with Craig and I said that we needed them.

'It's great to let young players play but because the league is so demanding and so physical, you just don't get a chance to breathe. It's not like the Premier League where people can get on the ball and play, you don't get that chance. It's the toughest league week in, week out and results didn't start happening. We started going down the table and the atmosphere, the fans were rightly upset. We were going into a situation with young players who were finding it hard.

'The likes of Lee Grant and people like that had been thrown into a situation, but you were treading water. All I was trying to do was what I'd always done and stayed professional and helped everyone out, along with the likes of Rob Lee to do the best we could, but we were treading water. The problem is we had five of them who would have made a difference who weren't picked.

'And let's not beat around the bush, a couple of them said "sod it, I'm not going to play, I'm injured" and they had that around the football club. That was hard to have because we needed them. There would have been a better atmosphere and some good players, good professionals and we might have bounced back. But that's the manager and the club's decision ultimately.'

Gregory's problems from isolating individuals would lead in part to his eventual downfall. Craig Burley had slowly found his way back into first team plans as Gregory grew in desperation. But come February and another stint out of the team, he revolted.

Already that week the manager was in the news for the wrong reasons, Aston Villa's Graham Taylor telling the press that Gregory had been in for some of his former players, the most notable being Juan Pablo Angel. But when the noise and vociferous criticism came from one of his most established players, things took a dark turn.

'I don't speak to John Gregory now,' Burley confessed in an interview with the *Daily Mirror*. 'I have never had a good relationship with him, but now I wouldn't give him the time of day. I won't talk to him.

'If the manager wanted me to play and came to ask me, he would have to be quick because I would be walking past him in the corridor as he said it. I had little respect for him when he started here and it has completely gone now. I will play for Derby County FC, but I will not play for John Gregory.'

Burley rounded off with a hit out at the financial situation, 'I have not been paid for the past five months, that makes ten months' money they owe me, and something has got to be sorted out soon.'

The *Mirror* was not the only media outlet he vented his side of the story to. One day later, BBC Radio Derby's Ross Fletcher was party to an interview conducted 45 minutes before kick-off against Sheffield Wednesday, in which Burley went on to further divulge his take.

Fletcher recalls, 'He didn't get along with John and it was pretty obvious, to the point that Craig ran his mouth off one too many times and he banished him to the youth team but also revoked his parking pass at Pride Park. He wasn't going to play games and he wasn't even made to feel welcome at the stadium itself but Craig being Craig decided to come on to Radio Derby on a Saturday afternoon 2.15pm slot and tell us all about his side of the story. It was this explosive 15 minute interview with Colin Gibson, visceral really, where he was ripping into John Gregory and making a few claims about where he thought it was going wrong with him.'

Opting to give Gregory a right to reply, it quickly became apparent he knew nothing of the interview, setting Fletcher on a path towards perhaps his most terrifying moment in journalism: 'He tried to shut it down really quickly and so I asked him another question about it. And then an even harder question because he hadn't answered the substantial allegations made by Craig, but he hadn't heard the radio interview. And he walked off, walked out of the interview. I'd never had and still haven't had someone walk off and he did.

'I wrapped up and took it back to Colin but John hadn't walked fully away, he'd just walked around the corner where I couldn't see him. He heard me wrap up, came back in and closed the door and then got in my face. He said, "If you ever ask me any more than one question on a subject like that again" and left it at that. He gave me a few more stern words and stormed off. I was pretty shaken up. But a week later, he'd forgotten all about it. He was under such extreme stress that he probably had so many of these run-ins.'

The Burley saga continued. 'There's about a thousand stories of John Gregory that I won't go into,' laughs the Scot. 'He thought I was swinging the lead and that I was putting on the injury so I didn't have to play. I went to the club doctor on two occasions for injections into my Achilles, tried to train again and it didn't go away. John got it into his head that I wasn't interested. I had to have it operated on so at the end of 2001/02, I went to a specialist at Chelmsford, had my Achilles opened and cleaned up. But do you think you'd have an operation if there's nothing wrong with you? Nobody does that.

'The club sent me to Lilleshall to rehab there, a place that is for players of clubs in the lower divisions that don't have the medical facilities or the nous or the personnel to cope with some of the injuries, not for Premier League clubs. They were happy to send me there though to get me out of the way. The management got it in their head that some of us were not trying or bothered and it was crazy.'

Burley was not alone. Branko Strupar suffered immensely during his time with injuries and under Gregory, two operations on his abductor failed to fix the issue. Burley continued, 'We all felt sorry for him because he was so depressed when he would come into the training ground. He couldn't get to the bottom of this problem so we missed his physicality and goals. He was another straight up and honest guy who would not shirk his responsibilities.'

Isolating senior players and losing control of the squad, it was the beginning of the end for Gregory.

* * *

The final days and weeks of John Gregory's time as Derby County manager were a sad affair. Already difficult enough with abuse from his own players, sales of his star assets and the fact that he wasn't even being paid, the ending only made the situation ever the more depressing.

Neither Gregory nor Keith Loring wanted to speak on the matter. Gregory explained his reluctance to damage the reputation of the club when it had nothing to do with those currently there. For Loring, the mention of Gregory's name was swiftly cut off with, 'I don't want to talk about that.'

Without even factoring in the Burley abuse, Gregory's name was being dragged through the mud in December 2002. The FA confirmed it had launched an investigation into Gregory over his transfer dealings back during his days at Villa Park. The investigation was launched after Villa conducted one of their own, signalling a flurry of transfer activity that they deemed to be worthy of further scrutiny. Gregory denied the allegations.

The highest-paid manager in the division (when he was being paid at least), it would be little surprise if the opportunity to remove Gregory on a cost-cutting basis would have been thought of at the time. Gregory was on an income of £20,000 per week and as the club's debts spiralled past £30m, it was an amount that simply could no longer be afforded.

Then when Burley's comments are considered and as Gregory began to turn on his own squad, the case for dismissal mounted. Burley went in search of legal backing after claiming his injuries had been mistreated by the manager. Alan Walker, an expert in rehabilitation, built the case. As well as claiming Burley's problems were worsened by the regime, he made a case for Strupar too. Gregory had claimed Strupar wouldn't partake in a reserve team fixture because he 'didn't fancy it', supporting Burley's earlier claims on Gregory questioning whether players were truly injured.

By the time Burley was back fit, personal vendettas stopped Gregory selecting senior individuals. Burley said, 'I'd won more than 50 caps for my country, I'd played at World Cups, I'd won a title with Celtic. When it gets to that level of stupidity, you're only going to make people angry. I ain't got an issue now but it just doesn't help. Getting into fights with senior players, it always ends badly for the manager. He ended up getting in these fights with players, things got messy off the field and extremely messy on it.

'I'm a very fair person and not political, but once somebody starts digging in against me, I'll dig in and fight them. That's what happened and it did nobody any favours. John got on my wrong side, I got on his wrong side and it was survival of the fittest.'

Burley, Strupar, even Ravanelli were blacklisted. Burley recalls one particularly standout level of pettiness, 'Ravanelli and I pitched up one Saturday morning at Pride Park to get on the bus to go to a game and we were told to go home. I think John had just left; he was suspended but I think he was still passing instructions. We arrived and we were just told to go home. Ravanelli was just like, "This is incredible, I've never seen anything like this before." I went back to Rav's house but he couldn't get his head around it because he'd never seen politics like it before.'

The relationship between Gregory and the board was by now non-existent, so it was merely a matter of time before Pickering bit the bullet, particularly as a drop to the Second Division was growing in possibility. One reason would have been enough, but there was a rap sheet forming including players turning, allegations of bungs, allegations of mistreatment and a broken relationship with the board. Gregory was suspended on 22 March. A club statement simply said, 'These allegations have had a major adverse effect on the club and, in the light of these and in order to expedite a thorough, fair and objective investigation, the club has decided to suspend John Gregory while the investigation is undertaken.'

It was another sorry end to the tenure of a man with such a storied history with the club. Smith's end was acrimonious, Todd's time in charge a disaster for both club and individual. Now came Gregory, a symbol of Arthur Cox's great side, who would lose the legendary status he had built up 15 years previously.

But removing Gregory wasn't straightforward. Originally suspended pending investigation, there was never any prospect of him returning. He wanted no return; neither did the club. The issue was that Gregory would still be owed hundreds of thousands of pounds. What began from there was a long, complex legal battle.

Warren Barton witnessed the sad ending first-hand. Having been the voice of the changing room as the PFA rep, he'd worked a bond with Gregory and understood his frustrations at the direction of the club. He said, 'There was supposed to be a new ownership coming in and I think John had been promised that early on in his contract negotiations. There would be money but it didn't materialise. Then there was frustration. And the coaching staff he had behind him were brilliant, they were trying to generate a good atmosphere and be positive, but John was a big character and a big personality.

'Things would be starting all over again and we didn't have the financial side to do that, we didn't have the atmosphere in the club to do that, and it was trying to get to the end of the season to regroup and refocus. Then the ones who are out of contract would leave and be wished well and we'd try to survive with some of the parachute money to get a promotion push. You see what happened with Leeds, clubs like Ipswich who fall out and never ever look like they're going to bounce back again. John wore his heart on his sleeve and wanted to do the right thing. He felt for the club but obviously from what he'd been promised, it hadn't materialised.'

Of those on the staff side, Billy McEwan was later brought back to the club upon Gregory's suspension, Derby claiming his dismissal a month before was 'unmerited'.

* * *

Next would come a successor. Derby needed a man able to steady the ship until the end of the campaign and for that, they again turned to experience. 'They were looking for a caretaker manager at the time as John Gregory was in dispute with the club. I don't know all the details of that, but they asked me to come along, they were near the bottom of the table with a few months left,' said the chosen man, George Burley.

Burley's capture was enormous for a First Division side in dire straits. Though he'd struggled to take Ipswich back to the top flight, his record offered hope. A sturdy head, respected in the game and able to utilise the experience at the club, Burley was installed on an interim basis until the end of the campaign.

'It was more of a short-term opportunity for us and I knew little bits about the club. Craig [Burley's nephew] played there and they were like Ipswich in terms of size. I fancied the opportunity so I took it over in the short term and it was a case of just keeping the club from getting relegated,' he said.

It would be a task. Taking over a week after Gregory's suspension, Burley inherited a side who had lost five matches on the spin. November hopes of the play-offs had spilled into April ambitions of merely survival. He arrived into a side six points above the bottom three with seven games left to play.

He didn't waste any time. His first two games brought victories over Norwich and Wimbledon and despite rounding the campaign off with three straight defeats, Burley had done the temporary job. 'I suppose there was always the possibility of it being extended but it was an opportunity for me to get back into managing and progress, so it was an ideal situation that didn't tie me for a longer period. I was lucky to then be enabled to be extended.

'I spoke to Craig, but I knew Derby were a top club beforehand. I played against them as a player so many times, Brian Clough as manager and Roy McFarland and Colin Todd too. I played at the Baseball Ground loads of times and between myself and Derby it was always very competitive because we were both going for league titles and playing in Europe.'

Burley signed an extended contract. That was one aspect Pickering could find peace over. But he still had Gregory to deal with. It took until the end of the campaign for Derby to conclude their investigation and to the bewilderment of absolutely nobody, Gregory was sacked. He chose to appeal – and then to sue.

Barton left early in the following campaign but, surprisingly, amid all the turmoil and at that stage of his career, it's a spell he has no qualms over: 'I never regretted joining Derby. I had chances at Charlton and Aston Villa as well, but I really had a good feeling at Derby. I was proud to be their captain, proud to play for the club and when George took over the following year, he didn't want me for whatever reason, but that's life.

'To go and play for someone like Derby was a privilege and an honour. If you'd asked me if I'd rather it was better circumstances then yeah, no doubt about it, but I enjoyed the club. The fans had a different situation, but I tell you what, it was the biggest learning curve of my career being in there, particularly the last eight or nine months, and the fans don't hear that.

'They voiced their disapproval against me and Rob because we were the senior players, but we took it on the chin. People have got to realise though that every single day we were dealing with difficult and different situations.

'It was just putting fires out, and I was supposed to be a player. Not a counsellor, a footballer, not a secretary. But that's part of being a senior player.'

The end of the campaign marked the early days of Gregory's case. His defence centred around the club looking to save money through his sacking, presenting a 400-page document in his defence. His solicitors said, 'The decision to dismiss John Gregory for serious misconduct was clearly premeditated and dishonourable. It was done despite compelling evidence that he had done nothing wrong whatsoever.'

It took almost a year for the case to conclude, culminating in a settlement for Gregory and an amicable final statement from the manager unceremoniously humiliated by the club. After accepting a sum to be paid in instalments over several years, a statement on his behalf read, 'The club has agreed to pay the settlement sum in order to enable the club and its present board to concentrate on football matters and in particular the present fight against relegation. John Gregory bears no ill will towards the present board, the club or its supporters and wishes them well.'

It was an unusually amicable end that left Gregory in the clear, his sacking shone up as more of a cost-cutting measure, although with his relationship with the squad by now toxic, it was an understandable move.

The reason for the pleasant statement was clear though. By the time matters had been concluded a year later, there were new men at the helm. Lionel Pickering was ousted for the princely sum of £3 and Derby were under new ownership.

DERBY (TWINNED WITH PANAMA)

TAKE TWO for a shot at the Premier League and this time, in much more comfortable circumstances. John Gregory's disastrous spell was a thing of the past and so was the iconic Raynesway, finally replaced by land on a par with the modern bowl that is Pride Park. Moor Farm opened its doors for the first time in the summer of 2003, the early stages of a plan to develop Derby County's facilities into one of the finest across Europe.

It would be only one fraction of the changes achieved over the coming months, alongside a new permanent manager in George Burley, an entire new set of players, a new ownership and a new pathway to disaster.

Burley had steadied the ship and was rewarded with a two-year deal for his work. His weeks in the interim role allowed him a look into the squad but he was all too aware of the restraints he would be under. In the final weeks of 2002/03, he promised Craig Burley a one-year contract as he stepped up his return from fitness. But as the midfielder recalls, 'I got a phone call from someone at the club saying I would be getting a free transfer. It's not what George was told. Ultimately it was the right decision to try and get some of us guys out because it had been a bad time and it needed freshening up.'

The former Celtic man wouldn't be alone in leaving. Georgi Kinkladze and Fabrizio Ravanelli went too, the latter after agreeing to a 25 per cent pay cut to his wages in the final six months of his contract. He continued to be paid what the club owed him years after his departure and even his retirement. Branko Strupar, Rob Lee and Warren Barton followed. In their place would come experience, paired with a long, endless list of disappointing loan signings.

Michael Johnson arrived to fill the defensive hole. In front of him was a new skipper. 'My contract was coming to an end at Villa, I was getting to the ripe old age of 33 I think and had a few injuries which was frustrating for myself, because when I was fit, I played,' said Ian Taylor, the key capture by Burley. Still good enough for the Premier League, his signing would go on to significantly benefit the youngsters quickly integrated into the first team.

He continued, 'Villa didn't renew my contract, I got a few offers but I had a young family so really wanted to stay local. I had offers from Reading and QPR, but it was just the locality of it and the prestige of the club. I spoke to George and there were a lot of changes going on, but he wanted me to come and be one of the old campaigners to help steady the ship because a lot of big hitters had gone. They had to start playing some of the younger players so they just needed a few old heads to come in and steady it.'

Of the younger players Burley was forced to inject into the first team, Lee Grant had already enjoyed a taste of first-team life, 'We saw it as a natural progression. It wasn't like it is now where if you make it through it's a huge achievement, it was our rite of passage and it was what was going to happen. When we suffered relegation, it almost forced their hand to play younger players. That first year after relegation there were so many exits out the door, it felt like I was in the first team with 50 per cent guys I was used to playing with in the reserves, if not more.

'We all moved up together. At one stage I remember playing in the Championship with myself, Pablo Mills, Lewis Hunt, Izale

McLeod, Marcus Tudgay, Tom Huddlestone, which is already more than half a team that has come through the academy. That would be amazing now but it felt quite normal at that time, but the club was obviously going through a huge amount of change after relegation.'

They would be the core that Burley would build his side around. 'It can be difficult to build your own side,' reflects the Scot on his summer months. 'There had been a difficult time before I arrived but people like Kinkladze I got on really well with. Kinky, Ravanelli, there were a number of players there that I enjoyed working with, but it turned out the finances had to be lowered and the type of money they were on, the club couldn't afford to pay.'

Even with the incoming Taylor and Johnson, Derby's first team was thrown together and there was no bigger evidence of that than the opening day. With a handful over 20,000 within Pride Park, the enormity of the task at hand was made painstakingly obvious as Stoke City eased to a 3-0 win. Stoke had just finished 21st.

Derby crashed to the bottom of the table. There was perhaps no clearer indication of the situation of the club than a glance over kit numbers. Derby had no strikers of any substance, so Johnson took the number ten shirt. Johnson was a central defender. In came Matthias Svensson on loan, arriving within days of Junior.

Junior was a strange specimen. A quick turn of the head could have led you to believe Ravanelli was back, albeit with more of a blonde tint. The Brazilian struck a hat-trick against Derby in his final game for Walsall, more than enough of an incentive to bring him to Pride Park. Originally, this international pairing worked. Not wonders, but it worked.

Junior's goal against his former club handed the Rams their first win of the campaign six games into it. Then he scored in a victory over Watford and a draw at Nottingham Forest, hinting at a man capable of providing the firepower necessary to drag this young side forward. Then he got a cruciate ligament injury, Svensson was recalled from his loan by Charlton Athletic, and the problems started once again.

* * *

Derby were in the bottom three at the start of 2004 and they deserved to be there. Burley may have still been popular with supporters, having provided more stability than Gregory, but that was not transferring into results. Loanees would come, loanees would go. In total, 36 players wore the black and white in the campaign, Burley struggling to find any fluidity in a side lacking quality.

His saving grace came after Christmas. The academy had bolstered his side and as Huddlestone and Grant grew in confidence, their effect on the side became stronger. Huddlestone may have been 16 but his influence further forward began to impact matches, while ahead of him the growing Marcus Tudgay saw more match action.

It was experience the side needed though. Youl Mawene was still only 24 but having been reinstated under Burley, he became the calmness at the back alongside Johnson. The Frenchman said, 'I was fortunate because if Derby had a budget, they would have just told me to go and find a club. While the season wasn't as glorious as beating Man United, it had to be done. George had a look at what was there after John and instead of scaling down, he piled some players on. Johnno, a couple of Spanish and Brazilian lads. George found that right balance that was about good, well rounded professionals, people who knew how to run a changing room like Ian Taylor, it brought togetherness and camaraderie. Six months earlier, I'd have been gone.

'I had to lead a little bit to some extent more than I was used to, you'd let Ian Taylor do the talking on the pitch, but I had to now do some talking. We had to talk, to coach the youngsters like Pablo [Mills], be more hands on with some of the lads and I loved it. We were still playing in front of 20-odd thousand and no it wasn't the Man Uniteds we were playing but it was still crazy. I have a good memory of that season. It was like a rebirth, where I grew out of a young man's shell because before that, it was all up for grabs. I could have never returned to football from the injuries but that season,

I needed it. I was so grateful to George for looking into me and seeing potential and I'm fortunate that I was able to play my part in keeping the side afloat.'

Mawene would go on to be crowned player of the season before leaving for Preston. He continued, 'I remember the club appointed a technical director that came in who oversaw recruitment and there were a lot of free agents in summer. Big Martin Keown was rumoured from Arsenal and there were a lot of players that I heard they were in for at the time.

'The summer for me was a shambles. I remember leaving Derby for Portsmouth to head across the Channel to my home town Caen that summer without an agreement with the club. We hadn't agreed on anything. I had a feeling that it wasn't going to go well because the relationship with my agent and the technical director was at breaking point. He thought they could get more for their money, I think I was on £2,500. Very often when you look at those things, it's a case of the player thinking he can get more, the club think they can do better. Both are double bluffing each other to the point where the player ends up losing.'

Before Mawene was crowned, he would be joined by individuals who would make his life a little more comfortable. Burley added Jeff Kenna from Blackburn, but four additions at the top of the field mattered the most. Bundesliga winner Marco Reich joined in January from Werder Bremen, then came Manel, the towering Spanish forward from Espanyol who struck three times in a white shirt. His capture filled the Junior void after months of trying and he was soon able to unite with a man of a very different stature.

'I heard rumblings that Derby were interested, Michael Johnson gave me a ring to say, "What's this about you coming to Derby?"' said Paul Peschisolido, who had made quite the name for himself in English football over the years. Sick of being labelled as a super sub at Sheffield United, the opportunity of a permanent starting berth appealed to the diminutive Canadian.

He continued, 'I saw that Derby were struggling in the bottom half, but I'd spoke to Johnno and he said how amazing the facilities were, "It's a great bunch of lads, we're bringing in players and if you come, we'll stay up and this place will rock." I met with George Burley, he sold the dream of the club and it happened very quickly. I signed on the Friday in time for the Saturday match, scored early and then we had the big derby which was something else.'

Peschisolido scored four times in his first three games. In terms of league goalscorers, he was already fourth on the list following a winner against Rotherham, one in a defeat at Watford, then two after calling upon a favour from the footballing gods – the Kenco cup.

In the previous season, Peschisolido had ended Nottingham Forest's hopes of reaching the Premier League with a goal in the play-offs. This time he compounded their misery.

'Aside from maybe Darren Bent's goal with the beach ball [for Sunderland against Liverpool in 2009], this was the strangest. It's a windy day, there's a bit of debris, but taking all that away; it's against Forest. The ball is lifted on to this Kenco cup and poor old [Forest goalkeeper] Barry Roche kicks three-quarters of the cup,' said Peschisolido of his bizarre goal.

Taylor had opened the scoring and Peschisolido added a third before half-time. Forest got two back but a late strike from Tudgay sealed a famous victory.

Manel, Kenna and Peschisolido were all astute captures by Burley. The experience was needed. But creatively, there wasn't much for him to work with in the first five months of the campaign. For all of the importance that these three had, it was an unassuming youngster from Merseyside who saved Burley's job.

'Leon was a fantastic player. From day one I always felt he had the potential to be a player at a top Premier League club,' recalled Taylor. The addition of Leon Osman is still the greatest loan capture to arrive at Derby. 'He was just a young lad in from Everton and nobody had heard of him,' Taylor laughs. 'But his close control and creativity in training was just fantastic and the longer it went on, the more you thought, "How can this lad not be in the Everton first team?" But, and I can't remember how old he was, you could only put it down to his age. You knew he was a real player straight away.' Michael Johnson wrote in *Match of My Life: Derby County*, 'Leon was the main reason we stayed up.'

Osman was the difference between relegation and survival. His intricacy and comfort on the ball was a perfect foil for the slower pace Taylor and Huddlestone operated at, offering a calmness well above his years. Three goals in 17 appearances came in two vital victories and a draw.

The blend of youth and experience captured by Burley in those closing months were the difference. 'You need that balance,' he says. 'Of course, you want to bring those young players through, but they learn from experienced players. Being a manager, you're trying to develop the squad and working within your range as far as the budget is concerned. But I always think I enjoyed bringing them through and my strength was bringing them through. It was that fine balance that young players have to learn off good experienced pros which was the case.'

Though within the changing rooms it was a far different place to the one a year before, it was still a horror campaign. A last-day defeat at the soon-to-be MK Dons meant that Derby had survived by a single point. It was their closest scrape with the Third Division since dropping down two decades earlier.

* * *

On the face of it, the centrally located English city of Derby doesn't have much in common with Panama, the nation linking Central and South America. Sure, we can claim Derbados all we like, but it doesn't quite stack up. In the autumnal months of 2003 though, the two became intertwined; we just didn't know it yet.

Lionel Pickering was broke. His debts had topped £30m, payments to staff were hit and miss and financially, he had no way of achieving what he had in his first six years as chairman. Having taken the club he loved back to the upper echelons of English football, he was at risk of now guiding them right to the bottom, if they would even exist at all.

The financial situation was so poor that Pickering put the club on the market in the summer for £8m. 'If you've got £8m, you've got Derby County – but I'd listen to £5m,' he was quoted as saying in *The Telegraph*. 'We could be very close to a deal, because someone rang me yesterday and they are seeing their bank today.'

There was clamour for Peter Gadsby, by now out of the club, to make a play for ownership. Rumours had started to swirl in the summer of 2002, for a reported fee of £15m. 'The significant thing was we were running out of money,' Gadsby recalls. 'We all knew it. Andrew Mackenzie was then the finance director who Lionel relied upon, but he was not helpful to Lionel. They were negotiating and before we knew who they were, they were going to buy Lionel's shares. We had said, me and John Kirkland, that we wouldn't put any more money in because you won't give us these shares and the club is going downhill.'

Pickering had to sell and having failed to do so at £15m, and then at £8m, slowly faced a reality where the decisions would fall out of his clutch. And that became the reality on 20 October 2003. With a debt to the Co-Operative Bank topping £27m, the organisation called in the receivers. Within hours, Derby County were under new ownership. Immediately, suspicions began.

Jim Wheeler became a prominent figure in Derby circles. A lifelong supporter, he made it his mission to find out more over the coming years. For now though, he simply felt sorrowful about the situation the club had worked itself into. He says, 'There were a lot of people who expressed an interest in taking over the club and a lot of them, when we looked into their history, were extremely dodgy. People like Bryan Richardson who had been involved at Coventry, and they were the sort of people who had no history with Derby County and to us, we saw them as opportunists to make money out of the club and supporters.

'Lionel, bless his heart, was a true Derby supporter and bankrupted himself to try and do the best for Derby County. But he made bad business decisions towards the end. He could have left with some of his fortune but I think he both wanted to get the best deal for him and do the right thing for Derby County. He still wanted to go along to games and he was reluctant to make decisions which in hindsight, would have been the best for the club. It just spiralled out of his control to the final point where the club could not meet its debts and the bank foreclosed and found a buyer themselves. And unfortunately, the Co-Operative Bank didn't make the best decision at that point.'

Derby fell into the hands of the new chairman, John Sleightholme, a barrister from Yorkshire. The frontman of a new consortium (named Sharmine Limited), Sleightholme had little history in business but possessed a clean reputation to present the new project.

In a hastily arranged press conference, he told the waiting reporters, 'There was a very substantial indebtedness to the Co-op bank, over £26m. There was an indebtedness of £4.75m, approximately, to Lombard Finance. The position is we were enabled to arrange finance through a group of individuals who wish to remain anonymous that wish to support the current board and Derby County and with the benefit of those sums of money, we repaid Lombard the full amount of the indebtedness to them. We have paid back the Co-op £10m, we have restructured the loans with the Co-op into two tranches, each of £8m and we have arranged for a £4m overdraft facility from the Co-op.'

All well and good by this point. Derby had new owners; the debt was to be sorted. As the club fell into receivership, checks were done on Sleightholme, and his fellow consortium members, Jeremy Keith and Steve Harding. 'They have been well satisfied that the new consortium consisting of myself, a barrister by occupation, Mr Keith, who is a finance expert and business strategist, and Mr Harding, who is a marketing and communication entrepreneur, have the necessary combined skills and acumen to take this club forward,' said Sleightholme.

Harding was a closed book, with little information on his background. Keith had been involved with Portsmouth years earlier, leaving the club a day before a winding-up petition was drawn. He also had a string of failed businesses behind him. Sleightholme's only involvement in sport was with an organisation in Edinburgh named Finance for Football. There he worked with one other director, a man named Murdo Mackay, who we will get to in a couple of seasons.

But first to the money, where there was just one hitch; nobody knew where it was coming from. Luckily, one man did. Journalist David Conn had already made a name for himself working for *The Independent*, investigating the murkier, hidden world of football. Two weeks after the takeover, he got to the bottom of just where the funds to take over had come from: Panama.

* * *

It was a fact Sleightholme had been keen on hiding, until registering details with Companies House. The ABC Corporation had previous in English football, the mystery financiers of QPR at a similar time. Conn wrote, 'The Panamanian Consulate in London proudly advertises on its website that a principal advantage for people registering "offshore corporations" in the country is that the Republic operates "the most secure confidentiality laws to be found anywhere". Companies must name officers, but these are usually lawyers working for the owners, whose identity does not have to be disclosed, and the companies do not have to file accounts or regular financial information.'

It was a startling discovery and the first inclination that Derby's new owners were, well, skint. None were millionaires, none had the significant monies to support a football club and none really knew a thing about the sport. Suspicions would only grow and it was at this point that Derby supporter group RamsTrust came in.

Wheeler remembers, 'Every time somebody expressed an interest in the club, we would send our talons out, talk to other clubs through the network and find out as much as we could about the potential suitors for the club and if it was in Derby's best interests or not. Now, Keith, Sleightholme and Steve Harding, were never public knowledge until the day they turned up at the ground and said "right, we've taken over for a quid each".

'At that point, we went into overdrive trying to find out everything we could about them. Sleightholme's only history was that he was involved in the legal side of the Hillsborough disaster as one of the legal guys on that. Harding had some involvement in clubs but not in a big capacity and never really did anything. I'm not quite sure why or how he got involved in this. Maybe he was easily led.

'But Jeremy Keith, if you look at his history, had a number of previous businesses which it's difficult to see any successes in. And that was the concern, none of them had the money. The journalists and us at meetings regularly asked, "How are you going to take the club forward?" and they always said the plan wasn't to invest. "The plan is to run the club well and not make the same mistakes that Lionel made." Now the mistakes Lionel made were putting too much money in to try and make a success and they made it pretty clear from the start that they weren't going to do that.'

Not only had they no background or money, they immediately drew the wrath of 1,000 supporters having claimed all shares in the club. Andy Ellis recalls, 'Lots of us long-term lads, going back to the 1980s, were actually shareholders at the club as well. That was one way of getting the club through the time. But overnight those shares became worthless and it upset a lot of people. People put a lot of money into the club just to say they owned a bit of it. Shares varied from £25 up to several thousand and they lost that money.'

Two months into 2004, Keith and Harding sat down with RamsTrust to discuss their situation. Had they put any personal money in? 'No.' How much had they paid for it? '£3.' Three pounds bought Derby County. For the price of a matchday programme, you could have bought the football club – at least if you had Panama-based connections.

The meeting got worse, with Keith and Harding drawing ire. They had already brought Murdo Mackay into the club, the soon-to-be-announced director of football. Five months into their regime, the consortium was being sussed out. 'Good luck,' the minutes concluded, 'you're going to need it.'

MURDO

FIVE YEARS had passed without a season free of relegation concerns and life had been increasingly sucked out of the club. Pride Park, for the most part, had experienced continuous turmoil after the initial success Derby achieved at their new home. And having barely clung on to their spot in the Championship – as well as enduring conflict that would only escalate in the coming months – it looked inevitable that the battle would continue into George Burley's second full season. Leon Osman, so pivotal in keeping the side afloat, returned to Everton where he quickly found a permanent home in David Moyes's first-team plans and with funds still low, things didn't look promising.

Then the summer of 2004 happened, a pivotal three months that provided the lasting memory of Burley's time in the hot seat. 'We had good contacts abroad and our chief scout Simon Hunt played a big part in bringing the players over and getting them on trial,' he said. Having seen stars of the world game attracted to the quiet city of Derby in the mid-to-late 1990s, fans were wanting that level of mystery again.

The signing of Marco Reich earlier that year was the catalyst for three more intriguing additions to make short-haul flights from the mainland. 'I was always interested by English football, so it was my agent who came to me with the name of Derby,' begins

Morten Bisgaard. A Danish international with experience at Euro 2000, his switch from Copenhagen was the first coming of a new wave. 'Because I'm from the 1970s, all I knew about Derby was Jacob Laursen. Mostly I remember his free kick against Peter Schmeichel [a Premier League goal in 1996]. That was my only knowledge of the club and I had to look to find out where Derby was geographically.' He pauses. 'It's a bit different to Copenhagen.'

Since the departure of Stefano Eranio in 2001, Derby were missing a midfielder with a cultured right foot, a mind made for unpicking defences and most importantly of all, a terrific head of hair. Inigo Idiakez ticked all three boxes. So when Hunt identified the Spaniard, Burley rushed him in to a pre-season friendly to peruse over the latest name passed his way. Idiakez, in his own words, didn't do well. Burley didn't care though; he'd already seen the tapes.

'I remember being in Spain and one of the agents phoned my brother saying, "We want your brother to do a trial and go to Derby County,"' begins Idiakez. 'I didn't know anything about Derby, so we checked the story of the club and it was, "Okay, I don't mind going there to be honest." I went there and I couldn't even say hello in English, it was so difficult. I had an agent here in England and his Spanish was actually worse than my English. I played this game, played really badly and was in as a number four. Ian Taylor was there, and we couldn't communicate at all. But after that they told me they wanted me to sign a two-year contract, which was a big surprise for me. I was terrible!'

Fresh from ten years in La Liga with Real Sociedad and Real Valladolid, Idiakez's capture hinted at a style of football Burley had been unable to fully commit to with his previous squads. The addition of Tommy Smith would prove to be equally pivotal. A striker turned nippy winger, Smith made the comparatively short switch from Watford. Bisgaard on one side, Smith on the other with Reich an able replacement became the norm the longer the season went on. A structure began to form for Burley.

Funds remained at a premium, with all three joining without a fee. But the choice in players and their respective styles, while alien to Derby supporters who don't normally cast much of an eye on the Danish Superliga, showed innovation. The bloating of the squad thanks to a chunk of loanees would be unnecessary this time around, and Burley was allowed to prepare his own group.

In the early season, there was still an imbalance to contend with. Forward options of Paul Peschisolido, Marcus Tudgay and a permanently sidelined Junior wouldn't be enough to challenge in the top half of the league and certainly looked like struggling when presented with those meaty Championship defences. Still having to operate penniless, Burley set off in search of a towering centre-forward.

Polish international Grzegorz Rasiak had only moved to Siena during that same summer but with the Serie A side unable to register him, his options were open again. 'I had been watched by Derby in a game against England in a World Cup qualifier. I checked a list of the players, looked at the stadium and came to visit. I saw the training ground and the people around and knew I'd stay,' he says of his signing, which was concluded in September 2004.

Rasiak, a beanpole of a forward at 6ft 3in, was an anomaly. Dominant in the air, he lived up to that shocker of a cliché, having good feet for a big man. The longer the campaign went on, the more comfortable he became with the ball at his feet. Any original fears about hoofing towards him for nod-downs to Peschisolido were quickly cast aside. Championship defences (particularly the one just down the A52) didn't know where to begin with him.

It's little surprise that the trio of Bisgaard, Idiakez and Rasiak clicked early on, finding a corner of solace in a largely English changing room. Bisgaard, boasting a strong knowledge of the English language, was able to find his feet with his new team-mates early on. Things took longer for Derby's newest playmaker to get to grips. 'I can communicate now but before it was so difficult for someone who comes over and doesn't speak anything,' said Idiakez, who had found in his first pre-season tie the flaws of not being able to understand his team-mates. Quite how he was able to star with such ease over the course of the season, still without a jot of English in the bank, is testament to the footballing brain he possesses.

He continued, 'The club didn't help in terms of the language. The second year they did but the first they didn't do anything. The trouble was the barrier, but I always remember every meeting with George was the same. He'd say, "You give the ball to Ini, give the ball to Ini" and I went home and said, "He's saying something, what does give the ball to Ini mean?" and so my wife told me. But George was amazing with me and looked after me.'

Burley was adored by players and fans alike, able to connect on a personal level. As a manager, it was about being a human first and foremost, a position that immediately endeared him to those missing home. Rasiak explained, 'From the beginning, George said if I missed my family I could get time off to fly back and arrive back here on Thursday just to make sure I'm okay for the games. But when I came with my two-year-old and my wife for the first time, it was so much easier. I never used to take the days off to fly. I wanted to be part of the team but that was very good from the manager that I could feel his support from the beginning.'

Rasiak's commitment to the side, bringing his family to Derby and making that effort of better engaging with his new team-mates, was the starting point for a three-month spell that saw him strike nine times.

* * *

Before Rasiak found the net for the first time, Derby were again at the wrong end of the table. Just four victories from the first 14 games led to early doubts over Burley's future and defeats to fellow strugglers Crewe and Millwall didn't point at a squad built for a push up the table.

The beginning to the season was difficult for Burley for another matter though. Away from the pitch, calamity and unrest continued.

Despite the new board being in place for almost a year by this point, there remained an unease around the club with the presence of a bulky Glaswegian. Installed as director of football during the initial takeover phase, the position of Murdo Mackay was murky. A delve into his background didn't shed any more light. FIFA registration as an agent aside, it was more the five companies being struck off the Companies House register that stood out in his biography. And from the moment he stepped into the club, the relationship with Burley was weak.

'It wasn't right my relationship with Murdo. I wasn't particularly happy with how it worked, and I made that very clear to the club,' said Burley.

It was a relationship that only worsened the longer it continued, but things were initially positive. Mackay told *The Telegraph* in October 2004 that they would be discussing a new contract. He also later revealed to *BBC Radio Derby*, 'George and I were never going to be bosom buddies because he's not that sort of individual. But he's an excellent coach and we had a healthy respect for one another – and that was proved with what we achieved.'

At that stage of the campaign and with Burley's squad beginning to click, things were rosy. The signing of Rasiak was pivotal to the more open football Burley was able to delegate to his squad. Paired alongside Paul Peschisolido more often than not, support came from skipper Ian Taylor and Idiakez, while the rapidly improving Tom Huddlestone and Michael Johnson held fort. In goal Lee Grant, by now an established England Under-21 international, had been ousted by the younger Lee Camp, another academy graduate.

Across the pitch were options for Burley and after 18 months of bulging squads and loan additions, he had a core. Just 24 players appeared in 46 league games, 12 fewer than the previous season. This was largely due to the use of those free agents signed in the summer, though some of the more senior players were able to thrive with better players around them. Peschisolido, who had such an impact in a struggling side the season before, was by now an older head. The opportunity to be part of a team with genuine quality was something he thrived on. 'When you look at what Inigo did in terms of his distribution, calmness and the set pieces, when you have someone 30 or 40 yards out who looks like he'll score every time, it panics the opposition and relaxes you as a team. I was then able to form a fabulous partnership with Grzegorz who I adored playing up front with, and it just fell into place.'

What became clear early on was that even on days when Rasiak and Smith failed to find form, there was an ace in the side. Today, 16 years after the signing of Idiakez, the Spaniard's name can be heard from the stands when Derby win a free kick within 35 yards of goal.

Idiakez scored from almost every position within the opposition's half. Penalties, headers, free kicks, even the odd corner. Nothing was beyond the realms of possibility for Derby's number 27, who recalled, 'I was a specialist in Spain too. The only problem is I played with one other player for ten years, my best friend Javier de Pedro who was an amazing free-kick taker. It was always a fight for who would take the free kick, so I didn't have the same chance like at Derby. On the left it was Javier and on the right, it was me back in Spain, so it was hard.

'From the age of about five I would practise the technique with my brother and when you have that and the time comes, it's just composure. The feeling I had at that time was that I was always going to score. It was 11 free kicks and 11 assists from the corners. And crossbar 11 times as well!'

And score he did, as Derby went on the charge. Two defeats aside, they were enjoying their best run of form in six years. A dominant 3-0 victory at home to Forest showed the side at their very best, with Rasiak netting twice and Smith adding the other.

Before 2004 ended came two important wins on the road, at Plymouth Argyle and most notably against a Wigan side who went on to be promoted as runners-up. The upturn in results surprised even Burley, who recalls, 'I don't think we expected it after a couple of seasons of the team struggling. It was always going to be a bonus to finish in the top half but the longer the season went on we got a good feeling. I remember we got beat in the cup at Fulham [4-2 after extra time] and we absolutely played them off the park. They were in the Premier League and to go there and play like that, you've got a real chance. It was extra time that one we took them to. We had some great performances that season. Those Forest games especially too, to win those games was tremendous.'

Ian Taylor had scored against Forest the previous season, yet he knew early on in 2004/05 that he was now part of an altogether better side, 'You can never tell how things might go at the beginning of the season. But you could tell with Idiakez, just like Leon the year before, you could see he was a quality player. George was allowed to bring in a couple of players that season that he wanted, the scouting system was pretty good because there were all these players that nobody had ever heard of. We didn't half have a hell of a team.'

* * *

Since making his debut on the opening day of the 2003/04 season, Tom Huddlestone had become a colossus. Originally touted as a centre-half, it soon became apparent that he possessed a skillset far beyond a traditional defender. Burley instantly liked the look of him, 'Tom was a great young player, about 6ft 4in at 16 and we had to keep working him on his weight because he was such a big lad. But his main asset was his passing ability, I always said he was like a Glenn Hoddle. He came through at 17 and was fantastic for us, which gave us a bit more dimension as well.

'He could do either centre-back or midfield but he wasn't one who would come and win it in the air because he didn't really enjoy heading the ball! But he was just one of these players on the training ground that I loved to watch train because you just think, "How did he see that pass or how did he deliver that?" Left foot, right foot, inside or outside, he could do the lot and he was a pleasure to work with. Just watching him training, it was great.'

And for supporters, it was a blessing to see a genuine prospect emerge. Aside from Lee Grant, it had been almost four years since Chris Riggott burst through by the time Huddlestone made the step up. Blessed with the finest eyes for a pass as well as the physical attributes that would see him reach the very top, he became an instant star.

Taylor, who sat alongside Huddlestone for most of the season, had the pleasure of playing with him as he came to the twilight of his own career. 'There was always a question on whether Tom would play at the back or in midfield because he flitted between the two under George, but he was very adaptable. You knew he had ability but it was just a question of whether he could get across the pitch,' he said of his colleague.

It became only a matter of time before Huddlestone was to be on his way to the top division but the manner in which the move came left a bitter taste. When Tottenham signed Huddlestone in the January window, the sum of £2.5m was confirmed, a steal at the time for a man who went on to appear in the Champions League and for England. That sum was not reinvested and even the end location of that money remained in doubt, with rumours it had been significantly cut to allow him to remain at the club until the summer. Burley, without prior knowledge of the sale, had been undermined by Mackay.

* * *

The first half of the season may have started slowly but by the end of January, the side had reached their peak. From 23 January until the start of April, they didn't lose a single outing and a top-six spot became ever the more likely. Rasiak struck twice in a memorable win at West Ham, followed by goals from Smith and Adam Bolder at home to Leeds. The run, which included consecutive away wins at Brighton and Rotherham, continued for ten games. Such a spell hadn't been seen since the promotion season of 1995/96.

But the difference between what life was like on and off the field was stark and probably the biggest tell of the management style of Burley. By March, the relationship with Mackay was almost at boiling point. Burley said, 'Jeremy Keith knew the way I felt because I'd told him months before the end of the season. I was working with a director of football and I couldn't keep going along with that. Jeremy knew the situation, I wasn't happy with how it worked and I had made that very, very clear to the club.'

The failure to show support to Burley was ultimately what led to not only the departure of the manager but in part, it added haste to the situation that would arrive in the summer of 2005. At the time, Mackay reflected upon a period of illness that saw his position significantly amended. In an interview with BBC Radio Derby, he stated, 'My role was changed. Nobody ever formally told me anything about it but it was changed in my absence and it made my position incredibly difficult. I went from leaving a George Burley who would stand at the bar having a beer with me, to a George Burley who didn't want to be in the same room as me.'

Burley, who won't be drawn on specific details of the exact occurrences behind the scenes, retains the same ill feeling towards the situation today as he did at the time. By the end of the season, the ties were severed.

But on the field, despite the unbeaten run coming to an end in a barnstormer of a game at Ipswich, things looked incredibly promising. Sat in fourth spot with eight games to go, Burley had his side four points clear of West Ham down in seventh. Automatic promotion was off the cards as Sunderland and Wigan had a 14-point gap, so the only remaining focus was on consolidating that spot in the play-offs.

Burley himself was a veteran of the end-of-season shoot-out, taking his beloved Ipswich back to the top flight for the first time in five years that way in 2000. Four consecutive wins against Crewe, Stoke (which included an Idiakez goal direct from a corner and a mesmerising finish by Rasiak), an inspired performance at Sheffield United in torrential rain, and Gillingham ensured that Derby were right on the brink.

'It was clear that things were going to be different,' Peschisolido says. 'Did I think that we'd be challenging in the play-offs? Probably not because once you've just staved off relegation, chances are it's a slow build-up. But as the season progressed, you could tell there was something special happening. We were scoring goals, we were solid at the back. Inigo would come up with these ridiculous free kicks and you could see something was going on. It was getting more and more exciting and was such an enjoyable season.'

By the final day, following an absurd 6-2 loss at Coventry in the Sky Blues' last game at Highfield Road, Burley and his side were preparing for the serious business. Derby had secured a top-six spot and they would end the regular season at home to Preston North End, the side they already knew they were to face in the play-offs.

While they recorded a relatively comfortable 3-1 win, ensuring they overtook the Lilywhites into fourth place and had the supposed advantage of playing the second leg of the semi-final at Pride Park, the result came at a price.

'The last game of the season I got injured and went for a scan,' recalls Idiakez. Forty-five minutes into our discussion at a remote pub just outside of central Leicester, Idiakez is heading into a part of his Derby career that he doesn't look back on with fond memories. That final day, he made one pass too many and tore his groin, resulting in an expected six weeks on the sidelines. Derby's one true game-changer was to miss out on the two biggest occasions of the season.

'The doctor told me I'd be out for 45 days and it would be impossible for me to play. I tried to explain to the doctor that I had to play in that second leg. He said, "No, it's 45 days, you have to watch it instead" but with my poor English I told him I was going to Spain. I told my wife to ring the club and tell them I had to go to Spain and I'd play or not depending on what he said. I went home and really believed in my physio in Spain. I tried to explain that to George but he didn't understand.'

The expected loss of Idiakez was a huge blow. The fact that Burley then learnt he would have to make do without Rasiak ripped the core of his side in two. Rasiak said, 'It was the first time I'd never had a winter break. I came from Italy so I played a lot of games plus some for Poland too. Unfortunately, I had a hernia injury in the last four or five games. Even painkillers didn't help. I just played but didn't train, but then I had to go for surgery before the play-offs. Thirteen days after the operation I didn't train with the team.'

The lack of a winter break, which has only recently been introduced to the Premier League, had a lasting impact on both players who had never played a full season without one. If Derby were to make it to the Millennium Stadium, they had to do it the hard way.

And that hard way meant coming up against Billy Davies. By now, Davies had made a name for himself in the Championship. His first campaign after replacing Craig Brown was remarkable and echoed what he would achieve at Pride Park a couple of years later. Ahead of a well-structured side with Paul McKenna the anchorman in front of Youl Mawene and Claude Davis, the talismanic figure of David Nugent was the difference in the first leg. Derby, who were dealt a further blow when Michael Johnson hobbled off six minutes in, conceded before the break when Nugent snuck in between Mo Konjic and Jeff Kenna before slotting over the oncoming Lee Camp. And it was the boyhood Ram who was left cursing midway through the second half when Richard Cresswell's feeble effort squirmed under Camp. The second leg at Pride Park was an advantage no more.

But miracles can happen in the strangest of places and on the night of the return leg, Burley served up two. Rasiak and Idiakez were both walking wounded, but both were back. Idiakez recollects, 'I tried to say there would be no injection or nothing, it would just be massages. It was a small tear but nothing bad. I had a meeting with my wife and the director, I explained that I'll have ten days there and then the day before, I would fly back to play. They didn't understand it was no injections and was just hands. Anyway, I flew to Spain and went to a physio and he said, "Okay, you'll play." The day before I went and trained in the morning with the physio and then played the second leg. Every day they were phoning to see how I was. The first few days were so painful but then the seventh and eighth day I could run and felt right. I went at eight in the morning to the physio and said I'll be playing. I did a couple of runs and nobody knew I'd be playing but the changing room was surprised.'

The return of Idiakez gave fans hope. The return of Rasiak gave them confidence. An almost sell-out crowd packed in to Pride Park, each and every supporter sporting the complimentary black and white wristbands and clappers urging supporters to 'join the charge'. But the longer the game went on, the more it transpired that the charge in Idiakez and Rasiak wasn't at 100 per cent. The Spaniard, so deadly from set pieces, was unable to find his range and Rasiak's missed spot kick ten minutes from time proved telling.

'If they weren't injured, it 100 per cent would have been different. We had more quality than Preston, the better team on paper and although they were organised under Billy, had we had a fit Greg and Inigo that would have changed it,' recalls Peschisolido.

Davies's Preston went on to lose the final 1-0 to West Ham, and in 2006 they capitulated against Leeds at the semi-final stage.

* * *

That defeat was the catalyst for a close season that threw every filthy detail of the club into the air. First came the departure of Burley, barely two weeks after the play-offs came to an end. When Burley's predecessor John Gregory had been suspended from the club, it was under a huge air of controversy. But with the Scot, matters were even messier. 'Jeremy knew the situation, but I just felt it was time to move on,' said Burley, who remains cagey on the details. The severity in his voice increases when the subject is brought up, even 15 years later. It's little surprise considering the subsequent allegations made against him at the time.

Within 10 days of the 0-0 draw at home to Preston, claims had been made against Burley. The theme was around his choice of training ground tipple, with murmurs coming from within that he had attended Moor Farm under the influence. Considering Burley's ever-worsening relationship with the board and Mackay at this time, it didn't take long for him to suspect where the talk may have originated.

These allegations proved to be the final straw for a man who had been through the mill in his 26 months in Derby. Backed by his entire squad when the question of alcoholism was put to them, Burley felt he could no longer continue and on 7 June he resigned.

Murdo Mackay, who left the club months later, told BBC Radio Derby, 'The issues were never going to get any better, so I met up with Jeremy Keith and Andrew Mackenzie in Edinburgh and offered to resign. But some hours later George announced he was going.'

The failure of the Derby board to back their man spoke greatly about their ambition (or lack thereof) for the football club they had inherited. Burley's record of 39 wins and 43 defeats from his time in charge may not read positively decades later, but his role under increasingly difficult circumstances not only helped to avoid relegation to the third tier, it put Derby County back on the periphery of the Premier League.

LOS AMIGOS Y LOS CABALLEROS

IF SUPPORTERS thought they had lived through the worst of it after Premier League relegation, impending financial ruin and the very real threat of dropping to the third tier, they were made to rethink. The hierarchy at the club, largely given a pass after the heroics performed by George Burley, soon found themselves at the brunt of supporters' fury in a campaign incomparable to any other.

The 2005/06 season should have built on the foundations laid in finishing fourth, yet the departure of Burley sparked impending doom and gave the footballing world a glimpse into just the sort of characters running the club.

Still there was little known about the men at the top. Jeremy Keith, the public face of the group, was a secretive figure with no background in sport. Listed as simply 'businessman' in most media reports, the West Indian-born chief executive had three months of experience in football with Portsmouth in 1998 and stated he 'always wanted to prove to himself that he could run a football club'. A BBC Radio Derby article in 2004 had the potential to investigate but, as results on the field were positive, instead it opted to find out his thoughts on cricket and the music of Bob Marley. John Sleightholme, a coroner, was the man who had announced himself as chairman back in 2003 and over time, emerged with at least a shred of respect. Then there was Andrew Mackenzie, brought into the club by Peter Gadsby to handle the finances of Lionel Pickering before rising to the position of finance director. Factor in Murdo Mackay and the perfect combination of greed, ineptitude and cunning was left to combine.

Losing Burley left Mackay and the trio with the task of finding a replacement. The 50-strong list of candidates did little to inspire supporters furious at the loss of the Scotsman and rapidly losing faith with the decision-makers. Yeovil's Gary Johnson emerged early on as the frontrunner, but the challenge of Bolton's assistant Phil Brown provided an alternative. Johnson, who had never managed above League One (aside from four years as the Latvia national coach) didn't set hearts racing and though Brown had six years of experience working under Sam Allardyce at Bolton, he'd never taken the reins for himself. Neither individual inspired a fanbase desperate to build on the solid foundations Burley had put in place. Ultimately, it was the latter who took the job.

'We still didn't know anything about George leaving, it was through the press,' said Inigo Idiakez, who was as much in the dark on the reason a new manager was in place as the supporters were. 'Players went to the board and although I wasn't involved, nobody ever asked me about George. I think he was sacked, right? I just didn't understand it.

'Phil came in and it was amazing really. It was always with a ball playing. He'd talk to me and wanted me to be here and said it would be the same, but it was different. He was a different character to George.'

Idiakez's opinion is shared by most, not least Paul Peschisolido, 'From day one, he was very, very good and really impressed all the lads. His training and everything he said was ultra-organised. He was just one of these managers who looks at every aspect of the club and would leave no stone unturned.'

Morten Bisgaard, another who had come so close the season before, was equally impressed, 'I liked Phil's ideas; he was a lot more tactical. I remember we were rehearsing how to defend the 4-5-1 [formation], how to show them inside and get the ball for counter attacks. I remember good football chats with him and good training.'

Brown was quick to win over the squad with his methods, but he was soon left with the difficult task of building on the work of his predecessor. The January sale of Tom Huddlestone was tough to handle for supporters but come the end of the summer window, dismay was replaced by fury. A promising start, with only a single defeat against Watford in his first six games, gave Brown a platform to build on. Within days, that platform was taken out from beneath.

'When we play football, we just focus on what to do on the pitch. We knew that the club was in debt because it was facts and reported, but at the end of the window it was quite an intense time because I didn't want to leave Derby', admits Grzegorz Rasiak. The Pole, Derby's most prolific forward in a league campaign since Dean Sturridge, was the final piece in Burley's jigsaw and was expected to carry on his fine form under Brown. Instead, he was moved on to Tottenham. The sale to a major force in British football was semi-understandable and it could have been a move that drew only disappointment. The problem was though, it was announced at midnight, too late to bring in any replacement.

He continued, 'I was only 11 months into the club and the dream of playing in the Premier League was always there but a couple of days before the end, I knew there were a couple of offers from the top league. I was at the national team in Germany and had a phone call to say an offer from Wolverhampton had been accepted. I had phone calls from the club, they wanted to speak to my agent and told me I was going to be sold to them. I said I wasn't interested in moving to the same level because it would just change the players and to be truthful, I didn't want to leave a place where the people liked me and supported me, so I turned it down.

'They offered much more money, a longer contract and some clauses for the future because Glenn Hoddle was the manager. I said, "I'm not interested, I'm staying at Derby." We had Phil come in who was very good to me from the beginning and I wanted to stay. But with five hours left in the window, the Tottenham offer came in. I had a phone call from the club to say it had been accepted and the club said again they would sell me.

'Of course, Spurs were in the Premier League so if the club accepted the bid, I had to leave really. On the last day of the window the club had big, big problems so of course it was a big move for me but at that time, I wasn't prepared to move. I would have preferred to reach the Premier League with Derby.'

The timing of Rasiak's departure was monumental and prematurely sounded the death knell for Brown. Undermined, just like Burley had been, he was left hideously exposed by the board as being powerless to their decisions. To take Rasiak's place in the squad, Brown turned to Dean Holdsworth, his 37-year-old assistant manager. Holdsworth, who had last appeared for Havant & Waterlooville in the Conference South, was an inconceivable addition to the matchday 16 and the first move in an endless line of bizarre first-teamers.

First came Stern John, roundly considered to be one of the worst loan signings in the history of Derby County. Trinidad & Tobago's top scorer went goalless in eight games, winning none. Next came a young Danny Graham, who later went on to impress in the top flight. He failed to score in his 14 outings, appearing on the winning side only once. The loss of Rasiak had seen Brown's side nosedive and even before Graham joined, Pride Park had descended into a song not heard for some time, 'You don't know what you're doing.'

The first rendition was the most vociferous. Two months into the season, an entire stadium turned on Brown deep into the second half of a home draw with Leicester. Journalist Nick Britten had been visiting matches for years, yet even in the darkest days of Robert Maxwell's tenure, he'd never experienced a day quite like it. He recalls, 'When you think back over your life as a football supporter, you remember moments, random moments. One of those moments that I'll always remember was in a game against Leicester. He made a substitution and the crowd turned on him and in all my years of watching football in general, I've never heard a crowd turn on a manager how they did on Phil Brown that day. The howling and the jeering, the abuse was unbelievable. This was a home crowd against the home manager and it was just awful. I think from that moment on, he was a dead man walking.'

As well as losing the fans, Brown seemed intent on turning an ally in the media against him. Ross Fletcher, who had to endure every second of the campaign from the BBC Radio Derby commentary chair, knew Brown was only making matters worse every time he was greeted with a microphone. He said, 'Phil was a very proud guy and at this point I was the commentator, so Colin Gibson was down at pitchside doing the interviews. After one game, he had a nine-minute interview with Phil after a defeat and he walked out, walked straight up to Colin and stood within about an inch and a half of Colin's face, clearly trying to intimidate him. I remember Colin not taking a step back and continuing to ask the questions with his microphone that was just about between his and Phil Brown's chin and getting on with it.'

Mounir El Hamdaoui aside, other additions were hapless. Central defender Andrew Davies was sent off three times before returning to Middlesbrough in January. Khalilou Fadiga joined his former coach at the start of the season, appeared four times and was never seen again. Emerson Thome recorded four games and zero wins. Yet somehow, none of these can compare to the man Brown installed between the sticks. Brown's strangest move? Handing the shirt to 42-year-old goalkeeping coach Kevin Poole.

Overlooking the reception desk at Manchester United's Carrington base, Lee Grant's hands rise to his head. 'That situation with Kevin Poole was one of the most baffling scenarios I've ever been involved with as a goalkeeper and I really couldn't understand what was going on,' he remembers.

Brown had at his disposal two of the finest young goalkeepers in England. Grant and Lee Camp had both appeared for England Under-21s and either would have walked into most other Championship teams. Instead, having begun the season with Camp, Brown decided to bring Poole, another of his former players at Bolton, into the starting 11. To reiterate again, Poole was 42 years of age and semi-retired. He was also friends with Brown.

Paul Peschisolido had by this point been frozen out, despite being one of few genuine goal threats. Banished to training with the academy, he saw the treatment of the graduates from a distance but remained equally puzzled. 'Phil immediately lost them both because it completely ruins a young kid. In training I can sort of see why he did it because Pooley was phenomenal. If you were at a five-a-side you'd want Pooley in there! I love Campy and Grant but at the time, they were going through a hard spell and in terms of training, it was probably a right choice. But you just can't do that, think it but don't do it,' he said. 'And then again with Dean Holdsworth. I'm with the kids and he brings his assistant coach up front.'

Holdsworth was also experimented with at centre-half for the second half of a September defeat at Leeds United.

'I was a popular guy with supporters, and it seemed like a snub and gave off the wrong feeling,' Peschisolido said. 'When I was brought back, I was ready to go and I made Phil look silly because every time I went back, I scored another goal. I think if he was to look back now he'd say, "God, I shouldn't have done that."'

The first to speak out publicly was Camp's dad. Livid at what he saw as the mismanagement of the club, he opted to vent his frustration in the only way many fans see fit; he called BBC Radio Derby the night before the Leicester draw – which followed that defeat at Leeds – and complained. The following day, his son Lee was replaced by Poole.

Brown, after being treated to that crescendo questioning his management, admitted at the time, 'There is a situation there, yes, but it will be dealt with in-house. The decision not to have started Lee had been made before any phone calls to radio stations.'

Within three months of the first ball being kicked, Brown had managed to leave not only supporters irate, he'd done the same to players and their families. 'I know Lee's had his say on it in the past but it was just really confusing and really awkward,' sighs Grant. 'It wasn't a situation I'd wish on any young goalkeeper either. Who was the manager then?' His voice deepens as he recalls. 'Phil Brown.'

He continued, 'I didn't get on with Phil and never have since that because I just felt like the way it was handled was incorrect. The first thing that came was Kevin Poole as the goalkeeping coach, then he's playing but he's meant to be our coach. We're working with him on a daily basis but he's obviously working with an eye on playing, so the atmosphere was impossible and how any manager can think that situation would work is beyond me.'

Come the end of November, Brown was staring into the abyss. His first 21 league games as a manager had yielded four victories, had him sitting only three points above the bottom three and left him with a squad and fanbase rapidly losing faith in his abilities.

* * *

In the changing room and the boardroom all control had been lost, both homing individuals that Derby County supporters felt no connection with or positivity towards.

After another poor month to close the year, the squad turned. 'I remember the Marcus Tudgay sale. He was sold to Wednesday and Phil stood in front of the squad to tell us, saying he had to sell him because Tudgay wasn't loyal,' recalls Morten Bisgaard. The Dane was another who, like Peschisolido, had been replaced by loan signings as the size of the squad continued to expand. 'He tried to be a tough manager and for me, it was not the best leadership to show. I never talked to Phil afterwards and I'd like to tell him you can be a leader who can lead by example, but you can also show respect to players and don't have to be a super boss. For me, he was a bad influence. He had good ideas and it was a more central European style of management, but he was too inexperienced as a manager, so it just didn't work out.'

Staring League One in the face, the board were forced to act. The final straws proved to be the 6-1 defeat at Coventry and the subsequent 3-1 FA Cup loss at Colchester United. Keith had to front up and as the transfer window slammed shut, Brown was put out of his misery after his first break. Keith's search for a new man in charge ended just down the Moor Farm corridor.

'It was a weird conversation. Normally you do the caretaker role for a month or they will have already lined someone up to take over. I've been caretaker three times and clubs usually do it during an international break. But they weren't actually allowed to bring in a new manager because of all the issues.' Academy manager Terry Westley had already been slowly integrated into the first-team set-up with Brown struggling in the role. When the departure was confirmed, it was he who took the call to steady the ship. 'They said to me, "Can you do it? We can't change you until the end of the season," so I had to live with the dreaded possibility of being relegated, all while because we had no finances not being able to bring anyone else in.

'We had Geoff Horsfield come in to join us on loan. Neil Warnock phoned me and said he'd do it on reduced wages because he wanted us to help him out by beating some of the top teams. Geoff came in on Thursday and agreed to train only. So, training finishes and Murdo [Mackay] tells me we couldn't afford the finance so couldn't sign him. I had to pull him in my office and say it was all off. He went absolutely fucking ballistic. He had driven all the way down and trained, and we never had any intention of doing it because we didn't have the finance.'

Westley, as if he hadn't already realised, soon knew how desperate things were and the individuals he was dealing with, 'It was quite funny because there was this phone-in and Murdo loved the radio. I was driving home from the training ground and Murdo was on. He said that "we tried to bring in Geoff but, in the end, Terry didn't want him". I pulled my car in and phoned the station and said, "This is just ridiculous." It was a really hard time because I couldn't just have the job for a month, it was until the end of the season.'

Westley, responsible for the progression of the likes of Huddlestone and Tudgay into the first team, resorted to his roots. Earlier that year he'd been equally responsible for the emergence of a central defender soon to be recognised as Wales's youngest ever player. 'I grew up loving Derby,' begins Lewin Nyatanga. 'I had the wallpaper, the bedsheets, everything. I was at the Baseball Ground for the promotion against Crystal Palace and was a real diehard fan. I even had a shirt with Chris Powell's name on the back.

'I think I was seven when I was first signed up. When I was younger it was amazing. I remember being given a Derby County jumper, I think everyone who was signed was given one and I wore it everywhere. Going to the supermarket I'd wear it, going out to dinner I'd wear it. You can just imagine this seven-year-old walking around Derby with a jumper saying "Derby County School of Excellence" on it.'

The youthful exuberance of Nyatanga was a calming alternative to the carelessness Andrew Davies had shown earlier in the campaign and, with the addition of the behemoth Darren Moore from West Brom, Westley quickly set about shoring up the backline. More than that though, he provided the club with an identity in uncertain times.

Westley explains, 'Bringing more youngsters into the team helped for sure. The pressure Phil was under just to win rolled out on to the team, they were doing a lot of set pieces and people were bored. For me to just go "we're going to have a five-a-side tournament today and the 18s are coming over to be part of it", there was suddenly a vibrancy injected.'

Peschisolido, more integral the longer the season went on, even came on board with Westley in a coaching position. 'At the time under Phil, there was such a lot of negativity and that was even among the players. Sometimes it just gives everyone a fresh start under a new manager, particularly players he's left out or annoyed, and everyone gets a new lease of life. Terry went back to basics; he brought a smile back and just tried to get us to forget about results.'

* * *

While Westley slowly turned fortunes around, the battle for ownership of the club escalated and fan demand for an overhaul grew in stature and anger. RamsTrust, the Rams Protest Group and sections were sparking across the fanbase in order to get the truth about the club and do what they could to save Derby County. Journalist and supporter Nick Britten likens the situation to the 'people's front of Judea' from *Monty Python's Life of Brian*, with new groups, largely fighting the same battle, appearing on a daily basis.

The formation of RamsTrust had come years earlier, one of several groups to emerge across the country as the game slowly began to shift away from supporters. With earlier investigations into those running the board, they already had a presence so Jim Wheeler, today the chair of the organisation, joined with fellow members to take a closer inspection. He recalls, 'We put together a lot of information from Companies House, other people who had dealt with them, and when it really started to worry us was when Murdo Mackay came on the scene because he was a nasty character. Murdo was an ex-agent, he had a history of making money out of football and saw it as a great opportunity to get involved.'

Pairing with journalist David Conn, the RamsTrust discoveries made unpleasant reading. Mackay had fingers in many pies but it was the Inside Soccer player recruitment agency that set alarms ringing. Wheeler continued, 'I spoke to people like Terry Butcher who had dealt with Murdo in the past. As soon as I mentioned his name, [Butcher replied] "Don't touch him with a barge pole. You don't want to go anywhere near that bloke, he ripped me off for thousands." And there was a betting company guy who Murdo had ripped off as well. They said, "If you can find anything that will stick on Murdo Mackay, I will pay all the legal expenses." One guy actually drove up to Scotland to look through records offices to find out more on Murdo.'

The murky truth of Mackay slowly started to appear the deeper they got. For Wheeler, a fan first and an investigator second, his pursuit of the truth saw him dip dangerously close, 'I actually had a phone call myself from Murdo saying, "Can I meet you?" and I said, "Yes sure, can I bring somebody else from RamsTrust?" Well he actually asked if I could go to the training ground one evening, and I said, "I can but can I bring a colleague and he happens to be a policeman" and Murdo just went, "Oh no, it's okay, I don't want to do that."' There was something in the way Mackay spoke that made Wheeler think he'd better back off.

The dossier, unveiled earlier in 2005 while Burley was still in charge and totalling almost 100,000 words, became the first warning sign for supporters, who had previously dismissed many of the RamsTrust's fears. Wheeler said, 'We started the dossier as soon as they took over and it took a couple of years before we'd got enough information and before the club had gone downhill enough that people would listen to us. We were asking questions but a lot of people were telling us to stop criticising and to get behind the club. And the local journalists had to maintain a relationship, so they couldn't go on an all-out attack. People like Graham Richards asked questions and they then found themselves being banned from the ground. They were a lot more subdued in what they could do.'

RamsTrust had done what they could in raising their very real concerns but relied on support to spread awareness. Utilising message boards such as Pop Side and RamZone, the word began to spread far and wide. Though Wheeler and his colleagues had been distributing flyers outside Pride Park, it only got them so far. But with results worsening and the exposé out in the open, similar groups unearthed. He said, 'I can't remember the guy's name but he put thousands of pounds in to make flags, banners, foam hands with BOARD OUT across them, and it was this big visual protest that really got the ball rolling.'

Even before the departure of Brown, it became commonplace post-match for supporters to begin gathering outside the main entrance to the West Stand. Hundreds would unite, brandishing placards and red cards, embarking on choruses of 'sack the board' as the television cameras gathered. Where had the money come from, where had the money from the sales gone and just who were the people in control of the club? Three questions that nobody could answer aside from those sitting within.

Britten, then working for the *Daily Telegraph* but by now living in Derby after years in Scotland, still had a weekly column in the programme but was well aware his readership were of a different mindset to months earlier. He remembers, 'There's a phrase that's thrown around these days into everyday language and that phrase is "toxic". People say "oh the ground is toxic, this is toxic" but you've not known toxic until you go through those kinds of days. Then you really understand toxic. There was complete disconnect between supporters and the club and the team for the first time since Maxwell. That was all pre-social media as well, so it was difficult to rally people. But to see the extent of the protests and the bitterness, the disconnect, not just among supporters versus the board but I remember a lot of infighting too.'

Andy Ellis, the official historian for the club, watched on, 'We had something similar for the Maxwell protest [in 1991] and the theory behind getting all fans together in that way was already set. But once word got around through local newspapers and Radio Derby that they wanted to do this, it became word of mouth. You hand leaflets out in the stadium and it becomes easy to get a few, then you get more and more. Outside the stadium after the game, regardless of the result, make a big noise and that's what they did.' That noise only grew come February.

If there's one thing that is a constant theme throughout the history of Derby County, it's the power it has within the community. A one-club city with those who live there almost entirely devoted to their club, there remains a clamour for people who have personal relationships with Derby to be part of their football club. A look at those who have gone into management shows Roy McFarland, Colin Todd, Peter Taylor and Steve McClaren all having stints in the hot seat. All four over the years had captured the hearts and supporters yearned for them back. Lionel Pickering, a local man turned millionaire, was adored for the work and the money he put into the club.

On the flipside, Robert Maxwell was despised like no other ever has been. Phil Brown never got to grips with the city and was soon out. And the amigos, with no reason to own the club and no explanation behind why Derby, were villains from the get-go. When a local group of businessmen declared their interest in the club at the start of February, the people of Derby grew louder.

'I got together with a group of people. Me, John Kirkland, Mel Morris, Don Amott and Mike Horton. We became known as the League of Gentlemen,' recalls Peter Gadsby.

The group of five set off on a mission to get their club back from foreign hands. Gadsby, part of the board under Lionel Pickering, was joined by four of Derby's finest minds and wealthiest accounts. Amott was no stranger to the people of the city, as the undisputed 'King of Caravans'. Kirkland had been a director at the Baseball Ground and Pride Park for 21 years previously. Morris now needs no introduction. Jill and Peter Marples too were both heavily involved. Horton was renowned for his work in saving and ultimately resurrecting the county's cricket club.

Speaking in 2006, he said, 'Local people may not be better than people who come from any other part of the country, but they've got a passion and a commitment. Does it make a difference if we've all played on Darley Fields or stood at the Racecourse Ground watching our kids play in minus-five-degree conditions? Of course, it does. It's part of it. It makes the fans feel more comfortable that whatever the decisions are, right or wrong, they are being made by people who represent them and feel it just as much as they do.' They were the people's choice.

But there was a second option, which emerged before the support for the League had even begun to gather. The name of SISU is by now synonymous with Midlands football and is a ghostly reminder of what could have been the fate of the Rams. Since their takeover of Coventry City in 2008, the Sky Blues have plummeted down the leagues, attendances have fallen off a cliff, and twice they have had to move away from their Ricoh Arena home. Year upon year, new investment funds have in effect controlled the club, each one intent solely on taking out what they can. Millions in player sales have been amassed from the likes of James Maddison and Callum Wilson, with not a penny put back into the club.

Many fans, following years of protests, have simply left. Generations have been lost and whether the club will ever recover is unanswerable with the current regime. The carcass of Coventry serves as a permanent reminder, only a matter of miles away, of just what Derby could have looked like.

'We were made aware that a leading hedge fund named SISU was keen on acquiring Derby,' says Gadsby. 'The guy who ran SISU in the UK was a big fan of Derby County. Probably a Derby person who had left the area and gone to the City and made money.

'Hedge funds like to acquire distressed assets. They were unsuccessful at Derby but they bought Coventry, loaded it with debt and where are Coventry now? Without a ground! God knows what would have happened if they had been successful in acquiring Derby.

'At this moment in time, Derby was in serious financial difficulties and was being supported by the Co-op bank. The "Three Amigos" had run the club into the ground. I was the leading shareholder in a local consortium including John Kirkland, Mel Morris, and Don Amott.

But while Mortimer and Gibson were delving into certain parts, Gadsby was doing the investigating for himself. 'Jeremy Keith, one of the "Three Amigos" running the club, came to see me at my house. We were closing in on our bid for the club. As was to be proved later he was not to be trusted. He said, "I can deliver the club for you." He wanted £500,000 and he'd do the rest. I said, "I don't work like that."

'I went to see Andrew Mackenzie, who was the former financial director of Derby County for many years under Lionel Pickering's reign. I knew him well. The "Three Amigos" were not allowing us to look at the books to enable us to make an informed bid. I said to Andrew, "I want to see the books as I am aware that £725,000 has gone with no invoice. I want to do the due diligence and I need your cooperation." He would not help. We could not obtain any financial records.'

Gadsby continued, 'He wouldn't give us due diligence, we couldn't find any figures and so the Co-op bank brought us together and said, "Unless you're prepared to make a firm bid, we'll run with somebody else."

'The club were in debt to the Co-op bank in the region of £38m. They demanded that we make a bid soon or they were going to pass the club over to SISU who basically would treat the club almost as if it was in administration.'

But Gadsby didn't become a multi-millionaire by luck. Any man with four fountains on each corner of his house has left nothing to chance and he soon found himself with the advantage.

He said, 'We had a stroke of luck. A very influential Derby person of some considerable stature had spoken to the Co-op board of directors outlining the strength of feeling for local people to run the club and that we would be in a very strong position.

'The meeting was held between the Co-op bank and ourselves at the Cotton Hotel in Lancashire. The Co-op hierarchy, chief executive and board members stated that our offer of £6m plus add-ons was an insult and they wanted £25m for it. The club was losing £2m a month. Two more Co-op executives arrived, and now the chief executive of the Lending Committee appeared. We were advised that if we didn't increase our offer we were out.

'I didn't like their approach, so I took a bit of a gamble and asked them just to confirm that we were unsuccessful so that I could go back to Derby and tell my family that I was out of the madness and let the Derby press know that we had tried our best and we got up to leave the meeting. They called us back and within half an hour the deal was done on our terms.'

Co-op's attempt at hardball had been seen through by Gadsby and it's possible that the people of Derby had some power behind their thinking. Wheeler recalls, 'The thing that made the big difference was when some supporters, not members of RamsTrust, glued the doors of the Co-op Bank in Derby. The Co-operative Bank is supposed to be a very ethical body and they had, at that point, realised the strength of feeling against what they had done to Derby County. They had a board meeting and knew they had to get out of it.'

Despite board support for SISU which would have resulted in a healthier final financial total for the bank, it would be the local consortium who would wrestle back control of the club and put the Rams back at the heart of the city again. Before the season was out, and with an almost full house packed in for a last-day defeat against Sheffield Wednesday, the club was under new management. The appointment of the board, who invested £25m between them and would put their own money into the club unlike the previous regime, was a blessing for supporters concerned with the club direction.

Throughout the process, Gadsby had reiterated his faith towards Terry Westley, who had steadied the ship during his tenure. 'All of them would have thrown you under the bus,' Westley comments in reference to the group known as the Three Amigos. 'I had quite a good relationship with Murdo originally and could say what I thought so we could talk openly. But it changed when I became manager and he started asking questions about who should play. John Sleightholme was a nice man, professional and did his best, but the whole thing had just turned into a complete and utter circus.

'Peter Gadsby's people were intent on bringing someone else into the club so you had "you must stay up Terry, we must stay up" so you were getting calls off them on a private number somewhere, and then you've got Murdo and Keith fighting for their lives to hold on to the club and everything they've got and you were the pawn in the middle. But you hear all the things going on and you know Gadsby is trying to take over, but just trying to win a game was enough. It's one of the most draining times professionally I ever had because I cared about the club. I did not want them to go down and you see people around the ground constantly and know what it means to people.'

For those wearing the shirt, the takeover was a welcome relief. They had been the victims of the fan anger during the season and were welcoming a day when they wouldn't be hearing a chorus of boos for 90 minutes. Paul Peschisolido, who had been utilised more and more after Westley moved into the caretaker role, says, 'You couldn't psychologically avoid that negativity. We never went into a game wanting to lose but, in most clubs, where there is supporter unrest, usually the team is struggling. It doesn't happen when a team is winning the league. We had supporters looking for things to go wrong and it affected us that season.'

Survival was one thing but there was still so much more to unfold at boardroom level. When inside, the true damage of what had been taking place behind closed doors was clear for Gadsby and the new accountants to see. Gadsby recalls a situation weeks after taking charge, 'Jeremy Keith together with his colleagues, had run the club into the ground, taking out funds and treating it as his own fiefdom. When we opened the books it was far worse than we could ever have imagined and we were on the back foot from day one.

'I recall one rather rewarding action where Jeremy Keith had taken his large car back home and we immediately sent out somebody to repossess it from his house. They turned up at 7am and asked for the keys.

'He had the audacity even then to say that he wanted to keep it for a while as his wife wanted to go into town that day with it and asked if we could come back tomorrow when he'd had the opportunity to clean it! Together with the other "Three Amigos" he was subsequently sentenced for fraud.'

It took three years but in 2009, the situation reared its head again. Mackenzie, Keith and Mackay were all imprisoned for their involvement in the defrauding of £440,625 from the club accounts. The trio, who all agreed to be paid £125,000 each without approval from the board, were revealed to have set up a plot in order to make away with the funds. As outlined by David Conn, a national newspaper journalist who covered the situation from the original takeover in 2003, payments showed £375,000 plus VAT paid to Streamline Management, a false invoice with the company having never worked with the club. David Lowe, a lawyer for the club, was also jailed for his role. Only Steve Harding and John Sleightholme emerged clean.

For Sleightholme in particular, his decision to depart before the takeover was completed unearthed battles within the boardroom. In a statement in April 2006, he revealed, 'Recently it has come to my attention that meetings have been held, important decisions taken and documents signed without my knowledge. Important information has been withheld from me.'

The man at the front of the consortium who took over from Pickering had lost the power from within and when Keith and Mackenzie refused to launch an internal investigation into the missing funds, it led him down a path that ended when he testified in court.

The moneys stolen from the club went into everything from holiday homes to trips to Malaysia. Mackay even remarked in court that his behaviour was okay in the footballing world. A year later, the club attempted to retrieve the funds. Mackay claimed he was living with his brother and claiming jobseeker's allowance.

It was a sorry, yet almost inevitable end. Murdo Mackay had never endeared himself to supporters with his meddling in George Burley's affairs, while Jeremy Keith's early comments about Derby being his "train set" were never likely to make too many friends.

One acquaintance he did have at the time was Nick Britten, who said, 'I liked Jeremy, we got on very well and he was never anybody who struck me as being involved in that level of criminality. I wondered if I'd been taken for a ride, but he struck me as a good bloke. He had a family, kids, a good strong stable life and he was very religious, a God-fearing bloke and he always seemed to preach, not literally, but walking on the right side of life. I would like to have a conversation with him over a beer and just ask him what the bloody hell went on and why? What did they think they could get out of it?'

Come the final day of the legal hearing, Wheeler took his seat at Northampton Crown Court. It was a position he never thought he'd get to, and one he certainly didn't expect upon the beginning of his personal investigation. 'Jeremy Keith and Andrew Mackenzie looked genuinely scared when they were walking out of court with their bags, Murdo I think saw it more as an occupational hazard,' he remembers.

'I had taken the day off work to go and I drove to court in Northampton, went in and I'd never even been in court before. Just being there was interesting for one thing, but sitting in the canteen before we went in, Jeremy and Murdo came in to get a coffee. They looked daggers at me because they knew exactly why I was there and I heard one of them say "the vultures are gathering". It finished on the Monday and I saw them going in with bags, so I knew they'd been instructed to take them because they wouldn't be going home afterwards.'

Despite initial contact over the course of several months, Keith opted not to speak.

A THREE-YEAR PLAN

BILLY DAVIES is complex. His personality is complex. His reputation is complex. Even the process of trying to speak with Billy for this book was complex. So complex in fact that after two years of trying to arrange a chat, we're Davies-less. But when the man himself first stepped off the private helicopter chartered for him by the Marple family, he was just plain old Billy; a short, relatively unknown force from north of the border. The man who had led Preston North End to successive play-off finishes and only missed out on a place in the Premier League when Bobby Zamora struck for West Ham, seemed the perfect appointment for a club desperate to rebuild.

'When we were interviewing for a manager,' Peter Gadsby begins, 'we interviewed three people and one of them was Martin O'Neill. We interviewed him in an Oxford hotel and we really thought we'd got him. But then he turned it down because his wife was recovering from a serious illness. We then interviewed Joe Royle and a couple of others.' O'Neill, a year out from his three SPL titles with Celtic, would go on to lead Aston Villa that season while Royle would be out of work for three years before taking on a final management role at Oldham.

'We were starting to run out of ideas and time was against us. Then Billy appeared,' continued Gadsby.

'An agent contacted us suggesting he had a top Championship manager with an excellent record. We asked them for a name, but there was all this nonsense saying we had to sign him first, then they'd reveal the name.

'At the time Charlton were the favourites to sign him as a successor for Alan Curbishley. But we began to understand that Davies didn't want to go to London and in an interview he outlined his vision but basically he was unsuccessful with Preston in getting to the final hurdle because the players with over 50 games ran out of legs when they got to the play-offs. We took him on.'

Davies's appointment rather cruelly spelt the end of Terry Westley's caretaker reign, a managerial position that he insists he had no interest in despite reports to the contrary. More brutal than this though, the arrival of Davies meant complete termination of his employment. 'We stayed up and I did the whole pre-season, organised friendlies and fitness programmes and had the interviews with players. There was forensic detail on my side, but then I got a phone call from Karren Brady. She said she'd been to a CEO meeting and Peter [Gadsby] was there and said, "Terry could be replaced when he goes back to work,"' Westley said.

'I didn't think it was true but when I went in for pre-season, Billy told me it was impossible for me to stay here. But having said that he also replaced the cook, the cleaner and every other member of staff. He was paranoid about anyone who had been there.'

Westley was first to go, and remnants of previous regimes were soon to follow. Early in the season, he opted to replace the two most recent players of the year in moves that only served to worry a fanbase still hurting from the asset-stripping instigated by the previous regime. Tommy Smith, roundly regarded as the best forward at the club, was sold to Watford and a day later, Inigo Idiakez linked up with George Burley again at Southampton.

'My relationship with Billy was bad, really bad,' begins Idiakez. 'At the beginning of pre-season, it was okay but then we had a silly argument. I was wearing a jumper in the changing room and he told me to take it off, but I said no because I was cold. From that point onwards he was horrible, shouting at me all the time. He tried to sell me and then George came from Southampton and told me he wanted me.

'I didn't want to go because I felt Derby County was my family, but I felt with the manager, he didn't want me there and George told me he'd heard the same as well. But at the end of August, they had the money at Derby, so I knew they were going to make a good team, but Billy didn't want me there.' Idiakez's time as a player with the club was over but, as legend now goes, he'd have more of an impact in the closing weeks of that season than any other individual.

Davies quickly got to work on assembling a squad and his intent to build the same foundations he had formed with Preston quickly appeared. At Deepdale, he built his attacking presence around David Nugent and the early addition of powerhouse forward Steve Howard emulated the one-time England forward, albeit with more of an aerial threat and less pace. Howard, who became the first £1m signing since Francois Grenet, had thumped 69 league goals in his previous four seasons at Luton and filled the gaping gap Phil Brown and Westley had struggled with a season prior. There would be no Dean Holdsworth or Stern John this time around, in defence or attack.

Davies, by no means a master tactician even at the height of his powers, has always built his sides through the centre and Derby were no different. That core was vital and a step further back from Howard saw him add Matt Oakley, who had spent the previous 12 seasons in the heart of Southampton's side. 'Billy had been on the phone to my agent when he heard that I was available and said that he wanted me to go up and meet him about a long-term contract. I met him, talked about the plan of the club and they had this real fresh impetus going forward which I could feel from him,' said Oakley.

Howard and Oakley were seamlessly integrated into what Darren Moore remembers as the 30s group, joining himself, Paul

Peschisolido, Michael Johnson and Marc Edworthy. One rung below contained Seth Johnson and the incoming Mo Camara, while the final level, the kids if you will, Davies continued to bolster. Already with the hype of Giles Barnes at his disposal, the additions of centre-half Dean Leacock, Arsenal loanee Arturo Lupoli and much fancied young goalkeeper Stephen Bywater were set to create the perfect amalgam of youth and experience.

Though Camara and Lupoli added necessary width, the core was Davies's philosophy. It was all about building from the middle, with everything else working around that structure aided by the experienced heads. In his previous season, Davies had overseen 23 clean sheets in 46 games and although the early results in his Derby days didn't start perfectly, he could be excused for feeling a little déjà vu. The first five games of his Derby life produced five points and one victory, the exact same return as his first full season with Preston. 'Don't worry about where we are now, it's where we are at the end of the season,' was the line Davies reiterated to his playing staff early on.

A 2-1 victory at Hull on the day Bywater signed ('the chairman was on the phone, so I spoke to him and he said he'd give me a free car if I kept a clean sheet') offered hope but it was Wolves away that set the wheels in motion. Howard, who had floundered early on without a goal, struck the only goal in the first of many 1-0 wins. Bywater, though situated at the opposite end, realised that night what the likes of Howard brought to the squad beyond just goals. He recalls, 'Steve was lively, straight up, funny and would bring the lads together. He was a rock and on the pitch, he was a target that we could all count on. But we had loads of alpha males who wanted to work together. It wasn't "all about me" it was more of "I'm an alpha male, I'm a dominant guy but I want to work together" and we were all dominant ones.'

In many ways, Davies's portrayal as an alpha quickly began to reflect in his squad; confident, up for a battle, fierce. But ultimately, winners. The third victory of the campaign again came on the road, 2-1 at Sheffield Wednesday. 'I came on as a sub, cost the team the goal because I didn't go with my runner and then tried to do something fancy from kick-off, lost the ball and dived in two-footed,' remembers Giles Barnes of that September afternoon at Hillsborough. Barnes's dismissal left the team light and only a late Howard winner saved him from the wrath of Davies.

'We were tying I think and then Steve scores and I'm in the changing room thinking "fuck, I've ruined it with him",' said Barnes. 'But we end up getting a win. Billy comes in and just says, "You better go and hug him and thank him that I've not come in here and fucking ripped your head off." And you'd be damn sure I went and thanked him by the way!'

By this point, the former Nottingham Forest youth product was coming into his own. Brash but with a lightning turn of pace and a skillset unmatched in the division, Barnes was growing into a boy touted for bigger things. He may have taken his original belief from Westley, but Davies enhanced that faith, outing him in 46 games in all competitions. It was a move which stemmed largely from a need for excitement. Tommy Smith was gone, Morten Bisgaard fell into the older bracket and Lupoli still had a rawness about him. From day one, Barnes was pinpointed as Davies's talisman, even if he didn't quite know it yet. He said, 'When we turned up for pre-season, I was that nervous about doing well with him that I came in under the weight. I started listening to conversations where boys would say "I'm not going to eat tomorrow because I know we're running, and we'll be getting weighed" so you do the same and it was the worst thing I could have done. I only had a multigrain bar for my breakfast and when we were running, I was horrific.

'After the session Billy sat us down and he went off on the young players. "Young players and young fucking midfielders especially. If you can't fucking run, you'll never be in my team. Fucking young boys not running, what is this?" and I was the only young midfielder in the group, so it was pretty obvious who he meant! The next day we did a different run and I had a regular breakfast and I tore the run apart.

'But he's one of the best managers I've had. He used to go and talk with my dad after games. My dad would watch every single game and Billy would go and sit down with him in the players' lounge and just talk as if he wasn't my manager. You don't get that in football.'

* * *

If you can, picture this scene. It's 8.30am on a cold Thursday in mid-November. Canadian Paul Peschisolido is tucked into a changing room locker, wearing an umpire's hat, as Italian Arturo Lupoli launches a tennis ball at Guinean Mo Camara, who is brandishing a small cricket bat. It's the environment that greeted each and every staff member who would walk into Moor Farm throughout the season and they all embraced it.

It's a scene you won't see in any British professional football environment today, as every second is snatched by psychologists, analysts and pilates instructors. Even in the mid-2000s, such an activity was rare. For Oakley, like the rest of his team-mates, training would be set for 9am but the fun, for grown men with families at home, would escalate well before then, 'I think Lee Grant brought in this set. It was this thin cricket bat with the outside edges cut off and you played with a tennis ball on one side and then on the other, a ball that had the fur ripped off, so it grips on the other side. We had everything!

'Pesch used to sit on the lockers at the back with an umpire's hat on and he used to say whether you were out or not. You'd come in in the morning and you could just hear this cricket game going on and over time, the lads used to be getting in at 8.30am and just had this togetherness that I've never seen before or even heard about in the game. The breakfast was another one. We had a chef called Mark who would cook us all breakfast in the morning and in the canteen, they had those big round wedding tables. They were set out, but we'd all be around one, so you just had 25 lads all sitting around telling stories or talking about the weekend, the papers or whatever.'

The squad was one like none seen in previous years at any club. Bywater refers to it as '50 per cent football, 50 per cent friendship' and Moore adds, 'Something I've never seen before or since. We would voluntarily and happily leave home early to get to Derby and have our scrambled eggs, omelettes, fruit shoots or whatever it may be with all kind of minerals in.

'Everything was always with an emphasis on the team, we all played our part and that was on and off the pitch. We used to have a lot of camaraderie in the dressing room and we'd play the pairs cricket. So, we'd all have our nations, England, Jamaica, Australia, and we'd have little tournaments in the changing room. After training we would all stay behind having dinner together and we used to have teas and coffees as a team.

'The girls in the canteen would bring out a tray and this tray had the biggest load of Jaffa Cakes and the biggest tray of fig rolls. Oh man, I loved these fig rolls. I was incredible at them. I worked it out and I used to consume 1,800 calories in fig rolls every day when I was at Derby. But we worked so hard that they would just be burned off.'

Moore waits, seemingly ready for the next question before one final reiteration, 'I would have two packs of Crawford fig rolls every day. It was incredible!'

The unity didn't end in the dining room. Squad meals out, go-karting sessions and days at the racing became monthly affairs, agreed upon by every member of the first-team squad. So united were the squad that genuine friendships were formed that still last today. Michael Johnson and Moore were both guests at Bywater's wedding; Seth Johnson and Howard remain best friends. But probably the biggest indicator of the affection across the club doesn't come from a player.

King of Caravans and club director Don Amott was no stranger to the group. Part of the 'League of Gentlemen' consortium, his role quickly adapted from within the boardroom to within the heart of the group, as relationships began to blossom. 'I still text and ring Billy once a month,' Amott answers from the comfort of a Portuguese villa he frequents monthly. 'I went to Stevie's wedding a couple of years ago. Big Mooro I get a text from twice a week, Paul Peschisolido I'm still very close friends with, Stephen Bywater too.' Bywater himself reiterated three times 'you need to speak to Don' over the course of conversation.

'I was on holiday with Matty Oakley in Portugal,' continues Amott, 'and we were on about Derby and he just said the team spirit was the best he'd ever seen. And do you know what he said to me? "Don, you never knew but you were part of it. The lads would have walked through walls for you because you're just a normal guy."

'Giles Barnes was in America at Houston and out the blue, he sent through his football shirt for my grandson Oscar. "Don, how are you?" and the shirt arrived at the front door. He went to Fulham and his dad came up, and he said to somebody, "Let me tell you about Don. I went to see Giles in London and there was a good luck card on his mantelpiece, and it was from Don!" It was the best changing room that squad had ever been in. They weren't the best players, but it was just wonderful.'

Bywater even has a recollection of Mel Morris visiting the training ground and enjoying the company of the squad during his early involvement at Pride Park.

Davies himself would admit his strengths lay not in the tactical work but in the psychological. A glance back at Claudio Ranieri's primary success in Leicester City's 2016 Premier League title win was down to the group he built more than the way he integrated them and the results that followed bore directly from that. It's a comparison Amott uses, but the similarities are somewhat there. Morten Bisgaard, by this point a peripheral member of the first team squad, adds to Amott's comment, 'The tactical work we did was just that he would point and show us where we were in the videos. But on the pitch, it was not tactical. He came to me one time and he said, "I know you do a lot more tactical work in Europe, but I don't think this squad is ready for that."'

Another mastery of the man's management lay in understanding the needs of his squad and the incentives that would appeal to them. A common misconception of modern footballers is that they are machines, designed to train daily and expected to maintain the same level over the course of a 46-game season. But Barnes and his team-mates were allowed a different rota to the 23 other Championship sides the longer the season went on. He said, 'Billy would reward you for your good play. If we had a Saturday-Tuesday and won, he'd give us two days off. It would be play Saturday, off the next two and play Tuesday. Little things like that and you're thinking, "This is a lot of days off here, boss?" but it worked, and he knew what made teams tick. In the run to the end, he'd be giving us days off left, right and centre. But it was a real incentive for us.'

Many things altered the longer the campaign went on, including the inner strength and insulation of the football club. Perhaps the greatest compliment that can be paid is that in creating that 'bubble' as Bywater describes it, the manager encircled supporters too. Long before being tagged with the paranoid tag, on-field success meant Davies's circle was wider than in later years. Peschisolido, having seen the good and bad side of the Derby County fanbase in his previous three seasons, recalls the importance of having the fans brought within. 'Billy brought in players who would find a connection between supporters and players, which was another success. Supporters become our 12th man. He brought back that much needed connection because the season before there was so much venom,' he recalled.

There was no need for venom this time around, with matters on and off the field providing more than enough reasons to smile. The paranoia at this point was okay, as Barnes says, because it was in among victories: 'People will say he was intense, and he was definitely paranoid about certain things. But he just wanted to win so much that he didn't want anything to disrupt that flow, y'know?

There would be times he'd throw spanners in and he'd go to a player and say, "I'm going to make it look like you're not playing all week but you are, I just want to see if they know my team." A lot of the time he would be right as well! He wasn't wrong in his paranoia; he'd come to me and tell me I wouldn't be training with the starting 11, but I would be in the midfield three. "I just need to see if the other team can guess my 11."

'But he was so intense at times and I know for a fact that he wouldn't sleep sometimes. He'd come in and show us a video or work on something and you're thinking between you, "Boss, you've not slept!" Not in a bad way at all but he used to wear it on his face. You know when people are tired and when Billy hadn't slept he had these heavy eyes and you'd know he'd been on the computer all night, watching games all night to figure out what went wrong.'

Davies controlled the side but whereas Phil Brown looked to do the same more through an element of fear than anything else, the Scotsman's methods worked because he had a squad who simply allowed them to. 'He wanted to control everything – what you ate, where you slept, everything,' Bywater comments. 'It's being a manager and he wanted to get the best out of his players because at the end of the day, he's the one who gets the sack. He oversaw everything: 9am massage, 9.30am chiropractor, 10am yoga. He pulled me in after a week and said, "Stephen, you're a fat bastard. Lose some weight."

'I got sent off at Ipswich [in a 2-1 loss] and Billy was going mad, saying "I can't believe this" and I assumed it was at me for getting sent off. Anyway, in his jacket pocket he gets this piece of paper out and he's shouting at all the lads, he unfolds it and he points at Jay McEveley. "And you McEveley, you fat bastard, eating a fucking burger at 12 o'clock at night." He didn't care about me getting sent off, he cared about one of the lads eating a burger at the hotel and pulled out the receipt he'd found in a bin.'

For the management team and the squad, they recognised they weren't the best team in the league. In truth, they probably weren't even close. West Brom had a side built for the Premier League, as did both Sunderland and Birmingham. Southampton boasted players well capable of the level above, namely Gareth Bale. What you can assume is that none of those sides boasted the group mentality that Derby did. Throughout the 46 matches in the regular season, 20 of 25 victories were by a single goal.

From November to February, the defence was only breached six times in 17 outings. Of those 17 games, 13 were won by one goal, with only a 2-0 victory at Luton bucking that trend. Oakley says, 'The togetherness is something that you can't measure, which is a difficult thing. But when you're on the pitch and you know you've got an emotional connection and a friendship with the players that you're playing with, you just go the extra bit further. I played in teams where we had players that are technically amazing but are very much individuals, they don't want to do the extra for the team, are focused on their game but the rest of the team comes second. I was part of that group at Derby where the team came first and that was what got us through a lot of those games. Talking about the 1-0 victories, in a lot of those games we never looked like we would ever get beat, it wasn't like we were hanging on. We were such a tight unit that they would never score.'

The united front largely came from Davies but he should attest it to luck too from the side he inherited. Moore is regarded as one of football's good men, Seth Johnson, a man that any side would want 11 of. Michael Johnson too remains one of those often overlooked for the part he played during the campaign but he was a father-like figure for many in the squad.

Forced to watch on from the bench for the majority of the season as Moore, Leacock and sporadically Lewin Nyatanga shut out almost every side in the Championship, Johnson's presence remained. The club captain may have been required on a minimal basis as the campaign went on but he was perhaps one of the most valuable commodities for those around him.

Oakley's first day back in August could have been a dagger to Johnson's career, as the former Southampton skipper recalls, 'I remember very clearly my first session where we went around the training ground at Moor Farm, just having a bit of a jog and chat.

'Billy sat us all down and said, "I just want to welcome Matt to the group, he's going to be your captain." I hadn't even spoken to Michael Johnson, who I knew was the captain at the time, and Billy doing that made me feel even more awkward. We continued to jog on our little warm-up and Michael, being the person that he is, came straight over to me and I thought "oh no". He just said, "It's great to have you with me. If I can assist with anything, just let me know." He was amazing.'

Johnson's humility saw him installed as almost a secondary manager, a voice for the club and a model of professionalism for those in that younger bracket.

'I loved them [Moore and Johnson],' remembers Bywater. 'They were ultra-professionals and I loved them to bits. They were the two who came to my wedding, that's how much I like and respect them. They had experience and presence on the pitch, but I looked up to them and I enjoyed their banter as well. They were slightly different characters, Mooro more serious but they bounced off each other in a fun way and loved helping people.'

* * *

In the first press conference delivered by Davies, he hammered home one specific point; this was a three-year plan. It would take three years to build a side, rather a club worthy of promotion. It was a point he would reiterate as a matter of defence a season later, the statement turning from long-term promise to short-term justification. Even years later in the rare instance Davies opened up to a media he remained so wary of eyeballing, it's quickly ticked off in Billy bingo.

On Oakley's first day with the armband he heard the exact same assurance, 'The brief was that he was given a three-year period to get promoted but in my first meeting, he said, "We're going to do this in one year. That's the target so get focused on it." That was where we started. Whether he believed it would happen in the one year or that was just his way of motivating me, it created an unbelievable desire to get there.'

Bywater adds, 'I knew it wouldn't take three years. I even told all my mates "we're going up this year" because we just kept getting lucky.'

It was perhaps bluffing on Davies's part to suggest this to his captain but if he had any reservations about the likelihood of the conversation coming true, by February those were put to the back of his mind. Two separate runs of 18 points from a possible 18 placed the Rams right at the helm of the division and expectations skyrocketed, as did attendances. The opening fixture against a much-fancied Southampton attracted fewer than 22,000 to Pride Park, but by early March, almost 27,000 ventured for a Friday night, live-on-Sky game against Colchester. That 5-1 demolition of the Essex side was another timely reminder of the viper-like strike players such as Lupoli and Barnes could administer, the latter saying, 'I had a really, really good game that night and we were on fire as a team. I don't really think about games, but it was that night where I thought to myself "okay, we are good".'

The biggest victory of the Rams' season took them to the summit of the division, with a three-point lead and a marker laid down for the weekend to many of the chasing pack.

With a side in prime position for the top two, Davies's decision to bolster the side in the January transfer window has long been critiqued by sections of the support but, contrary to belief, they benefited the side early on. Full-backs McEveley and Tyrone Mears seamlessly slotted in, the former particularly filling a left-back slot that looked to be the weakest section of the side. Going forward, Gary Teale, Craig Fagan and Stephen Pearson all brought different aspects to the side. Teale had promotion experience with Wigan, Pearson had played at the highest level with Celtic and Fagan was highly fancied at Hull. In the centre too there was the pivotal permanent addition of David Jones, who had delivered one of the key moments of the season when his 90th-minute free kick flew past Mark Crossley to beat Wednesday.

Bywater welcomed the arrivals, 'The January signings settled in just fine. We were all inclusive people helping the cause, they came and they were strong characters as well. They could see we were doing well, and it became natural. To be honest, if you sign for Derby County, I swear to God it's a big club and you know it is. The facilities, the people – it's just big and it's somewhere you want to be involved. As soon as you walk in as a player you get the vibe that it's a place where people want you to win, people in the canteen, everywhere.'

Davies, mindful of how his Preston side ran out of steam in previous years, went to Gadsby with his demands. Gadsby said, 'Things were going well on the field, I think we were second at Christmas. Billy came to us and demanded three more players. We told him money was tight and Billy reminded me that we had promised that he would not be in the same situation [as at Preston].

'We signed Stephen Pearson, Teale, Fagan and Mears. I recall vividly that he referred to Pearson as a lad that can run all day, and he'll probably score the [promotion] winner.'

But despite the squad strengthening, the finish line drifted further into the distance. Defeat against fellow automatic hopefuls Birmingham wasn't a disaster but home draws with QPR and Coventry were. Another point in between at Leicester provided further problems, as Moore reflects on a moment that potentially derailed any hopes of automatic promotion.

'I was accused to have elbowed Iain Hume in the face, but I never once took my eye off the ball. Seventy-two hours afterwards, Monday at 12, you could put a complaint in, and we had a complaint from two clubs about it. The EFL suspended me retrospectively for it and I remember one of the clubs who made the complaint were Birmingham.' The Blues and Derby were now battling it out for second spot behind Sunderland. A low blow from Steve Bruce and a hammer blow to Davies.

It was the final four league outings that did the real damage though. Defeat at Ipswich, in which Bywater saw red for brawling with Alex Bruce, was pivotal. A more suspicious person may at this point highlight the fact Bruce senior and junior had played significant parts in ensuring two vital components of the Derby defence would miss the final weeks. Although the returning Lewin Nyatanga stepped up to the plate with the only goal in a home victory against Luton, hopes of a top-two finish were over after a 2-0 defeat at Crystal Palace. After doing the noble thing of relegating Leeds United to the third tier of English football on the final day, preparations began for another shot at the play-offs.

* * *

Bywater looks back, 'We didn't care that we missed out because we knew we'd win in the play-offs. We just knew we were going up. Honestly, the mentality was so positive it was unbelievable. We didn't care who we played either, everyone wanted everyone to play. We were all going to benefit as players and people being part of Derby County in the Premier League so that was our goal. Billy was cool and just said, "We'll go up through the play-offs, it's a great way to go up anyway." And I'd already been up with West Ham and I knew how good it was to win it.'

Bywater, a man who has in the years since been outed as a character due to his penchant for erotic garden artwork and caravans, is as honest and open as modern footballers come. When he reassures his commitment and confidence of promotion at Wembley, it's crystal that he means it.

Perhaps the only other member of the camp who could rival Bywater's self-belief was Barnes. He recalls, 'I don't even know how we had that confidence but we literally all thought we were the best team in the league. If we messed up it was our fault, we never thought a team were better. Even when we missed out it was "don't worry, we're going up anyway". It was that cockiness, but it was an assured one.'

Having dropped out of the top two in the closing stages, the odds began to stack against Davies's side. Since the introduction of the play-offs for the 1986/87 season, only six of those finishing the highest of the four qualifying teams had gone on to win promotion. Given that few sides had come so close to automatic promotion as the Rams in 2007 and with an incredibly strong play-off quartet boasting the recent Premier League experience of West Brom, Southampton and Wolves, the doubts began to emanate about the mental strength of losing out on a top-two place. Although it would be the sixth-placed Saints to come in the semi-finals, a Wembley day out was anything but a guarantee.

Derby may have picked up four points against their opponents in the two league games, including a 1-0 victory at St Mary's, but so many side-notes came in to play that the win could barely be factored in. Southampton, managed by George Burley, boasted not only Inigo Idiakez but also Grzegorz Rasiak, the two men who were forced out of the all-important first-leg loss at Billy Davies's Preston in 2005. Idiakez had returned to the Southampton fray after being loaned out to QPR whereas Rasiak, after a nightmare stint with Tottenham that produced no goals, found the net 18 times in red and white, once more than Derby's Howard. On the Rams' side it was Oakley wearing the armband against the club he served and loved for 12 long years.

Leg one was almost perfect. After falling behind to Andrew Surman's goal, Howard took charge. Derby's number nine already shared many similarities with the great Alan Shearer, not least Howard listing Shearer as his hero. But the two finishes he displayed on the coast were well worthy of the Geordie great. The first, a header from a looping Oakley cross, saw Howard use neck muscles that the average human doesn't realise they possess. The second was a sweetly hit penalty after Pearson got the better of Pele. Howard's Shearer-inspired celebration, the one-armed salute, followed.

As it did for the supporters, victory sparked a reason to crack open some drinks for the players. 'Conversations were better after the first leg,' begins Bywater. 'It was a Saturday, next leg on Tuesday. We all got back on the bus and then the lads went out for a few on the Saturday.' Most except Moore, that is. 'Me, Stevie [Howard] and Mooro walked in on Sunday and Mooro's going, "I can't believe some of the lads were out last night. Massive game on the Tuesday, it's a disgrace" and me and Stevie are agreeing. Anyway, we were out and we celebrated that win,' he laughs.

'Mooro must have gone home and thought differently because I remember him being fuming, but they were massive wins and you still need to be human and switch off, because that's what we did. It was more of a release of pressure; it was so hyped. It was a beautiful hot day, by the time you're home it's eight o'clock or whatever, and you just think "let's have a drink together".'

The turnover before the return leg was short, with only two full days to wait before Pride Park hosted. Hope turned into expectation but whether you made the journey over the A52 footbridge, passed over the train tracks or even journeyed from right down in Southampton, nobody could have anticipated a second of what they were to witness that night.

'I scored the first goal from a corner to put us 3-1 ahead but within a few minutes they scored. It was pulsating,' said Moore, whose header inside the opening two minutes was balanced out immediately after Jhon Viafara pounced on a Bywater error. Into the second half, Viafara scored again to make the score 3-3 on aggregate. Moore adds, 'Don't forget that with Derby County, when you look at those play-offs, we were playing against two teams who had come down from the Premier League. Both teams dropped down, we had just survived the season before and come the end of the season we then have these two titanic fixtures when let's face it, nobody gave us a chance of even the play-offs.'

Sometimes a saviour can come in the most unlikely form and eight years before he would become a Ram, Leon Best made his most important contribution to the cause. His sliced own-goal finish from a corner re-established Derby's lead but, with so many contenders, the connections were soon to come into play.

First, Rasiak's 89th-minute winner on the night levelled the tie overall. 'It was one of the biggest moments in my career when I scored the goal. I always liked to play at Pride Park, it was a pleasure for me to even be back there against the club,' the Pole recalled.

It saved Southampton and put them firmly into the ascendancy with 30 more minutes to come, 30 exhausting minutes that produced no more goals. Pride Park Stadium, and all 31,569 inside, was about to witness history.

'We did all the preparations for penalties but people get nervous on the day and can't take the pressure. I've met loads who can do training ground penalties but ours on the night were just solid,' says Bywater, who was down to take number five. 'You'd walk up to that ball and think, "I'm going to score this. But if I don't, my team-mates are right behind me, they won't care because they'll put their arm round me anyway." When you have that backing, you go up there relaxed and you're on to a winner. I don't know what their camp was like but I know ours. If you miss, no problems. If you score, well done pal.'

Best fired the first kick wide, compounding his own night's work. David Jones and Steve Howard made no mistake from the first two Derby efforts, and neither did Barnes from the third. Rasiak, who missed in a white shirt in the 2005 second leg, found the back of the net this time around. A collective intake of breath met the fourth taker, the realisation that the occasionally wild-footed Jay McEveley would step up, but again he gave Kelvin Davis no chance. That set the stage for Idiakez, who had to score. Under the pouring rain, he missed. By a long way, and Derby were through to the final.

The Spaniard recalled, 'It was difficult because in the end, it was a penalty shoot-out against Derby County. I loved the club and the fans and everything I did there, so it was weird for me and for Grzegorz but that's football. I don't know how to explain it. I was the fifth and we'd already missed one. The day before that I think we missed one all day in training. Me and Leon Best were incredible at them but both missed. I was quite relaxed before taking it and knew what I wanted to do but ... yeah. But I really believed we should have beaten Derby.

'I was quite happy for Derby to go through though because I had ex-team-mates there. Some of the fans still thank me for it but I promise it wasn't on purpose! If there was one team I didn't mind doing it against, it was them.'

It's a night that has gone on to be recognised as the greatest in the history of Pride Park and remains a contender for one of the best encounters Derby have ever participated in. Oakley savoured the occasion more than anyone else, 'We beat them down there, went physical and it felt good to be part of a team where I had a group around me that could beat Southampton. The return leg was unbelievable for everyone, up and down and not knowing what's happening.

'The rain as well, it was such an amazing night looking back at the pictures. I think all of that emotion was building up because Derby had been in such a bad place in previous seasons. It was so good to finally just get over that line.'

As thousands took to the pitch, embracing the squad who hadn't managed to make it down the tunnel in time, chants of 'Que Sera' rang out. The next morning, thousands of those same supporters who were still wringing out clothes in the faint hope they would be saveable after being drenched, joined the snake around the stadium for Wembley tickets.

* * *

'You are potentially changing your life. You're 90 minutes away from the Premier League where it will completely change the outlook of the club, the money will change, it's the most exciting game,' Paul Peschisolido says. 'It's almost impossible not to get too excited but you do have to keep yourself level otherwise your emotions run away, so you have to try and play it down. Billy took us away to a spa where we had treatments, there was a training pitch there, he had the right approach just to come away from the circus.'

One masterstroke from Davies was in how he recognised the needs of every member of his squad. Bywater recalls how he was paired with Peschisolido, 'I shared a room with Pesch in the build-up and I loved it. I just remember getting up early on the day with Pesch and just chilling out, having a coffee and looking at the nice hotel we were staying in.

'We'd have a chat and banter and have a "can you believe we're going to win today? We're going to win today!" I was like his excited kid, but he would calm me down, which is probably why we roomed. Maybe it was strategic to put us together actually.' Mid-conversation, Bywater has a realisation, 'He was experienced and had been there, he was probably sent to calm me down, wasn't he? Otherwise I'd have been up all night like Tigger!'

Barnes's situation was identical. 'I'd been rooming with Mooro and it was the best thing that could have ever happened to me. I could have been in with Lewin or Nathan Doyle but they put me with Mooro and it was an eye-opening thing for me on a day-to-day basis. He used to ask me to make him CDs. He loves R&B so he'd be like, "Barnesy, we're in the room this weekend. Make me a CD. Slow jam."

'We had strict bedtimes, strict rules on what could be on TV before the game and it got me into a professional routine. If I'd have been in with a younger player, we'd have just been talking about girls and eating Haribo. But Darren is an amazing guy and it was great to see someone who played that many games in all leagues conduct himself in that manner and treat people as they were, not for what they earned. If Mooro walks into a room with 20 people who don't know him, he's going to say hello to each and every one of them and converse with every single one.'

The preparation for the final, in which West Brom would be the final hurdle to overcome, was meticulous. After original training, Davies moved his side from their Moor Farm base to Champneys Springs, but there remained hiccups along the way. The move may have been pre-planned but the paranoia of the side being outed ensured Davies's preparations went to extreme and often bizarre levels.

Bywater mentions one session that stands out, 'We were training one day and suddenly Billy goes, "Stop. Stop … STOP. EVERYBODY IN." He thought people were spying on us because there was a plane going over. That's when we went to Claridge's I think. It was around the time when Manchester United got a photo taken from above and he thought the same was happening to us.'

The fear of spies wasn't a first, Davies constantly wary. Peschisolido, who had played only once since the end of March, was barely expected to make the squad at Wembley, let alone the 11. In the play-offs, January signing Jon Macken was given the nod to partner Howard and with Barnes looking likely to up his return from injury, the Canadian looked like his time at Derby was done, with his contract running down. If anything, he would have been the last person any Rams supporter expected to see in the 11, but Davies's mind games meant he got the nod.

Peschisolido remembers, 'Billy told us the side very close to kick-off. He was ever so secretive about everything and almost paranoid about it. I was holding on to the secret of starting for so long, days in fact. Here's me thinking I'm not involved in the semi at all, and now I'm playing in the biggest game of this club's existence in recent years. Even when he announced the teams, the lads looked at me as if to say "really?"'

It proved to be the Canadian's final outing in a Derby shirt, released in the summer with no more than a letter of termination.

Derby, who were sporting a special one-off shirt for the occasion, found themselves up against it from the off. Despite finishing third, it was painfully evident that West Brom had more quality across the field. Relegated the previous season, Tony Mowbray's 11 still boasted a front line worthy of the Premier League, with Kevin

Phillips and Diomansy Kamara lining up ahead of Jason Koumas and Zoltan Gera. Even the likes of Nathan Ellington and John Hartson may have made claims for Derby's 11.

It was once again the task for Moore, who had left the Hawthorns for Pride Park almost 18 months previously, to keep out his former colleagues, 'I knew the squad and I knew every strength of that squad too. And I knew on the day that if we could defend properly, we'd get two or three chances in the game and we had to be ready to take one. Because West Brom played very good football under Tony Mowbray, I knew a lot of the players and things at the club, but on the day we were absolutely spot on defensively.'

There was little surprise in the manner of the afternoon, West Brom running the game without finding the net. The introduction of a barely fit Barnes early into the second half turned the tide though, albeit for 20 seconds. How he was able to take to the field though is a puzzle. He remembers, 'I can't pinpoint a date that I broke my foot because I'd been playing with so much pain and had just been on injections for a long time. I started to get the pain in my foot towards the end of the season but as a young boy, you get told it's fatigue and because there wasn't much swelling around that area, it was a case of "you'll be all right, take this".

'I had a stress fracture in my navicular but after Southampton is when it really started to hurt and it really started to feel like something was not right. I'd got a new crack in there where it was starting to split further and that's when I felt the pain. In the final was when I felt a bang in my foot and that was a crazy feeling because I was that doped up on injections. I had three before the game and one at half-time. When I could feel the pain and I couldn't walk at full time, I knew I was in trouble.'

Barnes, unleashed by Steve Howard down the right, squared for the onrushing Stephen Pearson. As Davies had predicted in a conversation with Peter Gadsby prior to his signing, he scored the goal that would take the side back to the top flight. 'Once we scored, I just knew we wouldn't concede,' Bywater says. 'Our mentality and our graft, we'd done too much throughout the whole year to not get through. I remember Seth [Johnson] struggling and nearly collapsing with his knee but he went on as long as he could. He would literally dive head first into that ball. He had one leg but we just had characters like that and when we scored, I'd just look at West Brom and think, "You ain't scoring."'

Graham Poll's blast of the whistle – the final one of his career – signalled promotion. Derby County were now £80m richer. From facing administration a year earlier, the bank account was bigger than ever before. Peschisolido, the man who made way for Barnes, was delirious: 'The feeling on the bench was unbelievable. We were just staring at the clock, they piled on the pressure, you just kept looking at the ref and screaming for him to blow the whistle. And when you finally hear the whistle it was euphoria. You can't describe the feeling because you lose yourself and you're kissing and hugging everybody, it was superb.'

Davies had completed his three-year plan within ten months of settling in, done with a group who really shouldn't have completed it. The afternoon was the final time Seth Johnson would ever take to a pitch as a professional, forced to retire after one injury too many. It was the final day for Peschisolido, released weeks later. Morten Bisgaard, Lee Camp and Paul Boertien all followed.

It was almost the final game for Barnes, too, advised by a specialist in the coming weeks that he should consider retirement. He recalls, 'Everyone was celebrating and I was in the room crying because I was in that much pain, I didn't know what was going on because the painkillers had worn off and my foot was just throbbing. I got an x-ray two days after and they tell me you've got a stress fracture and if this doesn't heal, you're in big trouble.'

Bywater, who celebrated by screaming 'get your rat out' into the live tv cameras and was next seen covered in powder, savoured a moment with his roommate, 'It was Powerade that Pesch threw over me in the changing room; you don't want that in your eyes. It's all crystal clear though now. I loved every minute of celebrating and they're moments you'll remember forever, I just wanted to hug everyone.'

Davies hadn't been awash with funds and he hadn't built a side that should have challenged at the top end of the table. The group he forged though had exactly what was required to get themselves over the line. Even come January, when rumours of a split over bonuses worked their way into sections of the media, that group spirit maintained.

Bywater continued, 'We had a big bonus to get promoted and we were given the option to keep it between us. But we decided to split it pro-rata with everyone so that even the subs got a part of it. We were all willing to go that extra mile and every player, even those not playing, were going to get a benefit in some shape or form. There were lads getting married in the summer, it paid for their weddings.

'We had a decision to make during the year; do we want to do the bonus between the first group of 16 before January or do we want to split it? And we all decided to split it. Nobody does that usually. The people who played way back in September, they got the bonus as well. They all got a slice of the cake. Holidays, weddings, houses all paid for. I don't think many people know that. We could have been selfish but we split the cake so everyone would still get the benefits.'

The bonus was split across the playing staff and after journeying back to Derby, there was an extra splash from the chairman, who looks back, 'Having been promoted to the Premier League, the team stayed overnight in the Windsor Hotel. We had a well-earned late-night drinking session and I personally put an extra £3,000 behind the bar as a request from a lovely, genuine person in Michael Johnson.

'I recall going out to the car park and Bob Malcolm was loading his car with six cases of champagne. I challenged him as to why he was doing it. His reply was, "You've got £50m now."'

Gadsby, who by that point in the day had far bigger problems to deal with than Malcolm's stash, was left to deal with the aftermath of what should have been a perfect day. The three-year plan had been completed in one, the club were now swimming in millions and Premier League football was back after a five-year absence. Things should have been perfect, but nothing ever is in Derby.

THAT SEASON

'I KNEW that we were in a very, very bad place.' Matt Oakley doesn't need the question to reach its completion before stepping in. 'We had the elation of getting promoted but as soon as that game finished, and with the dawn of what was coming, I knew we were in big trouble.'

The Rams' skipper had barely reached the sanctuary of the Wembley changing rooms before realising what was to come in the following months.

As the rest of his team-mates celebrated and 35,000 drank their way back to the East Midlands, Oakley contemplated the struggle that was to come. Yet even he, the voice of the group and with all of his years of footballing experience, couldn't anticipate the severity of the immediate future.

The precursor to 2007/08 began at full time when Billy Davies told Sky Sports he wished it was his Preston North End side he was celebrating with. Not the ideal time to air his frustrations and a turn of phrase that drew fury.

'We achieved success in the first attempt into the promised land at Wembley and Billy Davies made his infamous statement to the press coming off the pitch that it should have been Preston,' Peter Gadsby recalls. 'This was a complete downer as the press, the players and fans picked up on it.

'Mike Horton turned to me and said, "Fucking sack him now!"'

'I could almost see the headlines: "What sort of a muppet chairman recruits a manager when you've nearly been relegated with a limited squad and funds, gets to Wembley to the Premier League with a £50m prize and sacks him?"'

'Billy and the club never recovered from his outburst. I honestly believe Billy never saw himself as a Premier League manager. His success was always built on the underdogs and fighting everybody. He knew he could get £1.5m from us if he was sacked, just as we would have got £1.5m for him if he had been poached from us.

'He made life very difficult and he cleared off to Dubai for two weeks. His agent Jim Price was an extremely difficult person who was almost teasing us to sack Billy.

'As a chairman you want to explain many things to the fans so when we asked Billy for his budget and his list of players for the Premier League, his reply via his agent was, "You are never going to give him enough money," to which we said, "Well why don't you try us?" He then continued to frustrate us and the weeks were passing by.

'He eventually produced a list of players and one I recall was David Nugent who he had at Preston years before. Nugent would be available for £10m but his salary was way out of reach.'

It's difficult to fathom how the relationship between manager and chairman could sour so quickly. Just a year earlier, Gadsby and Davies proudly greeted one another as the private helicopter carrying the wee Glaswegian landed at Moor Farm. They had worked together to achieve the near impossible and as a duo had found the working relationship to take Derby County back to the promised land. It was the exact opposite scenario that Burley and Murdo Mackay had three years earlier. Yet less than 12 months later, they could barely bring themselves to converse.

On that day at Wembley, it wasn't only the Sky cameras who took the brunt of Davies' implosion, as BBC Radio Derby commentator Ross Fletcher recalls, 'He came over to be interviewed live by Colin Gibson and we had Ted McMinn as our summariser at the time, sitting next to me in the stands. Colin asks him the first question about his emotions and the day and instead of answering, he takes it as an opportunity to just rip into Ted McMinn! "All the things that you've said Ted, how about that now Ted?" and just talks to him directly. We could see him down on the pitch looking for Ted in the stands, wagging his finger.'

Whether Davies wanted to remain manager is a question only he can answer. Speaking with *FourFourTwo* in 2018, he said, 'I immediately called a meeting with the staff and told them that no matter what happens, it looks as if we're going to be out of the door come the summer. After the play-off final, what I said was, "I don't know if I'll be here next season." The press never clarified with me why I said that. I was trying to say that something's going on. They tried to make it out that it was the Davies Show, but it wasn't.' Except, it probably was.

Davies, in his regular way of speaking about himself in the third person, added: 'Davies had a knife in his back. Peter Gadsby was excellent and told me what was happening; that they were going to become an outgoing board.'

Conflicting opinions between the two key men at the club. But if Davies did want to remain, his pre-season business didn't point towards it. Somehow, early indicators of his transfer intent only made the task of Premier League survival even more unrealistic.

First through the door came Robert Earnshaw, an anomaly in the fact nobody knew who signed or wanted him. 'When Earnshaw joined, we didn't know he'd fallen out with his long-term girlfriend and he was shattered. He was banged up in some hotel and everybody said he was depressed,' recalls Gadsby. But as Fletcher remembers, 'Who exactly wanted Earnshaw? It certainly wasn't Billy.' His £3.5m signing, a club record that surpassed Lee Morris, scored one league goal, a consolation in a 6-2 home defeat to Arsenal in April.

Andy Todd, son of Rams legend Colin, was next in after making a £750,000 switch from Blackburn. 'As soon as I heard the interest, I wanted it to happen. I was born in Derby, my father had a great career at Derby and everything seemed right to go. Being a Derby boy, I just wanted to play for my hometown club. It didn't work out how I wanted but I was very proud to pull that white shirt on, mainly because of how well my dad did there,' he said.

Then there was Claude Davis, who Gadsby recalls 'could trap a ball further than I could kick it'. A £3m signing from relegated Sheffield United, he had previous experience with the manager from his time at Deepdale, yet became the epitome of the crisis Derby soon became embroiled in. Goalkeepers Lewis Price (from Ipswich Town) and Ben Hinchliffe (Preston North End's third choice) followed, lumbering full-back Andy Griffin the next.

There was a ray of potential light when one morning, *Derby Evening Telegraph* newspaper boards across the city boasted 'Rams sign international'. Unfortunately, the international in question was a 33-year-old Eddie Lewis, recently relegated to League One with Leeds. Fellow American Benny Feilhaber joined to replace Seth Johnson, but he would appear just ten times. Nobody really knows if he was any good or not. Rounding off the additions on deadline day was Kenny Miller, 'a nasty piece of work' according to Gadsby. Still, he did manage to provide the one positive of the campaign.

Oakley, slowly growing accustomed to his new team-mates, provides insight into how the changing-room dynamic can begin to alter over a summer: 'Players leave and then new ones come in and sometimes you're close to some of those leaving and you don't have a relationship with the new ones. Straight away you're thinking "why are they doing that?" Sometimes it works, sometimes not. I just knew that we weren't strong going into that season. It was always, always going to be difficult for us.'

* * *

Thirteen years have passed but the embarrassment remains. 'Sorry to bring this up' every conversation would begin before mumbling over the horrors of 2007/08, mentally questioning whether a trigger warning would be advisable. For you reading this now, just the mention of that season will provide gruesome flashbacks. Everybody associated with the club knew it would be a difficult 12 months ahead, but nobody realised the extent of what they were about to endure. That is nobody aside from those who were paid to wear the shirt.

'As soon as I got there, I could sense that we were just there to make the numbers up. You could smell the fear around the place,' Andy Todd sighs.

'There's no doubt in my mind that what was happening upstairs within the club impacted the team on the pitch, without a doubt. Suddenly from a positive year, the club became surrounded in negativity.'

Something seems amiss when Darren Moore mentions this. Roundly regarded as one of the friendliest men in football, when even 'Big Dave' opens the lid on the simmering anger slowly making its way through the heart of the club and into the changing room, the simple task of blaming Davies for everything that went wrong early on seems unfair. The new additions may have led to low morale from the outset but Davies himself had the same mindset as many of the players; he wasn't at a happy club.

A squad so united under Davies a year before wouldn't be divided, no matter what he spewed on the Wembley pitch. Against the club was where their attention started to turn as resentment grew.

Giles Barnes was a man in demand, the latest wonderkid to make his way into English football. From his first appearance under Phil Brown, rumours grew about where his future lay, with Pride Park simply not big enough for a player of his potential. It was hoped, or more likely expected, that his talents would be shown at the club he'd progressed through the ranks at, but from the summer he felt unwanted. 'You know what, fuck it. West Ham had three bids for me turned down in the summer. No, they had one accepted. I remember getting a phone call saying their second bid had been accepted for £8m,' he says.

'I was in a bit of shock because the club had promised me I was their future and then a few hours later I get another phone call saying Derby had changed their mind and they now wanted more money. I assumed that if they turned that kind of money down, surely, they'd reinvest? It said to me that they didn't need the money. And I never asked to leave that club once. I know a lot of people think I did and it would have been easy for me to ask because I'm from Barking, my uncle played for West Ham and my family is all from London. It would have been easy for me to force it, but I didn't want to leave Derby.'

By the time Oakley led out his new-look squad on the opening day, they'd already been dragged through the mill. Often unsure of who would be in the dugout and who would be wearing the shirt, it wasn't healthy preparation.

But the off-field drama wasn't reflected in those early weeks and within five minutes of the season kicking off, Derby sat top of the Premier League table and were on course for their first title in 33 years. The captain struck from Steve Howard's knock-down and although they fell behind, Todd's late equaliser secured a point against a strong Portsmouth outfit. The subsequent 1-0 defeat at Sven's Manchester City had positives too, even if Davies continued to insist that he needed extra financial support come the final whistle. Two games in and the Rams didn't look out of place in the division, acquitting themselves well against two sides expected to sit in and around the UEFA Cup spots. Matchdays three, four and five changed the tone.

'Oh Tottenham was a bit of a heavy one,' Moore chuckles. A 4-0 defeat was the first of many horror afternoons and really could have been worse, Derby having conceded three times inside the first 14 minutes. 'I just said to the lads, "Come on, we've got this season, we can do this, I'm telling you. This has been a right eye-opener for us all, but we need to regroup from here."' Moore's words fell on deaf ears.

The Spurs defeat could be passed off as expected. After all, Martin Jol was given the task of reaching the top four. The first real indication of the severity of the job at hand came at home to Birmingham the following week, Cameron Jerome scoring inside 32 seconds. Four games in, zero wins and a pending realisation that even home bankers against fellow promoted sides would provide unanticipated challenges.

'The only chance we would have ever had that year was performing at home and catching teams with a good crowd, creating an energy at Pride Park,' said Oakley, who with two goals in his first two home games had risen to the occasion as captain, even though he could recognise the cracks. 'That's probably what happened on that first game of the season, we surprised them and scored early and tried to hang on.

'But deep down, even then I knew that we didn't have enough quality. The team that got promoted were only just strong enough for the Championship in my opinion. Players that play in the Championship can get by, but if you put them in the Premier League you can quickly see that they're either physically not capable or technically not good enough. That's highlighted very quickly. Our squad was strong enough for the Championship but never anywhere near the level of the Premier League. It just amplified our weaknesses.'

A week later, Oakley and co were hit for the first of many sixes. Davies, opting to play Mo Camara and Bob Malcolm despite the fact neither were even in the matchday squad come the end of the previous season, watched on as his side were humiliated 6-0 at Anfield. When even Andriy Voronin scored, the severity of what was to come became horribly clear. Bookmakers Paddy Power paid out on relegation with 33 games to play.

* * *

It's sometimes difficult to remember that there was one good night among 37 other torrid ones during the campaign. Kenny Miller, unleashed straight into the 11 for the visit of Sam Allardyce's Newcastle United, rifled a half-volley past Steve Harper five minutes before the break. Slightly later than planned and having missed chances to extend the lead through Howard, Derby County had announced themselves back in the Premier League. 'I'm delighted with the players and they can take a lot of confidence from this victory,' Davies beamed upon full time, but he hadn't anticipated the next journey. Or maybe he had but was simply bluffing.

If anybody was preparing to get carried away and dream of safety, a 5-0 drubbing by Arsenal halted all thoughts. BBC Radio Derby's Ross Fletcher, like thousands of supporters, had travelled 684 miles for three away games. He had seen Stephen Bywater pick the ball out of his net 15 times without reply. He would have to wait another five matches before having a goal to celebrate, that coming when 4-0 down at Old Trafford.

Fletcher says, 'Arsenal away was just so painfully obvious. It was the game after beating Newcastle and they'd already lost 6-0 to Liverpool by then and you're thinking, "Okay, let's have a bit of faith here, we've just won." But then they went to Arsenal and got played off the park. In the first 45, they barely got out of their own half and it was embarrassing, hopeless. I didn't know how they'd recover but not quite to the extent that they wouldn't win another game the whole season. The defeat at Arsenal was soul-sapping.'

Pre-season hopes, already limited by off-field fall-out, had been destroyed. When they couldn't even beat Bolton Wanderers, the one side momentarily below them, the writing was on the wall – and it was still only September. Barnes, still recovering from the broken foot suffered at Wembley, was gradually introduced to the nightmare, 'When you start getting drubbed every week and things really aren't adding up after how well we did the year before, you think to yourself, "We're in the Premier League but we're not really a Premier League team." We were going to teams and we had the mentality of "let's just keep it down today". There were times, a couple of fives in a row and at those times you are only focused on keeping the score down. "Don't embarrass yourself" is what was being said among us.

'You began to see people go into their own agendas and look after themselves in that situation. You see people that aren't about the team and they didn't know what it meant to be a Derby player. I came through the academy so I can say that, but you would see certain things and you're just thinking, "Okay so he is just out here for himself, he doesn't give a fuck about any of us." When you get that in the team, that's when the cracks appear.'

The club became a sinking ship and as the horror began to unfold in front of their eyes, the board quickly reached for the lifeboats, leaving Gadsby on stormy seas. He said, 'We lost 6-0 to Liverpool and the rest of the board said they wanted out. We needed more money but they wouldn't put more money into the club.'

Funds had dried up and the Premier League dream had left manager and officials hankering for a departure. First Davies stated his intentions, then the people who saved it from the hands of Keith et al. Slowly things were becoming toxic and the ripple was being felt by the squad.

* * *

Adam Pearson contemplates speaking for a few days and even mid-conversation, he questions whether he has made the right choice to tread back down his Derby County path. Having made a name for himself with Hull City and later in rugby league, he became Gadsby's choice to take up the position of chairman as interest in the club rose from across the pond. He remembers, 'I went in there to start with hoping that we would stay up. At that point the aim was to finalise a deal initiated before my time, the GSE investment. It was hoped that would come as quickly as possible to help with additional finance to help the fight to stay in the Premier League.

'But obviously once I became immersed in the club it became very clear that the squad wasn't going to be able to compete in the division. So, I continued to search to try and finalise the deal that the board put on the starting block. That was my priority while at the same time hoping we could bring some extra players in in January to aid with the push.'

The interest from American group General Sports and Entertainment first took hold around October and with Gadsby looking to negotiate an opportunity to secure additional funds, he brought Pearson to the club to help get the deal over the line. But as much as he had to deal with the financial side of his position, he had a duty of dealing with Davies. As Pearson says, 'It was...' Impossible? Doomed? 'Difficult. I'm sure Billy feels as though I'd made up my mind and he should go but that was not the case before I joined. I really wanted him to continue to lead the club but it became clear pretty quickly that was not going to happen.'

Davies wasn't shy about his feelings at the time. Claiming after a 2-0 defeat at home to Chelsea that he hadn't exchanged a word with Pearson in three weeks proved to be the final straw. That comment, which followed on from telling the media that 'this team is not good enough for the Premier League, they know that', meant Pearson had to act.

The nature of Davies's final defeat was positive in comparison to many others. A fortnight before, a West Ham side missing 11 first-teamers arrived at Pride Park, struck five times and left the Scotsman staring at the biggest humiliation of his managerial career.

Giles Barnes, who started in the West Ham humiliation against the side he could have joined in the summer, stood on in disbelief at what was happening around him and offers an idea of the psyche of the group.

He said, 'There were some games where I can replay goals in my head but not the team and that is one of them. I just remember being out there and thinking "this is not good". You don't want to walk the streets, you don't go out for dinner with your mates and being 18 years old, these are things you should be doing with your friends and enjoying what I had been working hard for. I remember times where I couldn't even step out of my house, I'd be shopping in Tesco and people would just approach you. I'd understand their frustration, I get it. You think I want to lose? You think I want to look in the newspaper and see that we're being hammered again? I was one of you guys, I busted my arse to get there and it was not how I envisioned it.'

Davies's sacking was long awaited. Perhaps engineered by him, perhaps not. Regardless, it was a sad finish to the tenure of a man who delivered exactly what he promised. 'I remember losing 2-0 to Chelsea but we played really well and that night there we felt within the club we had turned a corner,' Darren Moore explains. 'I felt like we were clicking but when Billy left, that just knocked the stuffing out of us. He upped and left and it had a detrimental effect, a real lull on the club.'

Matt Oakley, handed the armband on his first day at Moor Farm and having worked closer with Davies than any other player, was left at a loss, 'Billy and I were very, very close. He pulled me aside before it happened on the day, just to let me know before it all came out. It was a sad day for me and him because we worked together for that season and went on such a journey, we were closer than I've been with a manager up until that point. I don't think we were turning it around though, there weren't many good moments so something had to give.'

Davies's 17 months in the East Midlands would, in the years to follow, roundly be forgotten due to the next move he made, but he remains the last manager to lead the club back to the top division. His 2007/08 points tally upon his departure was six.

* * *

Pearson's search for a new manager took just under 48 hours. 'We wanted somebody with immediate Premier League experience and Paul Jewell had kept Wigan there after getting them up,' he said. He wasn't the first man quizzed though, nor even the first Paul.

'Adam led negotiations for the new man, and we got down to three interviews,' Gadsby says. 'I can't remember the other but two were Paul Jewell and Paul Ince.' Ince, who was in charge at League Two side MK Dons, had just over two years of managerial experience to his name yet was consistently tipped for positions above his station.

Gadsby continues, 'I said to Adam, "How did you get on with Ince?" and he told me that he'd walked in, Adam said, "Hello Paul" and he replied, "It's not Paul, it's The Guvnor." The interview didn't last very long.'

Jewell, the jovial Scouser who had guided Wigan to the Premier League and a League Cup final, spoke years later about how he was first approached for the role in August, but was made to wait until November when Davies departed. He has also since discussed a call from David Moyes 'warning me not to go to Derby because they wouldn't win another game all season'. Foolishly, he laughed it off and took on the challenge, unaware of the damage it would do to not only his reputation but also his mindset.

'I knew before Paul had come in that the damage was done,' Andy Todd sighs. 'I felt sorry for him really because he inherited a squad that was losing and had got used to losing as a habit.' Working with a squad who mentally were absent and physically were incapable, the ex-Wigan chief couldn't have imagined the scenario he would encounter. Neither could his staff, of which Paul Winstanley was a part.

Winstanley already knew Jewell well, working with him at the JJB Stadium and providing him with information that would help to put in place the foundations of Wigan's remarkable rise to the top half of the division. Leading up the analysis, the expectation for Winstanley, today the head of recruitment with Brighton, was a scene similar to his last role under Jewell, albeit at a bigger club.

The scene that greeted them on their first day at the club was beyond imagination. Winstanley says, 'When he had the opportunity at Derby, he wanted a similar structure to what he had at Wigan. Derby were struggling at the bottom of the league but we recognised it as a great football club with great fans and an opportunity to be part of something. I remember at the time thinking we had a chance of staying up having not stepped foot into the building. But it quickly became apparent within a few days that the players had given up. They were dead. I've never witnessed anything like it. It wasn't a nice feeling and it was very difficult for Paul and his staff to pick them up. You had people like Darren Moore who were top characters but then you had one or two who weren't.'

Ask any career advisor and they'll tell you the first day in a new role is usually too early to tell how you'll settle in. You'll likely hide the full extent of your personality, provide the very best version of yourself and certainly won't let on your bad eating habits at lunchtime. But on day one of Jewell's reign, Oakley noticed some warning signs: 'I got on really well with Paul, let me just say that. But I do remember a kind of flag for me was in the first session. I remember doing a passing drill and he put a punishment on a bad or misplaced pass. I know why he was trying to do it, but he destroyed a lot of young lads in that training session, saying they weren't good enough and "this is why you're at the bottom, you can't even pass it ten yards". He was looking for a reaction but the way he did it destroyed a lot of the younger lads in that session. We needed someone to pick up the squad, not push us down and tell us we weren't good enough.'

Like Winstanley, Moore had worked with Jewell previously at Bradford and he 'knew if we developed that same tenacity and steel that he can instil in his teams, we'd have a real chance'. The early signs suggested he may be able to do that. He was seconds away from picking up a hard-earned draw in his first match away at Sunderland, but an Anthony Stokes stoppage-time winner hinted at what was about to come. The footballing gods, if they do exist, had only just begun to inflict their wrath on Jewell.

He was to experience no new-manager bounce and instead could only watch on as the situation got painfully worse. A solitary point from the next three – taking the tally from 18 games up to seven points, with four of those coming against Newcastle – left the side marooned at the bottom. It wasn't even Christmas and the gap to second-bottom Fulham was already eight points. In the darkest corners of Pride Park's executive offices, the side were already preparing for life after relegation.

Jewell could and probably should have had his first victory on 30 December. After being robbed of a draw by Steven Gerrard's 90th-minute Boxing Day winner for Liverpool, Oakley's opener at home to Blackburn had the Rams in the ascendancy. Had Steve Howard doubled the lead from the penalty spot, it's hard to imagine the three points would have been let slip and with a favourable run of games to come, things could have at least begun to turn a little. Instead, Brad Friedel kept his spot kick out and within five minutes, a potential 2-0 lead had turned into a 2-1 deficit, the way it finished.

Adam Pearson was left speechless, 'You can read the writing on the wall sometimes, can't you? You would put your money on Steve Howard to score against Blackburn and I thought in those early games under Paul we showed a great deal of hunger, of promise and verve but we couldn't get the points. That soon eats away at the morale and the unity and the passion of the team and it was a very difficult time.'

Morale was gone and soon so were the two key performers from the promotion season. Howard, inexplicably let go to Leicester for marginally more than the £1m paid, was hard to fathom. Without warning and having started him against Rovers only two days before, Jewell allowed the workhorse forward to leave. Within days, Oakley was making the same move.

Oakley said, 'I had a call from my agent going into January saying that Leicester had made an offer for me and I wasn't to go to the Derby training ground, I was to drive straight to Leicester. So that's what I did. I remember being about to sign the paperwork for the transfer to go through and it was all being done by Adam Pearson because he'd tried to recoup some money by getting rid of Steve and me. There was then a call from Paul to Ian Holloway and I remember Ian getting a mouthful from Paul and saying he wasn't happy about me leaving, he wanted me to stay and he knew nothing of it.'

Within only a month of being at the club, Jewell was having his warriors of the promotion campaign stolen from underneath him. Oakley continued, 'There was obviously a disconnect between Paul and Pearson. At that point I'd already had a medical and my head was there. Leicester were a club that wanted me, and Derby were one that didn't want me. I wasn't looking to leave at all though. I got the club into the Premier League and we at least then had a pot of money behind us where we could have bounced back up again with a stronger squad. But it was all Adam Pearson unfortunately, it was his decision to agree and sell me. Paul didn't want me to go.'

* * *

January 2008 was a dark, dark time for everyone associated with Derby County. The loss of Oakley and Howard perplexed supporters and the additions in their place did little to build back trust in the new regime. Early additions saw Danny Mills arrive on loan, play just three times, get injured and ultimately return to Manchester City before being forced into early retirement. Laurent Robert joined on a free transfer. If ever you needed a man for a relegation battle, the flamboyant luxury of the Frenchman was not it. Next came a £4m splurge on two players of very differing backgrounds.

First in was Emmanuel 'Tito' Villa, a forward signed from Mexican outfit UAG for £2.5m. 'We were convinced that Tito would come in and score goals,' admits Pearson. 'Or that if he didn't in the Premier League, he would in the Championship. That didn't work out. With overseas players they work or they don't and when they don't get an early goal they struggle and that happened with Laurent and Tito. Villa was an expensive recruit and we expected him to get goals, but it didn't happen.'

Villa fared relatively well. His three goals in half a season made him the second top scorer across all 38 games and had he had a full season, he would have been considerably out in front with six.

Five days later came one Robert William Savage, no stranger to the city of Derby. Hatred is a strong word but befitting of the fan opinion of Savage prior to his unveiling. Still largely despised for his tunnel-shaking days with Leicester City, the signing didn't go down well. The fact he would be the new captain? Even less so. Wearing the number 44 because 'four plus four equals eight', he divided an already exacerbated support. A minority were happy to see a player with fight and top-flight experience installed into the centre of the park. It was at least one step further away from Bob Malcolm returning to the side, after he'd been found asleep and drunk in the middle lane of the M1, having thought he'd parked up on the hard shoulder. Most, however, were furious because a) they didn't like the man and b) the club had spent £1.5m on a 33-year-old who couldn't get into the Blackburn team.

Pearson said, 'We knew it was a risk but we thought his enthusiasm and his passion would overcome scepticism and his previous relationship with the supporters. We then thought he would give us an injection of togetherness and unity and leadership and a desire we were lacking. It didn't work out that way. He was a very decent human being, but it didn't work as a chemistry with Paul or the team at that particular point.' Pearson, cheque book well and truly out, was signing off on deals of desperation.

And those new additions didn't gel, as Moore reflects, 'The dressing room was bound to change because Matt [Oakley] and Stevie [Howard] played a big part in taking the club forward. When they go and new players are coming in, you have people who think those new players are just going to take their spots. That was difficult to take at the time and so we were really disappointed, really low at that point.'

Further signings of Hossam Ghaly, Roy Carroll, Mile Sterjovski and Alan Stubbs rocketed the wage bill and somehow worsened the squad. Jewell's January was meant to inject life into the team and remove the negativity but only served to make matters worse, as Winstanley remembers: 'Paul tried to have a big impact straight away, but January is a horrendous market to try and do anything. Thinking back, there must have been nine players that came in that month and it was absolutely the wrong thing to do.

'The lads were already on the floor and the lads that were there, they figured they had no future at the club because all of these players were on their way in, so they became a problem. The players that were brought in just weren't good enough either. At that point, your short-term fix becomes a long-term problem and that was really the start of it. The scouts' hands were tied. Everyone was under pressure to bring players through at that point. January by its nature is a limited market, you overpay for players who are not that level. In hindsight it should have been a case of picking players off the floor and going with what we had, maybe bring one or two in rather than almost a full squad overhaul.'

Off the field, the takeover of the club had been completed late in January by the American consortium that was General Sports and Entertainment.

There was an initial wave of optimism with a 1-1 draw at home to Manchester City in the first game under the new ownership, followed a few days later by a draw at Birmingham thanks to Villa's late equaliser.

But those results were sandwiched either side by a 4-1 humbling at home to Championship side Preston North End in the FA Cup, and a 3-0 Pride Park reverse to Tottenham Hotspur in the Premier League.

The die was cast. Jewell's failed signings were damaging but by that point, relegation was certain. The incomings weren't good enough and for the current squad, they had sunken deeper under the new boss, as Giles Barnes recalls: 'He was great when he first came in because he brought a lot of enthusiasm and a lot of ideas. But something just turned, and I don't know what it was. It wasn't that he wasn't a great manager anymore or a great individual, it was as if the life had been sucked out of him. He was quite a lad's lad, he had jokes, cracked the whip yes but he had jokes and was a funny guy with a lot of charisma and banter. And then it became as if someone had just sucked all of that out of him. It wasn't overnight but it was pretty quick.'

Not only had the fight been taken from Jewell, Winstanley saw the man he worked so closely with descend into a shell of the one he recognised, 'I'd worked with Paul for five or six years before Derby and he was a vibrant manager and a lot of fun. He could give out a terrible bollocking now and again too. He's a very funny man by nature but those jokes and the vibrancy quickly dried up with the players.

'He was still that way with staff, but I noticed that he started to fly off the handle very, very quickly because the players weren't on the level. He recognised early on that this was a group of players who were going to go down, hence the reason he went straight into the market to change it all.'

By this point, Jewell's mind was perhaps aware of a bigger issue on the horizon. 'He'd been in the job two months and the *News of the World* ran a piece that said, "Paul Jewell's pants are going down quicker than Derby". He lost it. His family had gone, his wife had gone, he just didn't know what to do. He cared, he just lost it,' said Gadsby, by this stage looking on from a distance, barely able to believe what he was staring at.

Neither could academy product Miles Addison. 'When all that stuff about Paul came out in the news, the training ground was really strange for a good couple of weeks. In the corridors nobody was talking, nobody would talk about it in the changing room, you'd have to go to the gym,' he said.

On the back of dealing with the humiliation handed to him on the pitch every Saturday afternoon, Jewell's situation had been worsened by the *News of the World* article, which revealed that a sex tape of him had been leaked. A headline of RAMPANT and a well-placed club badge compounded the misery. Derby County had descended into a laughing stock.

* * *

From the closure of the January transfer window, 14 games yielded a beyond pathetic three points. Draws against Manchester City, Sunderland and Fulham were the relative high moment, in a second half of the season that was even worse than the first and before March was concluded, relegation was confirmed. That was the first record the club would set, with no other club ever mathematically dropping down this early in a season.

On reflection, it's difficult to pinpoint the key fault in the side. Evidently the talent didn't come close to matching the level required but was the mental side of the game the key factor behind the humiliation? To put where the heads of the squad were at during the campaign, Winstanley examines a February away day at Jewell's former employers, 'Giles Barnes was in central midfield and this epitomises how the group were at that point. We lost 2-0 and Giles had four passes, two completed in the 90 minutes.

'Paul said in the dressing room afterwards he was disappointed, "People said there was a player in you, but I just don't see it." Because typically a midfield player would have about 50 passes and he had completed two. When we looked at the game back it was apparent that the lad was just hiding, he was frightened to death. That was the group in the main and I don't mean to have a go at just Giles here. The group was frightened of having the football, they were frightened of playing it and the Premier League as it was then, the spotlight and media attention is on you and they were frightened to death.'

Full time prompted Jewell to again tear into his side in front of the press, 'I could take it if they were showing some passion and desire to perform but apart from half an hour at Sheffield Wednesday, they have been poor since I've been here. They have made my life uncomfortable today and I'll be making theirs uncomfortable during the week.'

Faced with an already humiliated and terrified squad, Jewell did as he promised, and he made Barnes pay. 'He dragged us in the next day and put on one of the hardest sessions you can think of. I don't know why he did it because we'd just played and it's not what you do. That's the session where I then did my knee,' said Barnes, who was sidelined until the following season and was again faced with the prospect of retirement. 'It's hard to say I won't forgive him because it wasn't technically his fault but I remember thinking during the session "this is an unnecessary session when we've just played" and the rest is history.'

Jewell has to take part of the blame for the culture of fear and humiliation, even if it was already instilled under Davies. Instead of supporting his squad, his desperate methods to inject life into his beaten players led to a blame game. After another defeat, he told the BBC, 'I'm embarrassed at the way we played. I can accept losing but not like that, it was a disgrace. Some players are not worthy of being here and the sooner we can get them out the better.'

The squad Jewell was dealing with surprisingly remained civil to one another, but mentally they were broken. The only saving grace by the end of March was that it was almost over. The season that is, not the defeats. The side were so bad that after a 2-1 defeat at Upton Park, Alan Curbishley's squad were booed off because they hadn't won by more.

'I remember the Aston Villa [home] game in particular,' Moore recalls, 'and I remember the home game against West Ham where we lost 5-0 too. I think Lee Bowyer even scored a couple and I just remember both games we started incredibly well, hitting the post and forcing the keeper into saves but we just couldn't score.

'Against Villa I walked down the tunnel at half-time and turned to Petrov, Gareth Barry and John Carew and just said, "How on earth are we 3-0 down?" And they just agreed and looked at me and went, "I don't know!" We were brilliant to start with and we gave everything early on but I just thought to myself "goodness me". I sat in the dressing room and we're there looking at each other and shaking our heads because we're thinking, "How are we behind this heavily?" We felt it, the opposition felt it early on and then we conceded. The Villa and West Ham games we were so disappointed.'

Villa was a catastrophic low among lows. With Derby already relegated and playing purely for pride, Roy Carroll shipped six goals – including a Stiliyan Petrov drive from the halfway line – against a mid-table outfit. 'The other game we felt disappointment was the last game at home to Reading,' continues Moore. 'We really thought that after a dour season, let's just send the fans home for the summer with a win at home and we had a real determination but when they scored, the feeling just set in. The losing mentality and that gutsiness to fight back just wasn't there, people were looking at just putting closure to the season and it was so hard mentally.'

Having conceded six at home against Aston Villa and then six more against Arsenal the next time out (in which Emmanuel Adebayor came on at half-time and scored his second hat-trick against Derby of the season), the campaign was confounded with a 4-0 loss at home to fellow relegated side Reading. A week before, 7,000 fans – likely more – had made the journey to Blackburn in the hope of seeing a solitary away victory, but left having witnessed a 3-1 loss. They did at least see an away goal, the eighth of the season on the road and the 20th in total.

The pain was over and having worked so tirelessly to reach the Premier League, fans paraded the pitch to celebrate the fact they would no longer be there. 'Thank **** it's over' was the universal motto displayed on one sign. That season concluded with a multitude of English football records. Lowest ever Premier League points total. Fewest victories in a season. Fewest goals in a season. Longest top-flight run without a win in a season. Most defeats in a season. Most goals conceded in a season. Worst goal difference in a season. There's probably more but that should do.

Still, it wasn't all bad. There were few who emerged from the campaign the same but by the end of the season, it was Moore who became the man who most resonated with supporters.

He said, 'I played every week because I had a real zest and a desire. It didn't matter if we were losing, are you giving your full 100 per cent? At my age, that opportunity was one you will never get again and it was the same for a lot of the younger players too. The opportunity to give your all, that's all. We worked our absolute nuts off over the 46 games and a final to get there, we deserved it and we were Premier League players.

'You could turn around in years to come and tell people you've played against the best, scored against the best. There are so many things you can say, that was my half-full cup. I've always had that. The fans gave me player of the year. What for? Was it skill or passing ability? No, it was just for effort and determination.'

Moore would leave that summer for Barnsley. By the time he'd face – and beat – Derby again within the first month of the new campaign, the club hadn't even come close to recovering.

POOR CHOICES,
CHEAP POPS

HAVING HAD barely a month to recover mentally and physically from what had come before, it was back to the grass for the beleaguered Rams. Paul Jewell would have hoped time apart in one of the many holiday destinations second-tier footballers seem to flock to would allow the squad to find themselves again. His answer to rediscovering the basics of football was to forget about it completely.

While Robbie Savage and co. topped up their tans, Jewell set about his second attempt at rebuilding a squad. As January had been, the summer of 2008 was never to be anything but a window of overhaul. It was arrivederci to ten first-teamers, most notably Darren Moore. He left upon the completion of his contract, but the desperately disappointing duo of Robert Earnshaw and Kenny Miller were quickly shipped out having been two of the key figures behind the worsening mood in the changing room. The pair had contributed five goals from a collective 52 league appearances and would never be looked at fondly, Earnshaw only worsening his position in the minds of supporters with a journey to the City Ground. Along Brian Clough Way he passed the exciting Kris Commons travelling in the opposite direction, the tricky midfielder becoming Jewell's marquee signing.

Commons, later to become a Scottish international, was one of 14 additions Jewell made in his second window in charge, added to the nine January signings. Tellingly, only eight members of the previous promotion side remained at the club come opening day. One of those, Tyrone Mears, soon departed for Marseille – although not through a window as the legend goes, Mears recalling, 'It was nowhere near the crazy stuff that was reported in the press.'

Giles Barnes also backed his former team-mate, 'If you know him, you know he's ballsy enough to walk out in front of you. If Tye has something to say, he won't shirk or hide, it's not who he is so I don't think he climbed through a window! If you told me he walked out with his boots in his hand and pushed Jewell away, I can absolutely believe that.'

Mears, by now one of the longest-serving pros at the club after 18 months, was told by Jewell that he would never play for him again after flying to France, but his desire to escape gives an insight into the lack of grip Jewell had over the squad he inherited. The departures of Earnshaw and Miller were countered by additions, ones which arguably left the front line going into the campaign stronger than it had been in the Premier League season. Proven Championship goalscorers Rob Hulse and Nathan Ellington arrived, backed by promising youngsters Steve Davies and Liam Dickinson.

There was even an injection of internationalism to the squad too, as Przemyslaw Kazmierczak joined from FC Porto on loan, as did Andrejs Pereplotkins, a man who has since gone down in folklore as one of the strangest Rams signings in recent history. Martin Albrechtsen arrived on a free to shore up the defence, with Paul Green plugging a midfield gap that was left after Matt Oakley's departure. Jewell had a squad to match the promotion promise he made the season before.

Yet despite the upheaval, the aura of negativity that arose from countless thrashings showed no sign of subsiding, the wage budget was still stretched and unless the manager could deliver the promotion he promised back in April, the future looked bleak both on and off the field. 'I felt that when we got relegated, we would be able to, with the squad that we had put together, compete around the top six,' starts Adam Pearson. 'But there was still such a hangover from the Premier League and we couldn't shake it clear. We had the nucleus of a decent team, but we couldn't throw off that defeatism and the losing mentality, even though we changed a dozen of the players. It also became incredibly difficult to get some players out of the club because you can't just move players on, so it became an expensive and very difficult process.'

Paul Winstanley recalls a pre-season outing that left him in no doubt of what was to come, 'In the pre-season Paul [Jewell] changed. He was trying to get everybody going again and was a bit more excitable and vibrant, more fun. He changed that mindset in the staff but there was a massive fear in the squad, the state of the squad meant you could smell it. It was just a mental fear. I remember playing Burton away in pre-season, we won 2-0 and Nathan Ellington scored. After the game all the staff were celebrating like we'd won the opening game of the season. I'm thinking, "It's pre-season against Burton Albion, why are we celebrating this?"'

If there's any one member of staff who knows the players better than the manager, it's the physio. Neil Sullivan worked under six different bosses during his eight years at Derby and quickly got to understand the state of the club he had joined, 'There were so many disgruntled players who were not involved from previous regimes, just waiting to get paid up and leave. You had Robbie Savage out of favour and he's obviously a bit of a voice. He was sitting in corners and not enjoying being with the group. It also meant loads of injuries too. People hide in the treatment room if there is no reason to push themselves.'

Savage was in the worst state of his career. In his autobiography *Savage!*, he recalled, 'Jewell pulled me into his office and said, "If you've got anywhere to go, go." I told the chairman [Adam Pearson], "If you give me £1.2m, I will leave."'

The bids didn't come and neither did the money. Instead, the Welshman was barred from the training ground, pinpointed as a bad influence and asked if he could train in Wrexham. Pearson also suggested he consider a retreat to Australia, questioning whether he could get a gig on *I'm a Celebrity...Get Me Out of Here.*

Players such as Savage and Roy Carroll remained on wages unsustainable for a Championship team. The former collected £23,000 per week. Andy Todd was another and along with Savage, moved out temporarily to League One as Jewell looked to blood his latest new faces and a select group of youth players. Alan Stubbs appeared once before retirement. Miles Addison was one of few positives during Jewell's duration and after being given a Premier League debut away at Blackburn, he was handed an opportunity to fill the void that Savage should have. In among seasoned professionals, plenty of whom still had sleepless nights over what came prior, Addison was able to cast a fresh eye over the development of not only himself but the side he was part of.

In his early Derby days, the England Under-21 international was a welcome sign of promise in a broken squad of professionals weighed down by bad experiences. As he sips an iced coffee in the Meteor Centre's Costa, he casts his memory back, 'He [Jewell] said to start with he wanted solid players so the likes of Green, Jordan Stewart and Paul Connolly came. Then he mixed it up with people like Tito Villa, Sterjovski, Kazmierczak. I feel he got caught in between getting fans off their seats and being a solid team and he really struggled with this.'

Addison was made to wait until the fifth league game of the season before taking to the field. Being blooded so early was the first step in the right direction for Jewell and a sign of faith in youngsters. But it only occurred after a start to the season that was as bad as anything that came before it. As it had been in 14 of the home fixtures the previous season, Pride Park was sold out on the opening day for the visit of newly promoted Doncaster Rovers. As it had been in 18 of the previous 19 fixtures, the atmosphere from the 33,010 in attendance come 4.45pm was glum.

A goal midway through the second half sealed it and after a spell of keep ball by the visitors, Pride Park's atmosphere turned venomous. No more was there an acceptance of losing every week, especially not now they weren't coming up against Premier League opposition. Jewell admitted it would take time to gel, but patience had worn thin.

Things only worsened. A solitary point at Bristol City was the precursor to two more defeats, Jewell's Derby with only one goal in their first four games. The rot had set in deeper than the post-pessimistic West Standers feared.

* * *

On Saturday, 13 September 2008, 361 days after Kenny Miller's clincher against Newcastle, the Rams won a league match. It came at the 36th attempt, 28 of which were under Jewell. The longest consecutive run of games without a win in the history of English football was finally over.

Miles Addison was integral on his first home start of the season, stifling a Sheffield United midfield containing Gary Speed. Paul Green opened the scoring in the first half before the Blades pegged Derby back almost immediately, but Rob Hulse, a £1.75m summer signing, opened his Rams account 18 minutes from time against his former club.

The win was also the first in the league under the stewardship of Pearson, who had moved to a role of executive chairman under the GSE ownership, not that he realised quite how long he had to wait for it. 'Was it really that long? That is an incredibly long time. How we survived mentally and physically that long, I'm not sure. I remember it was hard at the time and if I lived in the city it probably would have been impossible. There were some shoots of things going to get better on a short run in October, but it didn't kick on and the mental pressure that it put on Paul eventually just wore him out.'

The October that Pearson touches upon brought seven games without defeat. Jewell didn't get ahead of himself but there was finally promise for the first time since taking charge. Away wins at QPR and Norwich (the latter momentarily marred by reports of irregular betting) took Derby up to tenth and within reach of the play-off spots. But that was Paul's peak. Despite following that with another positive run, the game that sums up the campaign – and Jewell's tenure – came against Nottingham Forest. Or, as it has gone down in folklore, the Stuart Attwell show.

It marked the beginning of the end for Jewell, as told by Pearson, 'I think that game was when I knew it just wasn't going to work. That performance that day, from a very young referee, I couldn't understand those decisions and I just felt it was fated not to be.'

The day Pearson refers to is 2 November, and a Sunday game at Pride Park on Sky Sports. The first league meeting between the sides since 2005 was a big deal, as is every encounter between the two. So why the Football League decided to hand it to a 26-year-old rookie remains a mystery. Attwell was the official of choice for the PGMOL, fast-tracked into the Select Group of referees eligible to officiate in the Premier League. He had already been found wanting at Championship level two months before the East Midlands derby, awarding a goal at Watford despite the ball going wide of the posts and out for a goal kick.

The man who allowed the ghost goal took charge two days after Halloween and served up a horror show. But before getting to that, this was already a meeting with more spice than before. Forest had Robert Earnshaw and Lee Camp, the beginning of a timeless love affair between Rams fans and the keeper. Derby had Kris Commons; at least in body. Addison explains, 'I don't know if you remember that day, but Kris wouldn't even take corners. He got to the ground really early as well, he just wasn't feeling it. He had a bad day and I don't think he dealt with the pressure.'

The second meeting between the two in the FA Cup later that year saw Commons benched, before accepting the inevitable barrage in two consecutive victories over the Trent. Had he dealt with the pressure, things could have been very different for the season ahead.

A victory in a derby always has a far-reaching impact. This is where Attwell gets involved. With the game tied at 1-1, Addison powered home a header as the clock ticked past 90 minutes. But as the ball crossed the line, Attwell blew for a foul and instead pointed to the spot. Commons was on penalty duties yet passed up the offer. Instead it went to young Nacer Barazite, who saw his weak kick pushed behind. Camp flexed in front of the north stand. Game over, a point each and a chance wasted for Derby. Or so you'd expect.

The corner came in, Camp made another save, and from the next flag-kick Addison rose again to head home, this time without any foul in the build-up. Jubilation. Or so we all thought, and once again the goal was mysteriously ruled out.

'Every time I've seen Attwell since he apologises but the whole thing was so bizarre. Nobody understood what was going on. In the changing room the manager was kicking everything, we had to hold him back,' Addison explains.

From rising expectations, there would be only two wins from the 12 – including an uninspiring draw at a woeful Charlton that left Addison to add, 'I knew something wasn't right here after that' – culminating in successive home defeats. The precursor to that draw at The Valley was another desperately disappointing 3-0 loss at Wolves. 'I started that one in centre midfield alongside Ruben Zadkovich, who was just nowhere near the first team. When you start doing that and don't rely on what you're used to, you're in trouble,' said Addison.

Jewell called time on his spell in charge on 28 December, the ties severed after the first unanimous 'Jewell out' chorus in defeat to Ipswich. Twelve days after admitting 2008 was the worst year of his life, he was gone. 'We were both moving towards the same direction,' admits Pearson. 'We just said, "Look, this is just not going to work." I think we lost at home to Ipswich 1-0 and he was really down. He rang me the next day and he just said, "It's not going to work, is it?" and I had to agree with him. It was very amicable and sorted out very quickly. I believed in him. He had all the attributes to show he was a top manager and he was the right appointment. But mistakes and circumstance conspired against us and it just wasn't to be. It took a lot out of him. I think it hurt him that much. I think he felt players were changing as well and they weren't responding to a bit of stick every now and again.'

Jewell went on to have another unsuccessful stint in management with Ipswich, but his Pride Park experience changed the psyche of the once in-demand manager beyond recognition. Those same footballing gods found one more reason to curse him, as the defeat which meant dismissal at Ipswich came against Derby in October 2012. Cursed.

Retrospectively, Jewell was in no state to lead the club from the burning wreckage of the 11-point season. But who would have been willing to take on such a gargantuan task and risk their own sanity in the process? With a bulging wage budget and American ownership who couldn't subsidise further, Pearson set off in search of someone who could stop the rot and reunite not only a club but a city. The sat-nav was set for 22 minutes.

Prior to appointing Jewell's successor, Derby had two cup games that would be overseen by two different managers. First up came Chris Hutchings's solitary match, a fortuitous 4-3 win at Conference side Forest Green Rovers in the FA Cup, with Jewell's sidekick turning around an horrendous first half an hour before leaving the club in the following days, despite reportedly being in the frame.

David Lowe took control for the following fixture, a remarkable 1-0 victory over Manchester United in the first leg of the League Cup semi-final. The Rams had embarked on a surprise run all the way to the final four, edging past Premier League Stoke in the quarter-final, with Sir Alex Ferguson and his world champions next up. Lowe reintroduced Andy Todd and Mo Camara to the side, but most notably added Robbie Savage to the squad for the first time since he had been shipped out on loan to Brighton.

Savage, who had been sent back to the East Midlands early from his seaside retreat, looked for all intents and purposes to have been finished with Derby, yet this second lease of life led him into the captain's armband for two more years. But while a cup run was welcomed, there were more pressing matters at hand. Derby had slipped to 18th in the table and hovered ominously above the relegation spots. The change that Pearson was to make not only had to reignite Derby County for the sake of its fanbase, it had to be the right one to ensure Pride Park wasn't hosting third-tier football for the first time.

* * *

In the world of professional wrestling, a cheap pop is an act that is done to incite a positive response from the audience, like wearing that city's sports jersey. The choice made at Pride Park in January 2009 is the footballing equivalent. 'We (Peter Gadsby, Don Amott and I) felt that he would be the person who would give the club time to heal and repair,' said Adam Pearson. His first managerial appointment hadn't worked out and the second was arguably even more important. It was one completely out of the blue (Square Premier League).

Nigel Clough had worked wonders with Burton Albion in his ten years there, taking them from the Southern Premier League, via the Northern Premier League, and into the Blue Square Premier Division – the Conference in old money, the highest level of non-league football.

And when Don Amott brokered a discussion between the two parties, the Brewers looked odds on to move into the Football League for the first time in their history. But why did a non-league manager get the gig of taking over one of the biggest clubs in British football? Was he qualified for the role and if not, how did they come to this decision? That's what the man himself wanted to know.

'Nigel wanted to make sure he'd be given time and backing and it would be right for him. He wanted to know it wasn't due to his father's name, he wanted the job on merit and to know we believed in him, which we did. For us, he had the right history, the right personality, the right heritage and the right style of management to repair the club. He was big and brave enough to take on the club when a lot of other people wouldn't go near it,' said Pearson.

Where there's a Clough there's a Taylor. Martin Taylor, a goalkeeping stalwart of the early 1990s side, jumped at the chance to make the switch back to his beloved club. His Derby career had been marred by a serious leg break in 1994, so this was a chance to go back on his own terms.

He said, 'It was a whirlwind week because it was over Christmas so there were games with Burton, where we were on the verge of winning the Conference, and then there were the rumours. The gaffer called us on the Friday (2 January) and said we'd got the chance to go in. It was announced on the Tuesday and we started our first day of training with 50 players. Because there were that many players, we had to put two sessions on to work out who we'd need and not need.'

The fanfare that followed was extended beyond what even the PR team were anticipating. After the unveiling in the hours before the United victory, sections of the sports pages were dedicated to the Clough surname returning to Derby. The release of *The Damned United* two months later, a film that – although not entirely built on fact – chronicled the work of Nigel's legendary father Brian, only served to add a new layer to the Clough/Derby connection. Led by nostalgia, the appointment achieved the task of injecting hope back into the stadium and at least stopped Derby being labelled as the worst team in history. Now they were the worst team in history – but they were managed by a Clough.

It proved the most telling act of Pearson's role, with the former and future Hull City head honcho departing months later as GSE steered things in a different route. He reflects, 'It was the most difficult job I have ever had. In the middle of it, it was bloody hard. It was bloody hard. I learnt a lot and it would have been nicer if we could have put the club back into the Premier League. In the end I suppose it was from a success point of view pretty limited, but do I look back at it with pride? All I know is that I gave it my best. I was honest and we tried to do the right thing. We secured good investment that eventually led to Mel taking on the club and there's not a lot more I can say.'

Ultimately, Clough's first five months were good enough to stave off the threat of the drop. Although Derby fell into the bottom three early into his spell, results steered the ship towards the relative comfort of 18th place, eight points above League One territory.

The League Cup dream came to an end at Old Trafford despite a Giles Barnes salvation mission late on. Building a gap between the club and the relegation spots allowed Clough an opportunity to understand his squad, their needs and where he would look towards adjusting in his quest for frugality.

'There was an underlying belly [of negativity] even when we were doing well. If a goal went in you saw the confidence just leave and the team just went,' said Taylor.

His first five months in the role allowed him a glimpse into a confidence-sapped dressing room, 'In the early days we had to grind out anything we could and it took time but we had enough to scrape through that season with a week or so left. We had to rebuild that confidence in the team and the next season was very similar. It took a while to get rid of the players but the money wasn't there, so we had to buy the best of the rest players.'

Those few months were an opportunity for Clough and his staff to look at the squad they had inherited, but there was a flip-side to this; it allowed the players to encounter an individual like no other. He wasn't his dad and he never tried to be. But just what was he? To some, he was a father figure and the greatest manager they've ever had. To others, he was 'Non-League Nigel'.

NIGEL HOWARD CLOUGH

IF BRIAN Clough is your father, you're not born to sit on the fence. The greatest football manager of all time and the best orator the game has ever seen, not to mention the most witty and likeable man the city of Derby has ever encountered. Taking over at the Baseball Ground in 1967, the transformation Clough oversaw went beyond what Sam Longson could have ever imagined. Champions of England. Would-be champions of Europe had it not been for those 'cheating Italian bastards' of Juventus, in his words. The club he wished he'd never left.

The Clough name will be intertwined with the city of Derby forever more and when young Nigel continued the legacy in 2009, the media rounded upon the similarities. Brian was adored and detested in equal measure; Nigel too, albeit to a lesser extent. Adored by fans early on; less so the players.

Physio Neil Sullivan, who took up a first-team role soon after Clough switched from the Pirelli Stadium, got to hear all takes, 'There were those who thought he wouldn't last long, those who welcomed him because they were out of favour at the time and they thought they had a chance and there were those who were very anti.'

Miles Addison was one of those who leaned towards the first group, 'The foreign boys hadn't heard of Clough and the ones that were there already were a bit like "he's coming from non-league",' begins Addison, who was integral to Clough in his first two seasons in the role.

'I've not met anyone like him in football. Martin Albrechtsen and a few others didn't get on with him.'

Albrechtsen, momentarily taking a break from the weights that dominate his Instagram Stories, racks his memory. He simply states Nigel to be 'weird. I didn't like him.'

Addison continues, 'The established players, the way he talked to some people, they wouldn't have it because you're doing your job throughout a week and then Nigel Clough's calling you a fucking **** or whatever and they'd just laugh at him. We had a meeting about it early on and we all said it was wrong the way he was talking.'

But over the years, Clough went on to be worshipped by many of those he got closest to. At this point still a youngster in the early stretches of his academy days, Will Hughes credits his development to the man who gave him a first-team break, 'Nigel Clough had the biggest impact on me. To this day I'd say he had the biggest impact not just on a footballing perspective but as a person as well. He didn't only teach me a lot on the pitch and give me first team football, he taught me a lot off the pitch as a human being which is even more important.'

Nigel's style, as displayed through these two academy products, would leave some alienated and others admiring.

* * *

Giles Barnes is a difficult man to get hold of. From Derby to Hyderabad with six years in the MLS in the meantime, he couldn't be more apologetic for not seeing the Instagram messages, each one tinged with a growing sense of desperation. 'Hi Giles, not sure if you saw my previous message' they would begin. Finally, after a prompt from Addison, the reply came through. 'Don't take this the wrong way but I'm not sure if you want what I have to say on a certain individual in your book.' I did.

In January 2009, Barnes was back on the path towards greatness after a year on the sidelines. Two goals in a cameo at Manchester United showed the boy wonder was still blossoming after a mentally challenging 12 months in the top flight. He may have been one of Europe's most promising youngsters but early into Clough's reign, Barnes sensed the relationship may not work. 'After the United game, there were four or five Premier League teams who asked to take me on loan,' he said.

'I really hadn't spoken with Clough properly and I needed some sort of comfort. So I played a couple of games, Clough calls me into his office and he says, "Right, I've had a few offers from the Premier League. Fulham want you on loan until the end of the year with a clause to buy you. What do you want to do?"'

Barnes, whose 24 games at the top were accompanied by a squad simply not qualified to match his quality, wanted another bite, 'I told him that I felt I'd been robbed of the Premier League and I'd love to see if I could do it. He said, "Is that your last answer?" He'd not spoken to me at all since I got injured, so I said I'd like to go.'

With those words, little did Barnes know he would never play a first team game for the club again. 'He goes, "Fuck off out of my office then."'

The move to Fulham was the right thing for Barnes. The opportunity to work alongside a much stronger squad than he was paired with in 2007/08 was one he couldn't pass up. It didn't work out.

'I ruptured my Achilles while I was there after four reserve team games and I had to have surgery again which was mentally breaking. I still had two years left on my contract at Derby so at least I could go home", he continues.

'So I go back. I finally get contacted two days before pre-season for testing and I'm still not fit at all. I had a programme to follow but Nigel made it clear that if I didn't do everything that he said, he would treat me like shit.' Having been told to 'fuck off' during the first and only conversation between the two previously, Barnes's near future looked bleak.

'He'd have me running up hills when I shouldn't have been. Then he sent me with the second team. I'd be playing teams like Belper and he made it clear I wasn't in his plans. We got through pre-season and I'm still not feeling good, I think we had a friendly with Stoke. I told him that I still didn't feel okay and my Achilles was still sore from before, but he told me that "you'll be playing and you'll be fine". I was in pain, but I had no choice. That's when I fully ruptured my Achilles again. I get stretchered off, he doesn't come in to see me in the medical room, doesn't acknowledge me and it got worse from then on.'

Barnes would not return to first team action for more than a year and would never play for Derby again. He said, 'He'd make me come in at 7.30 in the morning to get my treatment and then I wasn't allowed to leave until 5.01 every single day. I was on my crutches and he'd make me go outside to watch training. I wasn't allowed to be in the treatment room with any of the other boys, I couldn't eat with them. When they were eating, I had to go into the gym because I couldn't do it when he forced me outside.'

Barnes, today with no intention of a return to the English league, is on the warpath. The longer he talks, the more he recalls, 'I had to wait until 5.01 every day and people would watch to see if I left early. I'll never, ever forgive him for doing that to me, a young boy at that time. Now, I'd tell him to go fuck himself but at 19, you don't. It went on for such a long time. That injury was his fault. I complained my whole rehab that I shouldn't be playing and I was still speaking to the Fulham physio at the time. He cannot believe what I'm being forced to do. And then what it turned into was a shambles. It wasn't just me. The way Jordan Stewart was treated was a disgrace as well.'

Stewart, a Jewell signing, was quickly transfer-listed before being swapped for Lee Hendrie. Barnes continues, 'I can't say to you some of the things that were said because they were very deep.

It was a sad one for me because he was a really, really good player but the way he treated human beings? I was on my crutches for the team photos and he told me to get out of it because I wouldn't be playing.

'I got back fit from my Achilles and this was when Derby were trying to get rid of players who were earning a lot; I fell under that bracket. The people that Clough picked on were the higher earners at that time. You knew what was going on but it was horrific how it went about. I made the decision that I wanted to leave the club because I couldn't take it anymore and if someone took me, they did.

'I'd had two years of hell and if nobody took me, I'd just do something else because it wasn't human how I'd been treated. We agreed a pay-off with the club which benefited them more than me because I didn't want to be around him on a day-to-day basis. The club I came through, that I played for with a broken foot, that I cared about. It took months of abuse for me to realise I couldn't do it anymore. I had enough.'

Barnes, a product of the Terry Westley conveyor belt, was no more. He did get his Premier League move after settling, making the short journey to West Brom.

Barnes wasn't alone in his experiences. While he and Miles Addison may have been younger and more susceptible to criticism, a returning Chris Riggott was not. Almost ten years after being forced out of Raynesway and boasting a career which included a League Cup victory and a UEFA Cup final appearance, the perma-injured Riggott came back for one last go in 2011.

He recalls, 'Mentally I was gone. I told Dave Jones [his then Cardiff City manager] that I'd had enough of the treatment table, so we cancelled my contract and I went back up to Derby in the January with family.'

Much like Malcolm Christie, the post-Derby years hadn't been kind to Riggott's body. His 148 appearances for Middlesbrough came in just over seven injury-ravaged seasons and after two appearances with the Bluebirds, it looked like his run was done at 30.

'I was with my now wife and we went out to the States for a month or two. I got a call when I was at the airport and it was from Nigel. He asked what my deal was and just said "if you get back and you're interested in playing or seeing the physio, the door is open". So I signed in the summer.'

By Riggott's return, Shaun Barker and Russell Anderson both had their issues. Riggott became the third central defender with considerable injury problems. 'I rushed back way too early and so it was a difficult environment. Nigel wanted me to play and he was getting frustrated with me for not being available. I remember having big issues with his assistant, Crosby I think his name was,' he said.

'In pre-season we went to Darley Park and they wanted me to run up and down hills when I'd just had surgery on my back. I said no, it was crazy.'

At this stage it's worth reasserting that this is not the Barnes story repeated, although the similarities are aplenty.

Riggott added, 'They thought that I was this guy who came in and was above the staff. You'd hear the same from a lot of players at the time who came into the club on big money and he'd clean them all out and get his lot in. They felt I was an old-school one who earned money at Boro, was this big-time guy and that couldn't have been further the truth. I just couldn't get fit though.

'Inevitably it blew up one day on the training ground and I just left.'

Riggott wasn't the first to incur the wrong side of Clough without so much as an explanation and by now, it was something the men at the top of the club had experience of. Tom Glick took the brunt of the complaints.

The Derby-born defender said, 'I spoke to Tom at Pride Park and he basically said "trust me, you're not the first one who's had this conversation with me. Whatever I can do to help, I will" and he put me in touch with the coaching group I'm now with out here in Vegas. I'm sure Nigel had his reasons for speaking to me and treating me like that but at the same time, I didn't hold back when I spoke to him either.

'I get on with just about everyone in life and in football; he wasn't one of them. He'd have people walking round and checking on what you were doing, reporting back to him. You had to be there at certain times of the day which sounds fine, but he would treat you like a kid. It was like you were back in the youth team for me.

'Look at someone like Giles, he'd had a good few years but Nigel wanted him out so pissed him off enough to force him out, the same with loads of players. It couldn't have been contract for them all because I was on pay as you play so it wasn't about money, I just didn't take to his management.'

Riggott would never again play a game of professional football. He does now live in Las Vegas though, which is likely an able replacement.

* * *

But not everyone is a Barnes and not everyone is a Riggott. One of the early indicators of Clough's direction for his playing staff came early in his first summer window, introducing familiar faces from his previous role, albeit from three divisions below his new one. Central defender Jake Buxton (who went on to become a club legend) and goalkeeper Saul Deeney (who made three appearances in five years) made the short switch from Burton, enjoying differing careers at Pride Park. It marked the first steps of a summer that saw a sharp contrast in the squad setup, as the recruitment team were set the unenviable task of slicing the wage bill.

Accounts from the close of 2008/09 showed that despite parachute payments, the club were operating at a huge loss. While revenue remained considerably higher than their previous campaign in the Championship, a wage budget that stretched to £26m left Derby in a financial position they wouldn't fully recover from for another four years. Three windows of absurd overspending had left the club in a dangerous position and yet again, the Rams' accounts were under scrutiny.

Clough, who later said he didn't realise the size of the financial problems, did the task of cost-cutting admirably. The £26m wages stated in the 2008 accounts had been reduced by £10m within two years. While this was still hefty in comparison to half the sides in the Championship, GSE and Pearson's decision to appoint Clough paid off.

Barnes, one of those players who benefitted from a rise following promotion, was one of many high earners Clough looked to remove. Albrechtsen was made aware that he wouldn't be staying before the season was out and his departure was followed by high earners including Roy Carroll, Claude Davis and Jordan Stewart. Tito Villa departed after nine goals in 53 games, the sale to Cruz Azul a £500,000 loss on Jewell's investment. Tyrone Mears had his long-awaited permanent transfer secured while Andy Todd and Mile Sterjovski managed to escape largely disappointing tenures.

A closer-knit community was being formed and the man who began to tie it all together was an occasionally bleach-blond central defender located in sunny Blackpool. Shaun Barker was one of the standout additions under Clough and a rare show of financial intent. His million-pound move, rehashed in the media as a 'Shaun Barker-type fee' in press conferences, was the highest Clough paid for a player until Conor Sammon in 2012. Joining the likes of Buxton and Lee Croft, Barker became the human embodiment of a Clough signing.

Barker said, 'Nigel's damning honesty about the club at the time, the players there, the state he felt it was in, was surreal really. Having that honesty from a manager who's trying to sign you, he's saying how poor the standard of players were, the age concern, the fact that a lot of the players didn't care enough about the club. He also guaranteed I'd just head and kick the ball which suited me down to the ground, I liked him from day one.'

Barker and Clough met at Morley Hayes, just north of Derby but easily accessible from Nottingham. For Barker, he had a foot in both cities. Raised a red, he soon had the decision to make between the two sleeping giants. 'As soon as Nigel turned up, he said "give him another beer" to get me to relax. We chatted for a bit and then we parted ways and said we'd sign in the morning. I had 15 missed calls from my agent when I left, I think Nigel had a sniff that Forest would go above what they offered. They offered more money for wages and signing fees. But I told my agent that I wasn't interested in what they had to say. I wanted to sign for Nigel,' he explained.

'Some players can like his honesty and many can't. You see with his teams, certain players he's had over his career as a manager, some players come and go and they're the ones that aren't as resilient. But a John Brayford, Bucko, we're more of the old-school type of player and he knew he could rely on us. There's a lot of loyalty and trust with him and the players he's taken around. I think Nigel has always been very comfortable in being who he is though, saying what he wants.

'He's not the easiest to play for but in terms of his ethos, his simple beliefs, they're very much married with how I felt football should be. So, in terms of, even though he wasn't the easiest at times, he was my favourite manager to play for in terms of just telling you if you were awful. If you were good, he'd tell you. Maybe less than when you were poor. But you wanted that little moment of him praising you. It'd often be quite sly, like on the bus after an away game and he'd turn round and say "well done today" and that was enough.'

Barker and Buxton became the first two of the core group that Nigel would build over the subsequent four years. They were joined in the following windows by a multitude of players from the lower divisions of English football and the middle section of the Scottish Premier League.

Each of those who contributed their time towards this book reiterated the same point: character. If you were to succeed in a

Nigel Clough side, you had to be the right sort of character. Paul Winstanley, by now one of the few remaining staff members to survive from the Jewell era, was part of the process in identifying who would fit, 'The thing with Nigel was that his values as a person were top class. He was a real family man and at the time, he was just what that club needed. He had to come in and run the club on a budget, a club who was just haemorrhaging money left and right.

'I remember Nigel having a conversation in the manager's office and him saying he was going to try and bring Jake Buxton in from Burton for about £100k. I remember thinking, "Oh my God, we're going to sign a player from Burton Albion?" This is what we'd become, we were Derby County, do you know what I mean? But it was about that character for him. The big part of Nigel's recruitment and what he recognised when he came in was that the squad weren't together, there was no team bonding and it was a big part of his philosophy if you like. Getting a group to fight for each other, on and off field.'

Clough's recognition of that fact kept the side in the Championship in his first five months and laid the foundations for the rebuilding project. The misfit squad assembled by Paul Jewell was filled with strong individuals but as a collective, there was no identity. Winstanley added, 'A lot of his recruitment was based on character because it was so big for him. He wouldn't take tricky characters, he tried to build a chemistry and togetherness between the players and he certainly did that. Shaun and Jake were the epitome of what Nigel looked for. They are not your typical footballers, they're just genuine people with great values who work damn hard for the team.'

Another man who knows Clough inside out is John Brayford. The attack-minded right-back joined a year after Barker and Buxton. He looks back, 'Nigel was and still is massive for me. Once I left Burton to go to Crewe, I thought that was my stepping stone but I didn't realise how much the relationship would progress once I'd left him the first time.'

Brayford, who has since gone on to follow Clough to first Sheffield United and then back to Burton, is another with that mindset and desire to be part of a unit, regardless of how things are going on the field. 'He has good morals and he wants people to give 100 per cent. He works out the character of a player and what they're like outside of football. They don't have to be the best, but he moulds them into the player he wants them to be and he'll mould the team into what he wants it to be,' he said.

Brayford, who by July 2010 joined a Derby County that was unrecognisable from the one Jewell built, is now a veteran of the game at the age of 32. He's seen the changes, even down in the third tier of the game, and the contrasts to the game he grew up in, 'A lot of football clubs now buy individuals, but the team gets a bond when they have Nigel. When I first joined Derby I remember people saying "why are we signing players from Crewe and Mansfield" and don't get me wrong I felt a bit of that too, but he knew what he wanted to do and he knew it wasn't just a quick fix. When they came down from the Premier League, they spent all the money and it was going round in circles. He knew he had a plan and it would take a few years to build that, but he had the right steps in place to build it.'

Over the course of the next four years, Clough would go on to divide many more individuals. For the Barkers and the Brayfords, he emerged as not only their dream manager but also a man they class as a friend. To the Addisons, the Barneses and more, they've never encountered a character like him.

THE CLOUGH YEARS: PART 1

IT'S HARD to believe that in among all the turmoil of the 2000s and the downright lunacy that was still to come in the following years, there were four seasons of relative nothingness at Pride Park. No courtroom battles, no promotion pushes and no relegation fears. Just nothing.

That's not to say it wasn't an important time, it's just when placed within the context of record lows, court cases and administration worries, the years of 2009–2013 offer relatively little in the way of front-page news.

The first task post-safety, one that would take up much of Clough and co.'s time over the subsequent 48 months, lay in cost-cutting. The Rams' wage bill come the end of 2007/08 sat at an eye-watering £23m and after a spectacular financial outlay in 2008 without removing many of the high earners, the club were significantly in the red.

'We didn't really know how bad it was when we joined,' goalkeeping coach Martin Taylor admits. From the outside, Derby had a side built primarily of higher-end Championship players but the extent of the financial problems left by Billy Davies and Paul Jewell remained relatively known. 'Take Robbie Savage. Nothing against him but why would you pay for him when you knew you were going to be relegated? It made no sense to spend money in that January. They were spending that money when they should have been preparing for the Championship,' Taylor continued.

'We get inside and find out how much they're all earning, and it was ridiculous really. And that's the problem with having changes of manager quite often. Each manager wants their own players and style of play. The board want to give the manager the best opportunity, but the only trouble is they're on that much money you can't get rid without paying them off. It's very different to my day when you were just told you were off. They're multi-millionaires now.'

The days of Taylor are far beyond modern football. Even in among the global pandemic of 2020, the gap between 'footballers and normal folk' was focused upon by the British government. Should something of that magnitude have happened in the 1980s or early '90s, the same focus wouldn't have been up for public debate. Football has changed beyond recognition though, often for the worse.

As Adam Pearson mentioned previously, that wild spending of January 2008, paired with players already on long contracts, was disastrous. GSE, unaware quite of the extent of matters when taking over, had little room to manoeuvre with budgets. The new management team had to find the balancing act between building a team and removing those high earners.

Taylor adds, 'It takes a while to get rid of the players, but the money wasn't there. We were having to buy players who were the best of the rest. We tried to sign Tom Naylor from Mansfield, but we had to wait three months to stump up the money. It was £50,000.'

Instead of the growth they hoped they'd be able to feed into, the new staff were having to reset every aspect. The £1m capture of Shaun Barker was the only opportunity to investigate what life would be like with a hefty budget.

The addition of Barker was grandiose in the context of the 2009/10 season. Without his signing, Derby could very well have been relegated. Having joined a club still reeling from the effects of dropping out of the Premier League and with a squad bloated beyond belief, Barker now reflects back on the state of the Derby County he arrived at, 'Nigel made it completely noticeable and obvious that there were certain ones that wouldn't have a future at the club. A lot of people would have thought Robbie Savage would have been in the not included but he was one of maybe two or three that were big-paid names, still in the later stage of their career that stayed part of it, and a lot that weren't. There were players that I hadn't seen because they were told to look for other clubs but there was a mix of Buckos and those there for a while.

'I didn't meet half of those who moved on because it was a ludicrous-sized squad; 35 having just come from 20 at Blackpool. One of the conversations I had with Nigel was, "I want that Blackpool mentality." Lower-paid players that were hungry to get further in their career and earn their money and adulation, rather than the old Premier League players who weren't pulling their weight. It was clear who he felt would be part of that direction.

'There was a divide when I arrived which wasn't easy and so part of that first season was just clarifying who would be going forward with it. To keep a squad happy, knowing that in the long term half of them won't be about, is a big challenge.'

Barker was and remains a warrior. Everything life has thrown at him, particularly after joining Derby, is proof enough. A watch of the *One More Time* documentary is recommended to truly understand the man. And the more he became part of the furniture in those early weeks, the more he saw himself reflected in others. Jake Buxton was almost a doppelgänger for Barker in all but looks. As a defender who had worked his way through the lower leagues, the signing of Buxton in 2009 was at first greeted poorly. His league experience was capped at guiding Mansfield down to the Conference before starring with Burton as they rose to the Football

League. He said, 'I played for Mansfield Town and got relegated as captain. I took an awful amount of responsibility for the team getting relegated because I was captain and it dented my confidence and affected me. I went into my shell, went to Burton and it was a bit like football rehab in a way. I went to an organised club and had a structure of play which suited myself. Nigel made it easy for me at centre-back and signing at Derby was a big, big turnaround in my career.'

Jake Buxton is a footballer like no other. Whether it be his regional twang, his desire to bring a carrier bag to training when all others have branded wash-bags or just the look of the man, he's something else. He remembers of his move, 'I was a cheap option and a free hit at the time, so I got the phone call from Nigel. I got the doubters straight away and I was tarnished with a tag of being basically "Non-League Bucko". I relished it though, it put fire in my belly. Even from team-mates, I knew they didn't really expect much from me. And bearing in mind I went into a club at the time as sixth-choice centre-back, I wasn't expected to play. But I wouldn't cost a great amount.'

In the departures lounge, Clough and GSE were able to successfully get rid of ten high earners. Taylor remembers, 'It was difficult because when you're trying to build a team spirit, some don't necessarily want to be there because they're not involved, and they become a problem within training. We had a group where they were put to the side and one of us would train them so they weren't spoiling the players who were selected. The owner understood there would be unhappy players and they always want to try and upset the happy ones. When you're not in the team, we want people who want other players to do well. When you're going in there and there are players already around the team who don't want to be there or are on so much money they don't want to do anything, it was a case of for the good of the club paying a certain amount for them to leave or go somewhere else. We just needed them out the way to build spirit in the team. It is difficult but that's part of being in management.'

Tito Villa, Mile Sterjovski, Roy Carroll, Claude Davis. The clear-out was vast and it was ultimately expensive, with major hits taken on most signings who commanded a fee in the first instance. Few survivors from the Premier League remained. In fact, of all of those signed in preparation for that season and midway through, there was only one survivor. 'First and foremost, Robbie [Savage] cared about football,' said Barker. Against all expectations, Barker walked into a changing room still captained by Savage, 'He was very funny, but I think he probably struggled with confidence a bit in himself. The louder a person is in football, the less confidence they've probably got. It's a bit of a coping mechanism. You've got 25 lads in a room that play competitively, and they develop ways to survive and that was his. We had a couple of run-ins, but we got on fine. He knew I could take criticism and he gave me stick the first few weeks. But he soon got a bit back from me, so he knew I wasn't a pushover.'

* * *

There were still some individuals of quality at the club, but those singulars were firmly replaced by a collective effort. Gaze through the back of a matchday programme from the 2009/10 season and Commons aside, there were very few players designed to excite; they would come later in Clough's management. For now, the task was simply to rebuild and generate a side worthy of showing enough fight to stay in and around the middle of the Championship table.

Barker recalls, 'Anyone that asked, I felt from day one there was a gradual progression and I didn't feel that it stunted at any point or slowed. It was organic in terms of how it developed through that time, there was consistent improvement. There were times in that first year that I felt we showed real quality and there were times that we were very poor and that was the inconsistency of a team still trying to understand Nigel and the ethos.'

After a slow start to the campaign, which the supposed sixth-choice Buxton started the opening day of ('I played Torquay away in my last game and was then against 33,000 at home and getting man of the match on my next'), Clough's workhorses grew, if not by much in stature then in numbers. The signing of the 5ft 5in, 36-year-old Paul Dickov provided something a little different. But it was another clear indication of the constraints Clough was under.

Barker says, 'Paul was the most reliable player you could imagine for a centre-forward. I played with him at Blackpool before and I always hated playing against him, I always thought he was a nasty, nasty man. He would leave his foot in, grab you, a horrible little forward. But he's a great guy, a great pro, always on the front foot and full of respect.'

Barker would later be joined by DJ Campbell, another former colleague. 'The gaffer asked about Paul and DJ because they were both at Blackpool with me and they were both good characters. But it was like we were asking for older heads to just get us a bit of a boost.'

Clough, who had already endeared himself to his new club with a double humbling of Forest within his first few months, now had the early-season opportunity to take a side more reflective of himself to the City Ground.

But of the six meetings Clough oversaw by the Trent, Derby conceded inside the first three minutes in four of them. You can excuse Taylor for thinking more of ways to have Stephen Bywater pick the ball out of the net than anything else. 'We always seemed to be 1-0 down after about 20 seconds against Forest. They always scored from the first attack.'

The August 2009 afternoon was no different and by half-time, Forest were three goals to the good. A valiant attempt at a fightback wasn't enough. In the context of all derbies around this time, the 90 minutes here didn't offer much in terms of going down for the ages. Each East Midlands derby has to have some basis for a story though and this one didn't begin to be told until full-time.

Nathan Tyson scored what turned out to be the winner that day and, having been forced to watch Robbie Savage's scarf-wielding antics months earlier, he felt it was time for retribution. The striker looks back, 'It was always fantastic to be part of those games. You come out of it and just think "wow" because the atmosphere was incredible and you'd love to have it week in, week out. For myself, I knew how much it meant to local people and the fans and you know how much it means to them. I remember Savage doing that twirl and thinking it was bang out of order.'

Come full time, Tyson exacted revenge, albeit unintentionally. His brandishing of the corner flag in front of a baying mob of away supporters sparked chaos, with punches thrown and fines aplenty being handed out. 'I wasn't intentionally waving it in front of the Derby fans and I hate when people say that, I was just trying to go to the other end. But I was stupid with it and I regret it,' he said.

'It's not who I am and it doesn't reflect it. I'm a good winner and a good loser so I don't condone that at all and I got punished for it.'

Tyson was banned for two matches and fined £5,000, while both clubs also had to make pay-outs as the violence escalated on-field.

He admits, 'Fans still come up and mention the flag and now it's "oh here we go again". If I was going to do something like that, I should have waved it in front of the A-Block and then put it down and just be done with it. There are not many things I regret in my career but that's number one. But the funny thing is I bumped into Robbie Savage that summer and he just laughed and said it was dead funny. He said he would have done the same and he got away with it!'

For all of the fan division seen in the later years of his time in charge, the first season was largely a bye for Clough. Fans recognised the need to cost-cut and GSE representatives weren't shy in confirming this. Shoots of growth, including a strong run in February, gave enough elements of hope to keep Clough on the right side of the support.

That period came off the back of a January that contained probably the worst home defeat since the move to Pride Park, at least in the Championship. A 4-1 reverse against Scunthorpe United dragged Derby down to 18th and a loss on their travels to relegation-plagued Plymouth Argyle only made matters worse. The side facing Scunthorpe contained only three members of the 2007/08 campaign, but it was enough for Clough to pass some of the blame elsewhere.

At the time, he said, 'This is as low as we have been for a long time. We just don't seem to have the character out there at the moment to get back in the game. Whether it is too much for some of them I am not sure. There are some players who have been here two or three seasons, who in the main have lost matches.'

It also sparked an infamous spat by Robbie Savage against BBC Radio Derby's Colin Gibson. Club captain Savage was angered at Gibson's suggestion that 'some of the players don't think the backroom staff are up to the job'. The debate, aired in its entirety, was an embarrassment for the reputation of the club and for Savage in particular, as he emerged worse off. He went on to berate Gibson, listing every accomplishment of the backroom staff in question. It was an excruciating listen and only worsened when he laid in to supporters, 'I've never known a local media who want the club to fail so much. The phone-ins, all people want to do is nail the team, nail the fans, nail the staff.' It was grim listening but somehow, Radio Derby only had positives to say over the coming month and a half.

Quite how that defeat sparked an upturn remains a mystery. First came Billy Davies to Pride Park. It was a familiar tale for the Scot, who had Forest second and with a 19-game unbeaten run as they sat a spot behind Newcastle. The Scunthorpe shambles somehow preceded a 1-0 win thanks to a Rob Hulse header, supplied by Kris Commons's free kick.

But the victory was slightly marred in the coming days owing to the fall-out from another post-match melee. Davies took to the media to allege that Clough had dug a knee into him, 'He came in and kneed me in the back of the leg. I said to him that I wouldn't have minded him doing it to my face but to do it to my back was a bit cowardly and that's why I never shook his hand at the end. He claimed it was an accident but he knows that it wasn't.'

The victory injected confidence and in a way showed the fluctuating levels of professional footballers. When Darren Moore took over as manager at West Bromwich Albion in 2018, he changed very little in terms of personnel but managed to completely rejuvenate the club after months of despair under Alan Pardew. It said more about the psyche of players and the run Derby put together during this month offers a little more insight into their heads.

From beating second-placed Forest and dismantling table-topping Newcastle United 3-0, to follow that up with a 5-3 victory against Preston North End was impressive. Yet it was frustrating just as much, a glimmer into the potential of Clough's early squad.

This lack of consistency made the 2009/10 campaign long, tedious and incredibly frustrating, especially for those brave souls who opted to make the journeys away from home. Just three victories from a possible 23 were recorded and when placed in among 6-1s, 4-1s and plenty of shut-outs, it became a trend that would continue long beyond this first full season. For some reason, Clough was never able to build a team worthy of even looking like competing on their travels. Formations would be vastly different to those displayed at Pride Park, built entirely around consolidating on the 0-0 they started with. Radio Derby summariser Roger Davies would routinely say 'you always take a point away from home'. There seemed to be a mindset across the club that simply 'that will do'.

Derby started the following season in stronger fashion but still only picked up five away wins across the whole campaign. Seven a year later marked an improvement but it was clear where many of the issues lay. Perhaps Clough was aware his side's focus on 'effort' wouldn't be enough to win regularly away from home but the set-up did little to endear the side to those travelling supporters.

Martin Taylor spoke of how he and the staff managed to eke that little bit more out of the squad when required, 'That's the first thing you try and do, create a winning mentality within players who just want to spend time together. We had a small amount of money and players to use and we just had to get everything out of them. You'd play players where they shouldn't play and ask them to do things that are not the norm for them, but they gave you 120 per cent on the pitch and they got the rewards during the week. You needed that togetherness to create so that when you win or lose it's still not the end of the world and you fight to put it right and not sulk about it.'

The issue was consistency though. Frustration grew as results were picked up against some of the bigger forces in the division but squandered against those in and around them. It was only late in the season that Derby put a decent run together, losing only two of the final ten to finish 14th. That marked progress on the season before but acted as something of a false indication of the year, as just four points separated them from 20th spot.

* * *

If that gave Derby a platform to build on, the first weeks of 2010/11 threatened to raise expectations beyond the norm. Luckily, before they had a chance to elevate, the Rams had done the dutiful thing and completely imploded. But even before that, the summer of 2010 seemed different around the club as the nature of the signings began to change a little.

Tomasz Cywka, who had impressed in the final third of the season after moving temporarily from Wigan, signed a pre-contract agreement. Looking back, he says, 'My first thoughts were that Derby is a Premier League club. Everything from the pitch that we train to the stadium, the fans, everything about the club was Premier League. Especially having been at Wigan, it was a smaller club that got promoted without being prepared. I had an offer from them to stay but Derby showed a lot of faith in me and so it was an easy decision.'

The focus soon turned to shoring up the back line and with Paul Connolly, Gary Teale and Jay McEveley all let go at the end of their contracts, there was some breathing space for additional finance. A swoop on Crewe Alexandra for John Brayford and James Bailey was Clough's first intention.

'Nigel invited me up,' Brayford says, 'and going from Burton to Crewe was a massive step but I didn't realise the jump and size of Derby. He explained the players he wanted to get in and I was incredibly humbled that he wanted me to be a part of it but he knew we'd build it over time and get to where we wanted to get in the end.'

Brayford joined having been transformed into one of the Football League's most adventurous full-backs, a two-time Crewe player of the year and voted in to the League Two team of the season. Bailey, a holding midfielder who was intended as a long-term replacement for Robbie Savage, was unveiled as part of the same deal, believed to be rising to £1.3m for the two. Gareth Roberts, a solid left-sided defender from Doncaster Rovers, was added to fill the void left by McEveley.

Nigel Clough rightly takes the credit for his work in transforming the set-up of the club but an individual who has flown under the radar is his brother. Simon, chief scout from 2009 to 2013, was the hidden factor behind the signings of Barker, Brayford and the rest of that core that grew over the years.

Analyst Paul Winstanley says, 'We had to go down the route of lower league but I have to say, Simon has one of the best eyes for a player that I've ever seen or worked with.' Some of the finds by Simon were remarkable and Winstanley was simply waiting to see who he would offer up next, 'He'd be embarrassed listening to it but he has a great eye for a player. People thought "oh, he's Nigel's brother" but when you work with Simon, you see his values as a person and how he goes about his work. I remember him going off to Scotland for one or two days to go and watch Johnny Russell and Craig Bryson. He tried to sign James McCarthy and James McArthur, he was aware of them early on but we couldn't get deals over the line. Gary Crosby got involved and was a good scout too.'

Winstanley saw it from the inside, Barker from the outside. The pursuit was long and with little money to play with, the scouting team went above and beyond to make sure it wouldn't go to waste. 'Simon is exceptional. When they were scouting for me, they told me afterwards that the analysts went to four or five games, Andy Garner went to a few, Simon had too. They did their research on me, my character, my family. They went into what kind of person you are, what kind of character you are, what background you have. They trust the person more than the player. He knew I was a local lad, had played lots and wasn't paid fortunes. They knew I'd got through injuries, all these little details so that there is no stone left unturned.

'Andy went to watch me at Bristol City when I had my blond hair.' That style is a time best left in the past, as Barker continues, 'We went down to ten men and it was 0-0 after 80 minutes, they brought on two centre-halves up front and he said he just watched me and I said, "I'll take these two." In the last ten minutes I always buzzed off a corner. I just wanted to throw my body on the line and Andy said he went straight back to Nigel and said we had to sign him. There's always a lot of detail and time and patience in it. They had five offers refused for me. It was like a car boot, just trying to offer and haggle.'

Though Garner and Crosby would help, it was always Simon who would identify players in the first place. The Clough brothers were almost inseparable and the attention to detail in finding the right type of player was forensic. It's difficult to imagine Nigel in many social situations but somehow, the thought of the siblings going over each minor aspect of a potential signing can come to mind. Sibling relationships often fade over time but if anything, the dynamic between the two was stronger than it ever has been during this era of employment.

'Nigel spent a lot of time with him,' adds Winstanley. 'You have to remember these are two family members who also speak to each other a hell of a lot outside of working hours.' It's little surprise too when you consider the insular nature of Clough's management. A quiet man who tends to sniff out outsiders, he's had the same coaching staff since Burton and even several of the same players. Nigel's management revolves around trust and even around creating this family, so why not incorporate his own family into it?

Much of the mastery of Clough's management lay not only in working with his brother to identify the right signings and the right personalities, but transforming those into reflections of the group as a whole.

Brayford knew the way he worked having been close with him at Burton and saw once again how his methods were designed to create unity, 'It wasn't easy to go into the changing room to start off with but after pre-season you get to know people and the gaffer loves his team bonding. Pre-season now has all these scientific ways but with him it was white-water rafting or the x-run in Nottingham, stuff like that. Just things to build the team mentality. It forces everyone to get on together.

'Nothing was done on an individual basis. He'd take us to a Chinese on a Wednesday night in Derby for instance, it breaks the ice with people. It's something you can look at and ask why it's happening but when you're in a game and in the last minute, it's that that keeps you together and means your mates stick up for you on the pitch because you break barriers down.'

Even Nigel's methods in training were designed to build a closer-knit feel. There would be no pre-seasons in Florida or intricate new tactics to work on, the side would simply train in full public view. The water rafting, the runs in Allestree Park, everything was almost within sight of Pride Park Stadium.

Clough is not a man who's ever strayed far. A look at his managerial career goes from Burton to Derby, up to Sheffield and back to Burton. Nothing north, nothing south. Even many of his signings around this time were local. Barker, Buxton and Brayford were all born within the Staffordshire and Nottingham area. There remains something instilled into Nigel's philosophy about finding success close to home.

Buxton, who starred alongside Brayford back at the Pirelli Stadium, is another who has followed him since his Derby days. Later he'll explain a little more about the relationship the two have formed over the years but by this point, he already knew the man well enough, 'Nigel's got an aura. I never met his dad so I can't compare but in terms of managers I've played under, he's got this aura that when he comes into a room, it just feels like the gaffer is there. He has an aura where everybody goes quiet and he's not afraid of the silences. He knows how people feel around him.

'But there's something deep down inside him that makes you want to run through brick walls for him. It's not anything you can put your finger on, it's just something he's got that no other manager has had who I've played under. It's just something he's got that makes you give when you've got nothing more to give. When you talk about a manager of a football club, or the gaffer, he typifies that.'

* * *

Derby's opening fixture of 2010/11, Elland Road. It had taken three long seasons for them to recover from relegation to League One and when they did, the BBC One cameras were on hand to capture it. Leeds v Derby still held significance in the footballing world. Hated rivals of the 1970s, the feelings may have dropped but they remained in some capacity. For Nigel Clough, it was about more than football.

Brian's 44 days in charge at Leeds after taking over from Don Revie need no explanation and the release of *The Damned United* only served to bring the story to a whole new generation. In the film, the young Clough has a presence around his father. Reality reflected the same and this, the first opportunity for Nigel to manage against the side he hates more than any other, meant more than perhaps any other game had.

John Brayford's first afternoon in a Derby shirt began like no other would, 'To get off the bus I think he just didn't want anybody to fear anything. It was a stick together mentality and obviously you take a bit of abuse and Nigel was walking at the front, but I tell you what, they weren't expecting it. We just did things differently.'

Clough, replicating the way his father would arrive at Millwall's Den stadium back in his Nottingham Forest days, requested an arrival halted 500 yards from the ground. All in attendance on the bus would then make that final journey by foot, a show of defiance. It was a game that still meant more, and Buxton recalls how Clough's desire to spoil the Championship return only intensified once inside, 'When we got to the ground, each time we played them they wouldn't let Nigel's lad on the pitch to have a look. That would always rile him up.'

The added intensity paid off for the visitors. Rob Hulse and Kris Commons forged a 2-1 half-time lead but when Russell Anderson was once again forced off injured, Shaun Barker was called upon from the bench. Still recovering from the first of several injuries over his Derby tenure, he remembers the process of taking to the field on barely one leg, 'It's one of my favourite moments of being in a Derby shirt to be honest. I'd been out, the boys had had six weeks of pre-season, they had Nigel's famous Allestree run where you're going through trees and round the park. I got to train on the Friday, which was my first session for four months or so.

'Just as I was leaving the ground, he said he thought it would be nice for me to travel with the team. As I turned to leave, he said how I'd feel about being on the bench, so I thought and said, "Yeah, that'd be great!" All the boys got in at half-time and [strength and conditioning coach] Steve Haines told me I'd be on. The gaffer said "look, I don't want to push you and you to get hurt" but I'd already got my shin pads and boots on.

'I had the full pre-season off, got back in for Leeds and was told to just train two or three times a week. After two months of the season I realised it wasn't okay and I was really, really struggling.

So, from October I trained maybe twice over the season. Playing Saturday, playing Tuesday, no training for 44 games in a row. All the lads used to take the mick because I would only turn up on the Saturday to play, very much Paul McGrath-like.'

Financial problems remained a burden on Clough's ability to forge a squad, though. Hulse, who was rumoured to be the subject of a £3m Middlesbrough bid a year previously, was sold to QPR for barely a fraction of that fee, leaving just the permanently hobbling frames of Chris Porter and Steve Davies. Instead of Clough delving immediately into the lower divisions or the British loan market as he did with Paul Dickov a season earlier, it was the turn of coach Johnny Metgod to offer a suggestion.

The role of Metgod had been largely overlooked by this point. Not as hands-on as Crosby and Garner, it was only in the summer of 2010 that the Dutchman's effect began to show on the side. After a World Cup where the Netherlands reached the final after operating with a more dynamic 4-2-3-1, Metgod set plans in place for looking to adapt it to Derby's side.

His influence wasn't just on the field though and with Hulse on his way out, attention turned to another part of the attacking quartet. Rather than raiding Forest or Feyenoord, Metgod went all the way back to a man who had just left the Bernabeu for the capture of young Spaniard Alberto Bueno.

The diminutive forward had appeared three times for Real Madrid, most often replacing Raul from the bench, before moving to Valladolid. Barker, who had assisted in the signing of Dickov at the exact same point a year before, began to see a very different side as Clough grew into the role. He recalls, 'Alberto came from Johnny's contacts. Where Johnny is in football, as soon as Alberto came in, we just had a different feel in the club. Kris Commons was fit again and back in the side, Sav was starting to find it harder to play but James Bailey turned up with Brayford at right-back and all of a sudden it didn't seem as old and robust, it felt more free-flowing and like it was growing organically.'

Admittedly it took time for the squad to fit into the demands of the new formation, but from the first minute it became clear of the intentions. Mark Lawrenson even drew a similarity in to the Dutch runners-up in South Africa.

'That season with Johnny, it suited more of a modern feel and for the first time, he started asking me to pass the ball. Me and Dean Leacock were splitting to play it from the keeper, but it felt like that first season was a little progress to bring the age and the wages down. I think Commo was a big player and more part of the side in 2010/11. Bueno added pure quality that we lacked beforehand. It had a European feel for the first time. It was probably Nigel feeling a bit more confident as well to go out, being comfortable with his set-up to try and create more opportunities. Before was all about consolidating and having that slow transition.'

Having seen Hulse leave and with no healthy replacement to fill his shoes, Clough was left plugging the gap. First came left-back Dean Moxey, who three games into the campaign was asked to move into a position he'd never played before. Leading the line at Coventry, he managed to find the net, but it was, as Barker tells, another timely reminder of the financial situation at the club: 'There were 100 per cent financial difficulties the whole time Nigel was there. There was no period where they could go out and spend money. I don't know if we made a profit on players sold. Dean was a very talented left-back and the gaffer had high hopes for him, so Nigel thought, "If he could do this and this, he should be able to play in this position."

'You see it when you bring a big centre-back on to go up front late on. That's all that is expected from it, Nigel simplified the game so much at times. Some coaches over-complicate everything and they want to have a defining say on everything that a player does. Nigel was very different to that. That simplicity allowed players to go and play and the more intellectual ones could play. To use John Brayford as an example, you could put him in any position on the pitch and he would perform. Left-back, centre-back, right-back, centre-midfield. If you stuck him up front he'd do well and Moxey was the same. He would maybe switch off defensively at times compared to other full-backs but he had pace, he had a nice touch and he did well in there.'

It was a temporary measure and soon Commons and Bueno would become the chosen two to rotate roles as the spearhead, tending to operate more as a false nine. Cywka and Paul Green would offer support, with Brayford quickly establishing himself as a new threat down the right. The football had become less lethargic and more modern, particularly with the newfound intent to begin from the back.

Early-season performances were encouraging, even if the results didn't indicate it. But the addition of another veteran forward in a whole different world to the Dickov mould would prove to be the puzzle piece that Clough needed. 'He was a character was Shefki. He wouldn't mind me saying this, but he was the worst trainer in the world,' laughs Brayford. The signing of Shefki Kuqi was a masterstroke, joining on a three-month loan deal from Swansea City and instantly elevating the attacking force of the side. His enormous frame became the focal point for those around him and gave even more allowance to the attacking trio to operate in new manners.

Brayford continues, 'He was a brilliant guy to have around, a real man mountain and even with someone like Shefki, you knew Nigel would have done his research on him as a character. If you look at him, he was probably a typical sort of player that the gaffer would sign really. He's not going to get you 20 goals a season but just this point where he can spearhead the team, he's a hold-up man and you can get the ball to his feet and be someone to hold the ball up. I think when Derby were doing really well, they had the likes of Chris Martin and you could see with Kuqi he was an earlier version.'

The Finn, who was joined days later by another loanee in Luke Moore, transformed everything. From his first home appearance, it became clear that things would click. A 5-0 victory over Crystal

Palace saw Kuqi and Bueno open their accounts and went on to spark Clough's first purple patch as Derby manager. Lifting the side from 22nd up to fourth, the new system was bamboozling sides home and away.

Kuqi's arrival also saw the best of Commons. Having endured an at times frustrating first two years at the club, Commons was allowed into a more central position and given a freedom to roam that suited his goal-getting ambitions. By the new year, he'd found the net on 12 occasions and was shining.

The unity desired by Clough was at its strongest during this period and he had a tactical set-up that allowed his creative first 11 to flourish. Savage, who for large parts of 2009/10 still looked jaded, grew and grew in the early months of 2010/11 when not required to go above and beyond as he had been the previous season. Matched with James Bailey, he was allowed to get back to what he was best at, particularly as the full-backs were now able to take over his attacking duties.

Not only was it his performances catching the eye but – and this is an indicator that vintage Savage was back – so were his off-field behaviours. Preparing to bow out at the end of the campaign, the skipper utilised the early days of Twitter to endear himself further to a fanbase eventually coming around to the idea of him at the club. From singing in bed with Kuqi and adapting So Solid Crew through to 'Ain't nobody, coming to Pride Park, taking three points, off the Rams today', Savage's final few months meant he would be going out on his terms. On his final day at Reading, he stripped to his underwear to say goodbye.

Brayford had just joined from Crewe, where Savage made his name after Manchester United rejection. He looks back, 'Sav was great to be fair. He was captain and you see this facade of him on TV but he's nothing like that as a footballer. He's the ultra-professional and I think the gaffer saw that in him. His dedication to work hard and that he was unbelievably fit for his age is why it worked; Nigel liked the fact he would run all day. He was a character but when it came to the serious stuff, he just wanted to win football matches and he would do anything possible for his team-mates to do that.

'You see this man on TV and that's not how I know Sav, I know the hard worker. Even back then you'd see him playing up on TV and on the pitch but that's not how I knew him on a day to day basis. It does him a disadvantage actually to say he's a hard worker because he was a good footballer as well and he was one of the leaders. People can lead in different ways, but he was captain not only because of his personality but his work rate as well. If a 35-year-old can run all day there's nothing to stop anyone.'

Barker too began to see a man who had grown into his role after initial rejection. The sulky, shy Savage as described by Sullivan back in 2008/09 had been rejuvenated into the beating heart of the club. 'First and foremost, he cared about football,' recalls Barker. 'He was very funny, a bit tough on the players that couldn't cope so he could be harsh. He wasn't everyone's cup of tea but he's the same as what you see on TV. I tell you though, he didn't like getting the yellow bib on a Friday.

'We used to have to give yellow bibs to the worst player and I'd made sure I'd speak to the lads and get them to get him. He'd always go for Greeny and would go "he's rubbish him, Greeny needs the yellow bib, you were awful Greeny" to try and get people on board. But he'd talk that much that it'd put the pressure on him. Some liked him, some didn't and he knew it and I think he does it on purpose. But what he did do was he cared about playing and to play as many games as he did, it says a lot. He was a better player than we saw at Derby.

'At times in games it would become a bit of a Robbie Savage show. I think because he probably realised he was running out of time and he loved the limelight. Every time we stopped on the bus on the way down to games he'd go "oh no, everyone will probably bother me here Barks" and suddenly he's laughing and joking as loud as he can so everyone could see he was there. He's one of the most unique characters I've met in football.'

* * *

Come December, the feel-good atmosphere was dissipating. From fourth to ninth in three games, a trip to Nottingham was to prove make or break for the season.

As the mist rolled in, it became painfully clear which way the campaign would go.

'I erased this game from my memory,' says Tomasz Cywka. The Pole started that night as Forest inflicted a 5-2 beating on a full-strength Derby. 'Maybe it had feeling for the rest of the season for us. Something like this can change the whole season and maybe at the time we didn't see this.'

The evening, in which former Rams Marcus Tudgay and Robert Earnshaw scored four between them, led Clough into one of his most infamous radio rants.

'It makes you very angry and upset,' he said. 'Lack of desire, individually and collectively. Especially individually. We thought we were a little bit further down the road in developing. It is a huge setback. We can't afford to have nights like this. I thought Dean Leacock, for an experienced centre-half with Premier League experience, and an international midfielder in Paul Green, offered us absolutely nothing. You are looking for those experienced players to show a little bit. They gave us nothing.'

The evening again saw Moore lead the line, a baffling decision after the victories picked up with Kuqi in the side. Whether he knew the bulky forward would not stay longer is irrelevant, but on an evening like this it cost him dearly. Then there was the baffling choice of switching Brayford and Leacock's positions.

Bringing up the night, Brayford begins on the changing room, 'The gaffer never really gave much advice on the team. He wanted me to play centre-half because I think he trusted me and thought I was the better option for the night. The gaffer would always say keep it tight and 50 seconds in we'd concede. There was an inquest into it after and I don't know how to explain it, but it was the worst night in a Derby shirt.'

Clough's annihilation of Leacock and Green was particularly cruel but acted as one of the first moments of cruelty dished out in front of the waiting press. If he was hoping to instil some fight back into his side, he was left wanting. From the 5-2 loss through to the end of the season, Derby won only three of 18 games. Within a month they'd been beaten at home to Forest again and were back in mid-table.

For Leacock in particular, something was amiss. From the calmness shown in promotion, he'd descended into a shell of the player he was. Martin Taylor digs into the mental side of footballers, 'You're more appreciative of the mental side these days but at that point you expect them to be able to handle big games. These are some of the biggest games for some of those players, but sometimes they struggle to handle it. You're looking for signs when you're speaking to them and showing them clips, do they know that, are they taking those instructions in.

'I remember Nige came in when Dean should have been the centre-half alongside Shaun Barker and everyone was excited about those two playing together. Dean was good on the ground and athletic, Shaun would give you every last drop of energy in his body and for whatever reason, either off the field bits with Dean or whether he couldn't handle the bollockings, he just couldn't seem to do it.'

There were issues away from the pitch too. Commons's fine form had attracted interest from Celtic and with his contract running down at the end of the season, Derby had a decision to make.

'On the day of the transfer I had no idea what was in store. I trained in the morning as normal and once completed was called into the chairman's office. I sat down hoping a new contract was about to be offered but he came straight out and told me that they had accepted a bid from Celtic and I was "free to go". To say that was unexpected would be an understatement.' Commons's comments in a Scottish *Daily Mail* column offered some background into the process.

But his recollection is different to that of Paul Winstanley, 'I remember it clearly. He completely ran his contract out to go, that was always his plan. If I remember right, he was coming out of contract that summer and in the build-up to the January, Nige tried his best to keep him. We played Ipswich away and I remember being in a hotel when Nige said he would go and have a chat with him too as he had a very good contract offer. He wanted to see where his mind was at and he came away from that meeting not feeling very confident. At that point they got an offer from Celtic and Kris knew it was coming because it had been there for a period. He knew that would come in and he had every intention of joining Celtic or running his contract down.'

Barker joins Winstanley in sharing that view, 'They knew he was going and it was very clear. With him not fully committed, he was one of those players where if he was on the right side, he was a very good player technically. He'd already got 15 or so goals and we had a lot of players who had to be consistent. You couldn't take Bueno or Commo out and bring an extremely good player in, we didn't have the squad or the money. We relied heavily on Commo and the creativity dried up.'

Commons's last contribution would be a penalty miss on an embarrassing evening at Crawley Town in the third round of the FA Cup. Facing the Conference leaders, Derby's task had all the makings of a banana skin. Woefully out of form and with few secondary options to call upon, Clough went full strength. Miles Addison's header should have been enough for a replay, but Sergio Torres's injury-time winner inflicted more shame than any other recent result.

Clough was left humiliated, Brayford too. 'Two thousand fans still travelled down and that hurts Nigel more than anything. He knows how hard people work and pay their money because he always says it. "The fans pay the money and they're the ones you have to produce for on the pitch." He just wants to be right with the fans and make sure you do right by them because they're the ones who are there with the club through thick and thin.'

Commons's departure, for around £300,000, was confirmed days later. Continuing in the same vein he began with, Clough's tried and tested formation began to falter as Kuqi and Commons were gone.

By this point too, Bueno was beginning to struggle. The early-season promise significantly dropped as those around him struggled and Barker remembers the doubts, 'We saw signs of that Spanish brilliance. I remember though we went to Burnley and it was absolutely freezing. I remember walking on to the pitch to play, his hands were up his sleeves, he was shivering, so I didn't know just how useful he would be in the middle of winter. But we saw the good bits and the bad bits of having a player like that.'

* * *

Play-off aspirations were replaced by murmured fears of relegation and Clough began to lose control. Results showed no signs of improving, creativity had been lost and fan irritation was moving to the surface again. It all came to a head after a 1-1 draw at Portsmouth, directly on to the head of Tomasz Cywka.

Clough's tirade following the loss at the City Ground was abrupt and it was harsh but when you compare it to Cywka-gate, it was a slap on the wrist. Having seen his side ship a last-minute equaliser, which Clough blamed on Cywka, the manager said, 'We'd like some players who – in the 89th minute – don't lose the ball 20 yards outside the box which leads to us conceding a goal, which Tomasz Cywka did. He's an extremely inexperienced and not very bright footballer. Despite being told – and he has been with us ten months – he is still doing things like that. He can go back to Wigan or wherever he came from, I'm not really bothered.'

Clough, never one to hide his emotions in front of the media, was lambasted. The PFA were quick to jump on his comments and for many, it sparked a turning point in their perception of the man. To claim a player is 'not very bright' is one thing but it was particularly the second half of the comment, which some saw as xenophobic, that drew the most ire.

It wasn't just in the media that Cywka was outed. Reflecting on the events at full-time, Winstanley says, 'That was the angriest I'd seen him [Clough]. He smashed the door down in the dressing room looking for him without realising he'd just smashed it on Tomasz's head because he was sat behind it.'

Speaking with Cywka, it's a surprise to find out just how inconsequential it was to his mental state. Still making his way into the professional game after failing to make the cut at Wigan, as well as mastering the English language in his spare time, he could only watch on in confusion as the drama unfolded around him: 'I found out about it from the fans because I don't really listen to the interviews, the most important time is in the changing rooms and that's where the most important things are said. In the world of football, what is said to the players, even criticism, stays in the changing room and that's how most managers work. He didn't say it personally to me so I don't know if I read or heard, but sometimes words can be changed in interviews.

'Maybe he was nervous after the game so that's what he said, maybe it was just another game me or the team didn't play well. I didn't really think about it too much. You know how it is with media, people like to talk about it because it doesn't happen every game when a manager criticises a player. I didn't even know he criticised other players because we as players don't read that much and we just focus on what's happening in the changing rooms. The media likes that kind of stuff and they had to talk about it.'

It proved to be one of the final straws for Cywka and Clough's anger towards the team left him searching for new options. Theo Robinson joined on loan from Millwall and Jamie Ward followed from Sheffield United. Ward, not too far removed from the Commons mould, was left unwanted at Bramall Lane after the arrival of Micky Adams and desperate for a move elsewhere. He recalls, 'I had a phone call from Nigel Clough, asking if I fancied going. It was a no-brainer. I had the choice between QPR and Derby, but Nigel rung me when my wife was in labour with our first child, so it was quite quick to sort once the calls had been made. It was an easy decision because we were learning parenthood every day so I don't think I could have just uprooted and left her to do it herself!'

The two had enough of an impact to be offered permanent terms come the end of the season and at least provided something different in the times of struggle. Goalkeeper Frank Fielding was warmly received in his two loan spells, particularly as Stephen Bywater had struggled and left for Cardiff, while the later addition of Brad Jones came at a time where the Liverpool loanee had bigger problems than football.

As he had done with Barker on his arrival, Clough outlined to Ward what was expected and found a player who was another to fit his personality. Ward says, 'The club was struggling towards the second part, but I always felt they would be safe. But there was still that element of having something to play for and I think the good thing with the man is he says it as he sees it. You don't get that much with modern managers, but Nigel says it and sometimes when he realises he's wrong he takes a step back and speaks to them after watching the game back.

'He knows when he's wrong. It's not his way or no way, he sits back. I really enjoyed working with Nigel because he's so open and honest. And he shook a little bit of fear into me. He's probably the only manager who's ever done that. So that was where I was.

'I rarely talked back to him and he soon shot me down when I did try to say something. There was that fear that probably helped me be successful under him. Some people don't like being spoken to honestly. I think some people like to have smoke blown up their arse, but some react to being nailed. You need to know your players and I'm happy to have a rocket and you go out there and prove him wrong or right. I'm one of them that likes to prove people wrong.'

Ward always felt that Derby would be safe and so it proved to be, finishing 19th and seven points above the bottom three. But for a season which offered so much until December, the drop-off was humungous. The early football provided enough of a glimmer to give hope going forward, but Clough continued to make enemies. His handling of the campaign, particularly his individual treatment of players, drew criticism. Heading into his third full season, he'd have to tone it down.

THE CLOUGH YEARS: PART 2

THE POST-ROBBIE Savage era had begun. The Welshman's final home game, a 2-0 defeat against Bristol City, was the final straw not just for Savage but for many of the squad too and as he had done for the previous two summers, Nigel Clough set off in preparation for another slice at the wage bill. Savage and Chris Porter departed, as well as a 35-year-old Michael Boulding, who had been brought in with weeks to go of the previous season.

The savings made on Savage were swiftly reinvested into the permanent captures of Jamie Ward, Theo Robinson and Frank Fielding. The trio, who had all experienced varied success during their loan tenures, arrived for a combined total of around £1m and marked another fresh era in the side. It became the era of youth and, with none of the players older than 25, the dynamic began to change.

The only remaining casualties from the Paul Jewell era by this point were Steve Davies, Stephen Pearson, Stephen Bywater and Dean Leacock. By January, all bar Davies had departed with their contracts cancelled. Even Miles Addison, who had continued to struggle with injuries, found himself out of the club on loan; even if he'd just signed for three more years.

He recalls, 'Before I went on loan to Barnsley, Tom Glick gave me another year deal and me and my agent were like "eh". He rang me and said, "I can't believe what's just happened, they're offering you a new deal, three years." It didn't add up because they said they were going to let me go, but then Tom Glick was saying they wanted to keep me but Nigel didn't, so they gave me that contract just in case they did get rid of him.'

Though the first three captures were known to the club, it was activity north of the border that would be even more transformative. 'It was so long ago,' the man concerned now admits. Having asked Craig Bryson to go back through nine years in a Derby County shirt, starting right from his first day was cruel. 'I think it was reported in the paper that at one of the games I was at Kilmarnock that Nigel was in the crowd. After one of the games I was doing press and a press guy told me Nigel was interested in taking me down to Derby.'

Bryson was relatively unknown in the UK. At a time where the television cameras were beginning to turn away from Scottish football, all that was really known upon his signature was that he was Kilmarnock's captain and, primarily due to much smaller funds in the SPL, he was cheap. Four years previously he had a trial under Billy Davies, yet it took until 2011 for Clough to rediscover his new diamond. A £350,000 hit was relatively minor at the time and come the day he would depart, the figure equates to around £1,286 per appearance. By contrast, Ikechi Anya's was £150,000 per game.

It was at this time that the Derby changing room began to populate with genuine leaders. Alongside Bryson, Jason Shackell, a dominant centre-half who joined from Barnsley, captained the Tykes and was another good purchase at £750,000. Factoring in Barker, Buxton and the loan addition of Kevin Kilbane, a changing room short on confidence was being filled with strong voices.

'Nigel would put people on low wages and shorter contracts to improve them as players and people,' John Brayford recalls. 'I think he liked the players that had something to prove and had been written off as basically an underdog. Okay, you'll never be an underdog as a Derby County player, but it had the underbelly and a hunger to want to do well for him.'

The 2011 signings ranged from the sublime in Bryson to the partially ridiculous. Chris Maguire arrived with high expectations but mustered only seven league appearances, Clough misreading the attitude of Maguire and swiftly moving him elsewhere. But on paper, there was no more ridiculous signing than that of Nathan Tyson.

Just two years earlier, he had incited a mass riot with a flag and yet, on 1 July, he joined on a free from Nottingham Forest. Tyson says, 'I'd heard rumours that Derby were interested. But Forest threw me under the bus. We lost to Swansea in the play-offs and I was sat there, and the chairman Nigel Doughty came around and said, "unlucky guys". The chief executive was going around shaking all the players' hands saying "unlucky, see you next season" and he gets to me and says "unlucky, all the best".

'I was at the time allowed to speak to Derby, had talks and stuff with two other clubs but I felt me moving away with three kids in Nottingham, I didn't want to be away from there because I want to be close to them and spend as much time with them as I possibly can. But going through that whole process and Derby knocking, it made logical sense.

'At the same time Forest sent me a contract offer in the post. They didn't phone or want any talks or invite me in, they just put out a flimsy offer which was a massive pay cut from what I was on and I thought look, I'd have been happy to take less money if they'd have been bothered to pick up the phone and phone me, meet me and have a chat. But that didn't happen and they put that flimsy offer to say they'd offered but I didn't take it. Derby were the only option that would be the right move and the best for me to further my career.'

Tyson's signature was curious in many ways. A proven player at Championship level and bursting with energy, he'd been dogged by injuries in previous years and even upon signing wasn't fully fit.

Rather than spending the time with his new team-mates, it was first-team physio Neil Sullivan who became Tyson's running buddy. Sullivan said, 'I don't think we realised how deep the problems were. It's always been a bit of a gamble when you recruit someone with a history. As a club you always back yourselves to give them a better opportunity than their previous employers to keep them on the pitch. But there's also an opportunity for a player to not let on exactly the extent of it and although you do your homework as best you can, it doesn't always work out. It was a shame because he would have been a real asset if he was fit for more, but not every player is as robust as the next one. It's just down to genetics, some people are more susceptible at a cell level.'

Tyson had to wait for his debut but watched on as his new side made their best start to a season in over a century. Twelve points from 12 was beyond expectations and victories over recently relegated Birmingham and Blackpool began to turn heads. Davies had found the net three times, Shackell and Bryson had both opened their accounts too and the side quickly gelled.

It wasn't only the summer signings who had begun in fine form though. While Bryson, Ward and company all had their best years far ahead of them and had a hunger, the real work from Clough came from within Moor Farm. From the pre-season of 2011/12, he began to introduce a fresh crop of talent, the likes of which hadn't been injected into the side since the days of Tom Huddlestone.

Martin Taylor, as well as the rest of the staff, paid a closer eye to the academy than any team since, 'We were massively tied in with the first team. Will Hughes was 16 when he came through, Mason Bennett was 15. He's in the side when he was 15 and has been around for seven years now. Me and Andy [Garner], we didn't have set tasks. When it was the under-21s, we were on the bench, but the gaffer would have been there and if they were good enough, they'd join in with us. If we'd had the money, they'd have probably been further down the order. That's where we were, they were given the chance, and most took it with both hands.'

Before Bennett and Hughes came the Irishmen. Jeff Hendrick and Mark O'Brien had been slowly bedded into the first team at different times and with injuries and departures, the two were highlighted as potential shirt-fillers. For O'Brien in particular, it was a long time coming.

The Cherry Orchard graduate was one of the first youngsters Clough opted to use. Back in 2009, his final-day appearance at Watford was a major step forward for the then 16-year-old and with the incoming Barker and Leacock to help bed him into first team football, there were huge expectations.

It's ill-advised to say O'Brien's career stalled in the coming years. When he should have been preparing to force his way permanently into the back line, a pre-season scan showed a leak in his aorta valve. He was soon told that he needed an operation within the next two weeks, otherwise he could 'drop dead' on the pitch.

Barker, still on the long road to recovery after his summer operation, saw O'Brien grow the longer he worked his way back. 'OB was a proper centre-half. Could head it extremely well, brave as they come and loved defending. He was very similar to me in terms of how he played. If there's a player that's been unfortunate with injuries that have curtailed a career it's OB.'

With O'Brien, Hendrick too had made his first-team bow and heading into 2011/12, Clough confirmed he'd become a more important part of his plans. It's a philosophy that has stuck with the manager since his early days with Burton and perhaps way back to his own debut as a 19-year-old at the City Ground.

Like O'Brien and Hendrick, it was at an early age that Brayford was brought through under Clough. 'Even at Burton now, the gaffer will always have two or three of the youth team players if he's watched them and if he thinks they'd be better, they'll stay on. When they come through and I first saw Jeff I thought he'd be a superstar because of his size, his comfort on the ball and I thought he'd be a top, top player. The gaffer with the young lads was harsh on them in a sense but for their own benefit, if that makes sense.

They wouldn't train with the first team if they thought he was rubbish and they might say "why's he always shouting at me", but it's because he liked them and he wants them to do well.

'Especially at a club like Burton, we can't pay loads of money for players but even at a club like Derby, if he could save money by producing a player rather than spending £2m, that's the way he saw it.'

It's not only at Derby he's produced players. A look into his Sheffield United days shows the emergence of Dominic Calvert-Lewin and Che Adams, now top-flight regulars. Money was a problem throughout Clough's Derby run but even today, he continues to prove his dedication to promoting from within and that's what happened the longer the 2011/12 season went along.

O'Brien's early partnership with Shackell was growing by the game. Hendrick, though seamlessly slotting into the centre of the park and offering an attacking intent that Savage simply couldn't in previous years, was biding his time before making the ultimate impression. And there wouldn't be a better way for him to do it than his feat on a September 2011 trip to Nottingham Forest.

But Derby's day did not start well as goalkeeper Fielding was sent off inside two minutes and Forest's Andy Reid stuck the resulting penalty home. Clough's side were already up against it.

Having come in very much as a number two behind Fielding, Adam Legzdins was forced into the action. Taylor had mere seconds to prepare him and little to say but 'good luck'. He now recalls, 'We brought Adam in because he was good enough to play and patient enough to sit on the bench, because it's hard enough to be a number two. He had experience but he was a cheaper option than having a more experienced one. Generally, your goalie doesn't get injured and plays the whole season, you try and save money so you can spend money elsewhere. But it filled me with pride that we picked somebody like Adam who comes on and does that.'

Legzdins, his first duty to pick the ball out of the net, could have been fearful of what was to come in the remaining 89 minutes.

But it was a Forest side low on confidence and the visitors were aware that if they could get a few opportunities, the fans could turn. There was nobody better, or more infuriating, to cause that turn than Jamie Ward.

An individual who thrives in the battle, his pre-match vow to get in the faces of those in Garibaldi red was to be achieved. When Chris Cohen went down after slipping, most would have expected the ball to be played out. But with Clough screaming at them to play on and with the sides now even, Ward took full advantage from the left. He says, 'It's unfortunate Chris Cohen was down injured and if I knew the extent of the injury, I'd have played it out. But the only other thing I'd say is it was ten v ten, they still had enough to deal with us and I had to just play on. Radi Majewski tried to nail me and then I've skipped away. When I got to the byline I thought, "I've got nowhere to go here."

'The only thing I could have done was roll it through his [Forest goalkeeper Lee Camp's] legs and he opened them at the right time. It actually hit my heel. It looks clean on TV but I never caught it clean which helped it go in. Scoring goals is great in general but it's even better in the derby.'

Ward's leveller, topped by a glorious celebration in front of the Trent End, was a thing of magic and those same supporters did turn. By the time Hendrick struck the winner, they were already in full revolt. Still aghast at a missed header from six yards, Ben Davies's touch fell into his path 20 yards out and capped off a day for the ages.

'To see Jeff score that goal after the header was massive. How he missed that I don't know but to react how he did and score the winner, that was incredible enough to see that. We'd have throttled him in the changing room if we didn't win but it was a great day all round,' says John Brayford.

One of the few survivors from the 5-2, the day meant as much to Brayford as it did to anybody, 'It was something which was really special. Before the game the gaffer said we'll keep it tight this year, nothing like the previous years. Then we went one step better by getting the goalie sent off too. That was talked about in Derby for weeks after, I saw all the t-shirts that were printed. Amazing.'

* * *

Away from football, marquee summer signing Tyson continued to struggle. Handed his debut off the bench in the victory at Forest, he soon found himself facing another lay-off. 'We had to be in on the Monday and I did a training session and was just breaking down. I couldn't kick a ball with it and I was in a lot of pain. It just spiralled out of control and I was thinking something needed sorting. The pressure got to me quite a lot because I was stressed out and I had people on Twitter giving me death threats and saying they wanted to chuck my kids in the Trent and things like that because I was still in the Nottingham area. So I always felt like I still had something to prove.

'I put myself under so much pressure. My first season I had an operation on my groin which looking at it now I shouldn't have had. The first went wrong and I had to go under the knife again, scar tissue had come out and moved. I was recovering from that and all the rehab work I had going on just wasn't working, it wasn't suiting the style of player that I am and nothing worked. There's then the factor of having not scored yet, not getting many chances, I'm in and out the team you know, we're sitting mid-table and not pushing, it was just mediocre all the way through that whole season.'

As Tyson recuperated, the story became all too familiar. Slightly earlier than the implosion of the year before, results began to fade away. A 4-0 defeat at Leicester was difficult to take and after a top-of-the-table clash with Southampton attracted a sell-out crowd (Derby were still third at this point), it all fell away. From sitting in the top three on 1 October, a run of six defeats in seven had the side down in 15th before November was out. In the midst of this, Clough and co were issued with extended contracts to tie them down until 2015. Even at this point, two and a half years into his management, the reaction was mixed.

Derby rewrote the record books again. Already blooding Hendrick and O'Brien into the first 11 – and with Callum Ball soon to be trialled at the top – Clough bypassed the under-18s. Mason Bennett was carefree. He was living the dream of representing his club while balancing his GCSEs in the process. The last thing he would have expected to be doing on a Friday afternoon was travelling to play adult football, but that's just what he found himself doing in mid-October. At the age of 15 years and 99 days, Bennett was handed a start in Middlesbrough, far surpassing Lee Holmes's previous record as the youngest to ever wear the shirt. 'He was ready and if you're good enough you're old enough,' said Martin Taylor.

Taylor, who had seen the Langwith-born lad mature under the tutelage of Darren Wassall in the academy, oversaw his introduction, 'We had to ask permission from his teachers if he could play and he had to have a room on his own because of his age for the CRB reasons. That's how it was. When he made his debut, we had to ask teachers to release him on the Friday. But it didn't matter how old in our eyes, they would play.'

Bennett, who struck the crossbar in a 2-0 loss, was part of the front three alongside a slightly perplexed Ward, who admits: 'That was the first time I'd ever seen him play. Never trained with him. The first time I ever saw him play football was that day and I think that's the first time I'd actually heard of him!'

It was another visible demonstration from Clough at the lack of funds he had to work with. Although his bench had the likes of Cywka and Maguire on there, and with the squad particularly stronger than it had been the year prior, he still wanted more. Loan signings began to filter through again, with Tamas Priskin and Ryan Noble failing to make a dent at the top end of the pitch, but again Clough couldn't find the right formula.

Hope had again turned into mediocrity in the middle and while form didn't plunge in the same way as it had a year previous, there was a pattern. Runs of victories would only provide further irritation when paired with long winless streaks, the seven from mid-January to early March particularly frustrating having worked their way back up to eighth.

With no promotion or relegation fears this time around, the focus had turned to Forest again. Already postponed due to snow – the first game ever to be so at Pride Park – it was another opportunity to condemn the Reds who, without Billy Davies, had descended under the stewardship of Steve Cotterill.

To the lows first. In a largely dull first hour, it was off the field that the headlines were being written. Forest's chairman Nigel Doughty had passed away a month before and Tom Glick was forced to apologise a day later in the aftermath of tasteless chants by a section of supporters. But there was a story unfolding in front of the south stand too and it was Shaun Barker at the heart of it. Barker, the boyhood red, had completed his journey back from the operating table. After a year of playing without training and the subsequent recovery from treatment on his bone crater, the now Alice-band-wearing skipper was forming a strong partnership alongside Shackell.

Physio Neil Sullivan remembers approaching Barker after Fielding's frame fell on to his skipper midway through the second half, 'As I approached Shaun on the pitch, he had a dislocated kneecap and because it happened so quickly you don't get that snapshot or those photos of his knee in the wrong direction. In that moment I just knew he'd had a collision and as we got on there, his kneecap was dislocated. So he was obviously in pain, it was relocated on the pitch by the paramedic and myself and then back into the dressing room and it was a case of packaging him up and off to hospital.'

Sport, just like life, is a tale of what ifs. What if it hadn't snowed for the original fixture? Where would Barker's career have taken him? He recalls, 'Every year we used to go to Cheltenham and that was the next day. The Forest game was rearranged so it shouldn't have happened on that night. I remember in the warm-up I was struggling with my knee at that point and I can't remember who I spoke to, maybe Bray, and I said I was going to have to pull out. Pretty much every sign you can think of was coming up. But after the injury I was coming off and telling everyone I'll see them at Cheltenham tomorrow and the physio asked if he could do anything. I just asked for a shoulder rub.'

The extent of Barker's injury needs no telling. He never again played for Derby and never started a first team game after that night. 'I knew the minimum it would be was four months because my knee was out on the pitch with a dislocation. They popped it back in and the best scenario was a patella dislocation. We had x-rays at Derby Hospital, saw there were no breaks and we thought at that point I'd be back for the start of next season, that was where my thinking was at then.

'Then we had the MRI scan and we knew I'd done two or three ligaments. We got the date for my surgery and I think when Andy Williams looked, we realised the severity. I was told I probably wouldn't play again because he'd never had one of these as severe in football before. The chondral defect was now 50p-sized in my bone and that was my concern. He knew he could fix the ligaments which would have to be ruptured and reattached with synthetics, but the crater would be a potential problem. You drill into the bone and it fills up with blood and then there's a crust. If you imagine ice it creates a puddle, the bigger the area the weaker it'll be. I was told it was like a car crash and I was lucky to walk. I was then told it'd be two years. And then a year down the line I'd had three ops and I couldn't walk properly or stand for more than two minutes. At that point you kind of know it'll be tough.'

Yet, even in immense pain, Barker would wait to go to the hospital. The injury was horrific, unbearable and sickening for all. One particularly affected was Jake Buxton. Now just a bit-part defender who had slipped back down the pecking order, he was called upon. It was a situation he was used to. Ten minutes towards the end of most games routinely became 'Bucko Time'. It was a cruel demotion for a man who had still been unable to prove himself as a first-teamer, three years after his signing. The season should have been one that saw him make that jump but injuries and moments put paid to it.

In September, Buxton was reported to have suffered a fractured eye socket in training. After missing the previous season completely and now finding himself pushing O'Brien, fate was against him and it was another cruel blow.

It wasn't the whole truth though, as Paul Winstanley remarks, 'We did an annual trip to Marbella that was organised by Nige, where it was a bit of a warm weather training camp that worked really well. There was one day they had an afternoon off, so the manager allowed them to go into the centre for a few drinks and they had to report back for 7pm. I remember we were all sat on the sunbeds, I was sat next to Gary Crosby and his phone goes off and it was one of the lads. "There's been an incident down at the beach," and you could see Gary's face change.

'Anyway, the boys had gone on a banana boat and it tipped, flipped them all out and Jake Buxton had crashed into Chris Riggott. Jake broke his nose, had stitches in his eye, cracked his skull. His face is an absolute mess. He's in a little ambulance hut, Chris is complaining about his shoulder so anyway, they both had to go to hospital. Chris had to go, Jake's refusing to go because he doesn't realise his face is mangled and he's smashed his skull open.

'Eventually he's made to go, they both report back later on that evening. Jake has to go back home but he can't fly because of his brain and a cracked skull, so one of the physios drives him back in a car from Spain, which takes two days. Jake wouldn't even go to hospital, even though he's had 50 stitches and cracked his skull open. I think the club had to say it was a training ground incident.'

So for Buxton, this night meant more than any other in his entire career. What he would do in the course of those final ten minutes transformed not only his season but quite possibly saved his time as a player. 'That night was the reason I done three or four successful years after that, all because of that night. I was just hoping to not concede really,' he says.

Buxton's injury-time winner, capped by an inability to de-shirt in celebration, created a hero. From that moment on, there was something about Bucko. A local lad come good, a person that fans could relate to. His moment, albeit coming in horrendous circumstances, was the catalyst for creating one of the most likeable men ever to wear a Derby shirt.

He said, 'I weren't on Twitter at the time or any social media but I can always remember my brother going "bro, you're trending worldwide mate" and I was like, "What, what do you mean!" But what's most important is Shaun could have gone off to hospital because he was in all sorts of pain but he waited until afterwards in the changing room to congratulate me for the goal, which was a class touch.

'I knew I'd done a big thing, but I didn't realise at the time or expect my life to change basically. We played Doncaster away in the following game and I came out for the warm-up and the stadium erupted basically. They erupted and that's where the football genius song came about and it's when I realised I'd changed a few people's lives.'

Waiting in the changing room was Barker, there to greet the man who would go on to fill his spot admirably in the coming years. Barker said, 'Jake never had the credit for how he performed before then. He was consistent in that first year and came out the team in the second season, but the first season he was outstanding at times. Maybe his pace let him down a bit because you could never deny his desire to defend and block and head, that first season people saw a player from non-league and he wasn't respected enough. They saw him as someone who wasn't valued enough to play for Derby County. But because I'd come from the Championship, people already make the decision before you join. But that goal changed everything for Jake.'

* * *

Once in a generation, a unique talent emerges. Giles Barnes in 2006 springs to mind as a comparison. How did a player of his quality and brashness, so un-British in his manner, come from within Derby County? Perhaps at a higher level it can be with more regularity and some can be incredibly lucky as Southampton did with Theo Walcott and Gareth Bale. But most clubs only have one. Will Hughes was Derby's one.

His start on the final day of 2011/12 was a 'were you there?' afternoon. Hidden in the academy, kept out of the squad for almost the entire season. Few had even seen Hughes before, and many had to double check the strength of their sunglasses under the May sunshine. Youngsters had come and gone, and the side had been packed with them that year. Hendrick would go on to start at international tournaments and be a Premier League regular. O'Brien and Bennett continue to have strong careers in the Football League. But Hughes was just different.

'In his first training session you could see he'd be a player,' says Martin Taylor, a keen observer of the academy. He recognised Hughes's talent early on because there was no hiding away from it. Hughes's debut at home to Peterborough was, considering that he had never started a game before, one of the great showings. Aged 16, he controlled the entire match and left supporters purring for more as he received a standing ovation off the field. Hughes represented hope.

'I'd say in the build-up to that game he was in and out training,' Jamie Ward says. 'He'd come down once every couple of weeks, then he was down more and more. We could see the ability that he had very early on. To see him play and take what he did in training, you knew what a player he'd go on to be. The most important thing was just to keep his feet on the ground and to be fair to Will, he was a very level-headed young lad. Some get carried away and think they've made it but Will didn't.'

Hughes, even at 16 and 17, was the best natural footballer outside the Premier League. Many before him, not just at Derby but across the sport, would emerge with his talents but find ego and expectation standing in their way. Hughes, unlike many who came before him, had the right role models. He says, 'I think Nigel Clough had the biggest impact on me. To this day I'd say he had the biggest impact not just on a footballing perspective but as a person as well. He didn't only teach me a lot on the pitch and give me first team football, he taught a lot off the pitch as a human being which is even more important.'

The now Premier League regular with Watford goes back through his memory banks. A week before Christmas of 2019, it's a long way back since Hughes made his first major step into first team football. By the time he left Derby aged 22, he'd appeared 187 times for the first team; it would have been more if it wasn't for a ruptured cruciate in 2015.

But still today, it's the same Will Hughes as the one who first stepped on to the Pride Park pitch in 2012. Still quiet, still humble, albeit with many more hours in the gym now behind him.

That he's managed to remain the same is largely thanks to those he shared a changing room with. Amid rumours of scouts from Manchester City to Barcelona producing dossiers on him, a group of senior coaches and professionals were on hand to keep him in check. 'At 15 or 16, it's easy to get drawn into those rumours when you're a young player making your way. But having Nigel as a manager kept my feet on the ground and helped me focus on my football first and foremost and anything that came after that was a bonus,' he says.

Clough, a father to one son named William, played a similar role with the other Will, spotting similarities to his own emergence. Nigel was pushed into the limelight very early on in his own playing career, earlier than most would be. Managed by the most famous football manager on the planet, not to mention his dad, he had to deal with the hype and the media expectation, the constant glare and the focus on his family.

Hughes may not have seen the eyes of the world on him, as well as a Football Manager-obsessed universe who had seen his development in the game, but he'd experienced that same level of expectation. It's no wonder Clough saw himself in Hughes. 'It is important he keeps his feet on the ground and that he keeps performing week in, week out,' Clough said at the time. 'The best possible thing for him at the moment is to stay with us, get a season or two under his belt in the Championship and just keep learning and improving.'

But beyond the impact of Clough in Hughes's development, his team-mates truly kept him grounded. The likes of Shaun Barker, who by now was watching on as opposed to getting involved, were able to mentor Hughes through his early weeks and months. 'Those players, people like Jake and Shaun, Bryson and Gareth Roberts, they had a similar sort of impact to what Nigel had for me,' Hughes continues. 'He had a group of players that first and foremost were good humans and that was more important than being footballers and he got a really good group there which taught me a lot. It was difficult with the rumours flying about and breaking into the first team so young but the lads I was around were fantastic with me and didn't let me get ahead of myself. They were seasoned pros, so they knew 90 per cent of the rumours were just made up in the paper and not to believe anything. I got along with them all very well.'

Hughes's development over his first full season was extraordinary. Had it not been for Richard Keogh's ever-presence, he would have claimed the Jack Stamps Trophy aged just 18. By November 2012 he was in the England Under-21s, the second-youngest player to ever receive a cap. New scouts from new teams across Europe were flocking to watch him in action. In 2013, Darren Wassall told ESPN, 'They are talents you cannot coach – certainly not coach to that level. He was born with those God-given abilities. They are the attributes all managers and coaches want players to have, but he is a freak in the way that he has them already.'

With Hughes, Hendrick and Bryson having all the makings of one of the finest midfields in the division, 2012/13 was always likely to spell more growth, even if it wouldn't ever be one for Derby to challenge the top six. New faces continued to emerge at Moor Farm, none more recognisable over the years than Richard Keogh. For all of the detractors and without taking into account the final days, the £800,000 spent on Keogh was a masterstroke and over time, potentially the best money parted with by Clough.

Jason Shackell, who departed for Burnley, was one of the leading lights the previous campaign, yet it was felt his character didn't fit the club, says Paul Winstanley: 'Jason did really well but as the season went on, Nigel felt like Jason didn't fit into the group as a person and as a character. Nige identified Keogh as a potential replacement and that was how it happened, Richard came in on the basis of getting Jason out. I was involved in a board meeting where he put that to the board and they were pretty shocked that we wanted to move Jason out.'

Keogh, immediately taking over the armband, was three years Shackell's junior and had missed just one game in his previous two seasons at Coventry City. With funds remaining scarce and Barker years away from playing again, the signature was based on reliability. James O'Connor joined from Doncaster, Paul Coutts arrived for £150,000 from Preston and promising winger Michael Jacobs came from Northampton. It was small steps forward and as ever, the outgoings outweighed the incomings. Chris Maguire left, Paul Green also after the completion of his contract. Miles Addison and Steve Davies were both sold after being placed on the transfer list. These sales marked the final two remnants of Paul Jewell's reign.

The window wasn't a total success, though. Derby were turned down by Kelvin Mellor, a full-back at League Two Crewe, who saw staying as the better option. And then there was Conor Sammon. The forward's record spoke for itself; one goal in 34 games for Wigan, for whom he signed on a reported fee of £600,000. Quite how that led to Derby paying £1.2m is bamboozling. Brayford says, 'Knowing Nigel I knew he wouldn't want to waste money unnecessarily. Whether there was more money to spend or not he'd still treat the money like it was his own and not just spend it willy nilly. However much he had, he'd still make sure the books were right at the end of the year. If he'd spent that money on a player, he'd have to feel confident it would be a success. I know with Conor it was like it didn't work out, but it would have been through no lack of thought or watching the player.'

There were moves upstairs too. Tom Glick, the figurehead for the GSE regime and someone slowly beginning to be accepted as results improved, announced he was departing for a similar role with Manchester City, leaving a gap in the chief executive role. Nobody, Clough included, knew at the time that the appointment of Sam Rush in his place would transform the entire football club. A respected head of football operations with global agency Wasserman, Rush's capture was heralded as a significant coup for a Championship outfit. With his contacts, business knowhow and desire to move Derby County forward, it represented a new era.

From early in the campaign, the talents of Will Hughes were again bringing supporters to their feet. One afternoon in August, in front of a crowd only just topping 20,000, he dominated an afternoon against Gianfranco Zola's Watford, the side he would go on to achieve his Premier League ambitions with. With a midfield trio of Hughes, Hendrick and Bryson, a new attacking outlet in Sammon and a reinforced back line, Clough again saw opportunities to press on in his vision for the squad.

But again, the group still wasn't quite formulated in order to make that next step. Signings like Jacobs failed to deliver – Johnny Russell remembers that prior to his signing, Clough had called him a 'League Two wanker' – and unlike the previous two campaigns, there was no need for an implosion as things hadn't ever got into a rhythm. The side never rose above ninth place, fluctuating between 15th and ninth from December onwards.

Signings like Jacobs and O'Connor didn't fit directly into the side, Sammon contributed only five goals before Christmas and at the back, the changing between the sticks of Fielding and Legzdins saw both fall out of form.

Nathan Tyson had gone an entire debut campaign without finding the net. From pre-season onwards of his second season, things would fare no better on a personal level as the management turned against him. He recalls, 'I remember we had a long summer – probably too long. We had like ten weeks off and it was the longest I'd ever had. We get back and we're doing the yo-yo test and me and Theo finished at the same time together, but I remember Nigel saying some players had come back looking like shit and I was thinking to myself, "Mate, you've given us ten weeks off? This is too much." Everyone put on a bit of weight and he's hammering us.'

Tyson struck for the first time in a 5-5 penalty shoot-out defeat at home to Scunthorpe in front of 4,724 fans.

'We got back into the changing room and Nigel just went to town on, well, me and Theo. He was saying we'd come back looking like shit and that's when I knew. Someone had warned me about this, that you have one season and if you don't do it, you're cut out basically. I thought "hmm, this ain't looking great". I start the following game against Sheffield Wednesday, score again and I'm finally showing what I can do. Then we go to Bolton away and he'd just signed Sammon and we were playing up front and he just drags me off. I get dropped after scoring two in three at Wolves away and that's when it started. I sat there and thought, "I know what's going on now."'

Tyson and Robinson would never recover, both loaned out as Clough again looked towards new options. One of those, coming later that campaign, was the loan addition of Chris Martin. Fresh from the back of a poor spell at Swindon, Martin was again seen as a cheaper deal for the club at the time. His initial signing was greeted with disappointment as his Championship record was in fact worse than that of Theo Robinson's. Robinson was loaned to Huddersfield in February, Tyson to Millwall a month earlier. Neither would appear in a Derby shirt again.

Tyson said, 'I don't dislike the guy, he's highly respected but at the same time his style is a bit much for my liking. We done some old-school stuff, stuff before I was even born. I just felt that it was a bit backwards. Things were happening that I saw when I was like, 18 or 19 and I just didn't feel it was acceptable at this time. The team needed more for us to progress further because we'd got good players, there's no doubt about it. We had really good players, it just needed that bit more coaching and it lacked in that department where it was more about, not so much discipline, but it was more old school and not with the times.'

There were moments though. Jake Buxton's resurgence continued, keeping the shirt after fighting away the challenge of O'Connor. He'd already struck against one rival and only cemented his status by netting an April winner at Elland Road. He recalls, 'I scored and then obviously the celebrations, I was over the moon for the supporters and for the history with Nigel's dad managing up there for 44 days, I knew those games meant a lot to the gaffer. When I came in at full time he bollocked me for over-celebrating so I was thinking "bloody hell". I was over the moon for myself, the fans, the team, but also I knew how much he wanted to beat Leeds as a Clough because of what they'd done to his dad. But all he was bothered about was that I was out of breath for four minutes for celebrating like a madman! I ran around the back of the goal and got spat on and a bit of stick. Neil Warnock got sacked after the game and he told Nigel, "Tell Bucko thank you for getting me the sack."'

The tenth-placed finish was Clough's best and marked another sign of improvement. New talent had emerged, unwanted players were out of the door and with the addition of Sam Rush behind the scenes, it should have marked a positive step forward for the management team. Things were beginning to bubble though, and a wariness had crept in.

Rush's influence hadn't begun until later in the campaign, but it was already threatening disruption according to Paul Winstanley:

'The relationship with Nige and the staff and GSE was very, very good. There was a genuine fear of Sam coming in with different ideas but to be fair, Sam came in in a very positive manner. He didn't try and change anything dramatically; it was very positive and you sensed that he was on board and appreciative of what had gone on before him. But I sensed that fear from Nige and the staff. Will he change things? Will he bring in his own manager?'

Clough would be given the summer.

DIVIDED

THE 2012/13 season was one which, although Derby again missed out on a top-third finish, signalled progress. Finally able to eradicate any trace of previous regimes, Nigel Clough went into the next campaign with the full support of Sam Rush as he continued his search for a squad capable of a play-off push.

As soon as the window opened, it became clear that if there was any time for the side to truly press the button on a realistic top-six bid, this was it. Four new additions joined and as ever, Clough's ability to work within a budget was exercised. Craig Forsyth and Chris Martin had both been steady additions during loan spells at the back of the season and signed, Martin on a free and Forsyth for a nominal cost. Lee Grant, recently crowned player of the season at Burnley, returned after six years away. He wasn't the only familiar face, John Eustace coming back following a 2009 spell on loan.

July 2013 also saw Johnny Russell sign. Russell, one of the most exciting young talents in the SPL after 46 goals in just over 100 games for Dundee United, made the switch south despite reported interest from Celtic and a handful of Serie A sides. The £750,000, subsequently countered by the sales of John Brayford to Cardiff and Frank Fielding to Bristol City, seemed good business and with the loan of promising Tottenham full-back Adam Smith, Clough had structure like never before.

'The squad we had and the quality meant we had a much more complete team full of young, hungry players,' remembers Shaun Barker, by now a regular feature at the training ground as he stepped up his rehabilitation. 'We had players who were eager to play for the club and a real team mentality. The squad felt relatable from the top to bottom and there was nobody there that was unapproachable. The two teams that got promoted that season, Burnley and Leicester, they both came to Pride Park and sat behind the ball because we were a good footballing team and they were there to stop us playing.

'Eight weeks into the season, that's a huge sign of respect because they turned up just to stop us playing. That only happens with good clubs and I think managers could see we would be up there that year.'

Clough's start wasn't the spectacular run of results seen in his previous two seasons but again, it was progress. Russell struck in the opener, while a Chris Martin double was enough for an impressive victory at Brighton, another side with major ambitions for the months ahead.

Sandwiched between those home defeats against Leicester and Burnley was a dominant 3-0 win at Yeovil. That match, featuring a scintillating 25-pass move for the second goal, was the clearest indication that the four years of squad building could all be about to be worth it.

The September win at Millwall was the first time Derby had scored five away from home since September 1997 at Sheffield Wednesday and even more impressively, Craig Bryson became the first man to claim a league hat-trick since Paul Simpson in April 1996 against Tranmere Rovers. A day of records was sealed when Mason Bennett, two years after his bow at Middlesbrough, became the youngest league scorer in Derby's history. There was little to suggest that would be the last victory under Clough's management.

Although it looked like things were starting to click after four long years, off the field there were other factors at play. Derby have always prided themselves on being a club of the city and even in 2007/08, the stadium sold out on a weekly basis. But following years of stagnation, interest had dropped. An opening-day crowd of 21,188 was the lowest league Pride Park attendance in a decade. That barely increased for the visits of Leicester and Burnley, both registering slightly above 23,000. By the time of Clough's last home game against Reading, the fall back to 21k hinted at a fanbase who had simply tired of obscurity.

Speaking in 2015, Sam Rush said, 'I think the Blackburn game was announced at 21,000. One of the concerns was that only three or four games later at home to Reading was about a 20,000 crowd that was officially announced. But we were also aware that about 20 per cent of season ticket holders weren't there [taking it down to around 17,000].'

With Rush largely brought on board to help guide the club forward into the world of wealthy new sponsors, something had to give.

* * *

The sacking of Nigel Clough, even more so eight years later, divides opinion across supporters. For 50 per cent, it marked a step forward for the club. For the other 50 per cent, it marked a loss of identity. Jill Gallone, a columnist at the *Derby Evening Telegraph*, declared that she was 'off to support the Brewers'. Robbie Savage, whose career was saved by Clough, tweeted, 'Ludicrous, diabolical, ridiculous, stupid can't think of any more words to describe the sacking of Nigel Clough.' Craig Bryson had one to add, simply tweeting 'poor'. Throughout the process of interviewing for the book you have in your hands now, there was one topic that drew more ire than any other. Here's how those at the heart of the club took the decision:

Jake Buxton
'I played the early kick-off [a 1-0 defeat at Nottingham Forest, Clough's final match] and I'll always remember I went to Matlock

Bath in the afternoon with my little lad who'd just been born. I got the phone call off the club secretary. "Just to let you know, we've sacked Nigel." Wow. It was up there with … I don't even know. I felt alone. Nigel had brought me into the club, he'd put his faith in me and I just felt I was back to square one. I felt like I was just alone.'

Craig Bryson

'I don't know if we were on the bus on the way back from Forest. We were devastated because we'd just lost to them and the last thing you want to hear is the manager's been sacked. I think for the players that he brought in like myself or Bucko and people like that, we were devastated. We had Ipswich on the Tuesday where we were 4-1 down at half-time. Everyone could see that it affected us because I don't think anybody saw it coming.

'We all were so behind the manager and felt he was doing well considering the circumstances and what he had to work with. But I always kept in touch with him. If I ever need any advice in the future, he's the first person I'd pick up the phone and speak to. It was all about team spirit.

'Whenever he had the chance to take the lads away and get everybody together, they always thought it would be worth a few extra points in a season and after games, instead of a recovery session we'd play snooker and crown bowls, we'd go and get an ice cream, it was all about being together and being a team, whether you win or lose.'

Paul Winstanley

'The squad took it bad; nobody saw it coming. I got the call on the Saturday night I think it was, a call off Nigel. I was up in the bedroom and saw my phone go off, and it was unusual to get a call at that time from him. I thought he wanted some stuff on the game and so I was absolutely flabbergasted. We went in on the Monday morning and the shock in the squad was incredible. There were phone calls between everyone in the build-up to seeing each other and we were all shocked.

'You were a little bit disappointed in the group at the time because I remember Sam came in to tell the players what had gone on, that the change was happening and Shaun was very vocal in that meeting, letting them know that everyone really believed in what Nigel was doing. As was Jake. But when they were looking for support from the rest of the group, some of them stayed quiet and were just genuinely upset, Jamie for example. But Shaun and Jake were very, very vocal.'

Jamie Ward

'That was a frustrating time. I don't think he deserved the sack. He was putting a team together to challenge and every year was progression. It was crazy to sack him so early in the season but unfortunately as players we have to move on quickly. Fans were divided about Nigel being sacked; players weren't. We didn't think he should have been. But once the decision was made, the club maybe thought that sacking him after losing against Forest would be okay and people wouldn't make such a fuss. But there was division with the fans. Football is football.'

Neil Sullivan

'I was at home that day and I saw the news on Sky Sports News. I was stunned. I thought it was unbelievably harsh. I thought regardless of what happened I expected the team to make the play-offs that season under Nigel. We had a couple of defeats in a row but it wasn't enough to make that happen at that moment. He was at the club for five years and that's the thing that mattered the most. Because he was a long-serving manager, everyone is very familiar with what it was and they could see how the team had progressed over the last 12 months into something that could compete in that league. Nigel came in on Monday to clear his desk and every player went up to him and said thank you for the opportunity and it's sad to see this happen. Not everybody likes their manager, but they knew what they had and that collectiveness that they had together, they were disappointed to a man.'

Martin Taylor

'The game was a midday kick-off so I think I had a missed call. I had one from Sam Rush and then my son phoned me and said, "I think Nigel's been sacked." And so, I spoke to the gaffer. We went back the next morning, emptied our desks and Sam [Rush] was there at the ground to say Nigel's been sacked and we'd all been put on gardening leave. I would say if it wouldn't have been that season in the play-offs it would have been the one after. And given the investment as soon as we left, it may have been that year. But definitely the following. We wouldn't have spent a quarter of what they've spent now and we would have been promoted. We were not far away. Look at what we did with Burton against them since then.

'I've still got friends at Derby. I look at their results and like to see them win. I won't say I hate them but it's not like it used to be. But it is getting better. It's not like it was three or four years ago but it's still there. The majority of fans say it was too early to get sacked but that's the way life is. We'd done what was asked, built the team and they then changed us when we thought we had a chance of getting in the play-offs that season. It left a sour taste.'

* * *

Not since the treatment of Jim Smith in 2001 had supporters been so split. As with Smith, Clough had that connection with many of those in the stands. Every interviewee from the 2013/14 squad and management team shared the same opinion; Clough's task was drawn to a halt too early. New signings such as John Eustace and Johnny Russell commented on their disappointment at the way Nigel was treated, Russell still sore at the fact he didn't get to learn from him beyond those first three months. And for those who still felt passion at hearing the Clough name, the move came as a personal attack on the club they had known for decades.

But the divide was vast and no amount of reasoning would change that. Still spoken about at length on forums such as DCFCFans, those who held one opinion on 28 September 2013 tend to hold the exact same years later. A December 2019 topic, over six years after the parting, titled 'GET CLOUGH BACK, MEL' produced collective eye rolls.

Clough himself hasn't been shy around the situation, even going as far in his post-Derby years as saying he never should have joined, further adding, 'We worked our socks off for four and a half years down the road and got kicked out anyway.' Never one to mince his words was Nigel, his bitterness towards the end of his tenure is one that seeped through whenever the Brewers played, and inevitably beat, his former employers.

Four years and 233 games after walking through the Pride Park doors, the Clough era had come to a halt. He'd built a team worthy of a play-off push but wouldn't be allowed to see how that group would fare. While the next man to be unveiled didn't hold the same personal connection as the Clough name, he was a very familiar face and had overseen many of Derby's best days.

It was time for the return of the Mac; you knew that he'd be back.

RETURN OF THE MAC

SOCIAL MEDIA was in overdrive. No sooner had the news broken of Clough's sacking than images flooded through of Sam Rush alongside Tony Pulis during the defeat against Forest. Clough, who had created a side of footballers capable of playing their way into the play-offs, had not left considerable height within his squad. There was Conor Sammon who stood well over 6ft, but his name provided a false indication of his leaping desires. Beyond that, there was no similarity to his Stoke side, the one that had bullied their way to top half finishes. Fears were cut short when it proved there was no coup, as a new front-runner swiftly emerged, one without a baseball cap.

'Nothing really came up in the summer and I decided to go and work with Harry [Redknapp] at QPR for a few months,' begins Steve McClaren. By this point in the conversation, after reminiscing about his career progression alongside Jim Smith and working with world stars at Manchester United, he's halfway through his coffee. Back in Derby to visit family, his Christmas return to the city took in more than a handful of visits to the Starbucks on Little Eaton roundabout. So, it came as little surprise when he decided to switch the chat upstairs, as well acquainted with the seating arrangements as he is with a training pitch.

He continued, 'I loved my three months at QPR, but I'd always kept an eye on Derby. My agent got a phone call from Sam Rush saying they were looking to change and would I be interested. I wanted to get back into management, so I went to watch them at Yeovil. They won 3-0 and scored this goal, and I counted it being 25 or 26 passes, a great goal. I just went "woah". I said to my agent, "If they want to change, I'll take that team." I'd come back from abroad and I felt when I came back, I'd learnt so much. I knew nothing about football before that and I wanted to bring methods over to the Championship.'

McClaren, who had two spells in Europe, winning the Dutch title with FC Twente and experiencing the Bundesliga with VfL Wolfsburg, escaped the British focus and adapted as a manager since his last dismissal at Forest.

Rush identified McClaren early into the campaign as a man to drive things forward in a post-Clough world. The initial chat between the two may have occurred while Clough was still under contract, but it wasn't the first time such a discussion had taken place. Igor Stimac revealed in an interview with Croatian television that he had been offered the role a year earlier.

McClaren said, 'I watched it [Forest vs Derby] at QPR as it was the lunchtime game, but I remember thinking that they didn't deserve to get beat. Then it was announced on the night that Clough had been sacked and I have to say, it was a surprise to me. I got a phone call and on Sunday I met with Sam, Monday it was done and Tuesday I was watching them at Pride Park.'

McClaren's return drew discontent from the off. His reputation, after success with Manchester United and Middlesbrough, had crashed in England. Tarred by his role as England manager, mocked for the Dutch accent he adopted at Twente and with a less than impressive stint at Forest the most recent English section of his CV, the media agenda on the man who helped Sir Alex Ferguson transform United in the late 1990s was bitter. His success abroad should have counted for more, but no amount of PR would ever change the one abiding memory of McClaren in England; the umbrella.

If there were doubts over McClaren in the fanbase – and there absolutely were – these were reduced when he appeared at Pride Park with his new coaching staff. He said, 'The best thing I ever did was get Simmo [Paul Simpson] and Steeley [Eric Steele] on board. I gave credit to Nigel Clough because I thought he built a good squad, good footballers. What I wanted to do, and I said this to Simmo, I wanted to play like we did in Holland. It was ambitious and took a lot of courage from myself and the staff. I felt we had the players to do it though, so it was really exciting, and coming back to Pride Park? It was a natural step. Player to assistant manager to manager. Only the kitman to go.' How about chairman? 'Steady.'

Eric Steele, so trusted by Ferguson and the man who helped David de Gea transform into one of the leading goalkeepers in the world, was the first call McClaren made. Second was a Derby County playing legend.

'I hadn't spoken to Steve for months, but he just called me out of the blue and started talking away,' revealed Simpson. 'It was about eight o'clock on the Sunday night and he said, "Simmo, I've had a phone call and I'm going into Derby tomorrow for talks with them." After about 15 minutes I told him I was really chuffed for him, "But what are you telling me for?" "I want you to come in and work with me." "Perfect, when do we start?" He said he hadn't agreed anything yet, he'd just had a phone call today, was going in tomorrow and he wanted me to go in and listen to what they had to say.' Simpson, a hero of the Baseball Ground having made 207 appearances for Derby, had mixed success in coaching, but it mattered little to McClaren. What mattered was what the football club meant to him.

He said, 'I loved my time at Derby as a player, I always felt I had a real good affinity with the supporters and really enjoyed living in the area. We were living in Stockport at the time and myself and my wife just put the house on the market and decided to get settled back in and throw ourselves into it. Steve asked if I had an agent, I told him I didn't need one because I'm agreeing to it. I don't really know how the other two felt but for me it was brilliant to go back. Everybody looked at Steve, myself and Eric as having Derby County history, hoping we would bring a heart to the football club and pick things up from what the previous management team had done. It was a no-brainer.'

Announced two days after Clough's sacking, McClaren took the reins of a side who had so far flattered to deceive despite considerable additions in the summer. His first task, before formally meeting the players, was to endure the Tuesday night game against Ipswich Town at Pride Park. He didn't know it at that point, but it was to be the night that laid the groundwork for the next 19 months.

Darren Wassall, another former Derby player himself and now responsible for the academy, was in caretaker charge for the visit of Mick McCarthy's side. The idea of course was to tide things over until McClaren but after 45 minutes, his tenure was over. The 11 he selected that night were a frozen mess of a side, evidently reeling over the dismissal of Clough. Jake Buxton, a man who put every fibre of his being into the club, openly admits he was a disgrace. Paul Winstanley, by now a confidant of Buxton having seen his progression over the years, said that Buxton's 'mind just clearly wasn't there'. But there were bigger issues going on for the centre-half than simply struggling on the night.

'I didn't like the way the club had gone about their business in sacking Nigel and I was a bit naive to the fact of how football worked. Steve had obviously been tapped up and it felt sneaky to me. Being a bit naive and being an honest lad, I didn't like how it all panned out and that Ipswich game it just all came tumbling down on me and frankly, I didn't care. I didn't care one bit and it's the only time ever in my career I just didn't care because of the amount of emotions running through my body. It was awful. I was awful.'

Buxton, a dominant force in the air, lost his man from corners twice within the first 30 minutes to gift goals, his body language painting a picture of a man who wanted to be anywhere else but

Pride Park Stadium. The Rams trailed 4-1 at half-time and at this point, the sacking of Clough seemed to have ramifications beyond any expectation.

'I captained the side that night and just thought, "Fucking hell, what is going on here?"' says Bryson. The new coaching staff had seen enough.

'Steve made the decision before Ipswich that we weren't going to be involved because we hadn't worked with the players,' recalls Simpson, who sat with McClaren in the padded seats of the West Stand directors' box. 'We introduced ourselves to the squad before the game but this was Darren's to run, so we were sitting in the stand and they got off to a shocking start. I said to Steve at the time, "I don't know about you but I don't want to sit and watch this for the next 45 minutes." He asked what we can do, and I told him we needed to change it. We spoke about what he'd do if he was in charge now, he said, "I'd make a couple of subs, change the shape" and I just told him, "I think we need to start doing something now."' What happened in that changing room between 8.32pm and 8.47pm was a mystery at the time, but you just knew it wasn't pleasant.

To the outsider, it appeared there was a tactical tweak. John Eustace sat in front of the back four and Mason Bennett added further attacking impetus, but there was more to it. 'Paul came in and hammered a few of us, then McClaren came in, told him to be quiet and dealt with it. He stamped his authority on it from that moment on, made a couple of changes at half-time and that was a game-changer,' said Jamie Ward, one of the scorers in the second half to rescue a 4-4 draw. He thrived under the early instructions.

So did Buxton, albeit driven by an entirely different circumstance, 'Paul Simpson called me a shithouse.' Harsh but seemingly fair having only ever seen him play 45 minutes of football. Johnny Russell remembers 'sitting there as Simmy went on and thinking "this is fucking mental"'.

For Buxton, it was maniacal on a different level, 'Call me what you want but I'm not a shithouse, I'm not having that. I'd turned to Paul, who I'd never met before and just said I was done, I wasn't in the right frame to go out there in the second half and I wanted to come off. He said to me, "If you make us replace you with Jamie Hanson, a 17-year-old, if you make us bring you off here, you're a shithouse, Bucko."' Those words saved Buxton's career in a Derby shirt.

Bryson, who struck the late equaliser, was one of those closest to Clough but his performance in that second half best represents the immediate impact of McClaren's words. He recalls, 'If I'm honest, we were sat there thinking, "I don't care what you say mate, I just wish it was Nigel giving this talk." But we were also thinking, "Well, we're getting embarrassed here. We either go out and get pumped or we step up to the plate and show a bit of pride that we are still representing Derby, no matter who the manager is." Looking back, we did step up and I'm thankful for that.'

* * *

The new staff took charge the following day, fresh from 45 minutes that had left the squad with a new-found belief in their abilities. Their impact, already instant from the Tuesday evening, was fully felt from the first training session, as each player was presented with training methods alien to what they had experienced anywhere else.

'His first training session blew everyone away and the players came in from it absolutely buzzing,' says Paul Winstanley, whose ears rang more and more the longer the season went on with praise for the man in charge.

'They all bought into it instantly. He told me "these aren't a 4-4-2 team, these boys don't look like they can play that" and he knew John Eustace was someone to rely on so he made it more into a 4-3-3 with one controller in front of the back four, which was John. He just gave the team a bit of life, a bit of structure and a change of formation that brought everybody into it.'

The changes made were subtle but telling. Eustace, signed with the intention of being a secondary option rather than a certainty for the 11, suddenly found himself as the glue, holding his position in front of Buxton and Richard Keogh, which allowed any combination of Bryson, Jeff Hendrick and Will Hughes licence to roam forward. That left Chris Martin at the helm as the recipient of better service, the full-backs with more permission to move further downfield, and even provided the goalkeeper with a regular outlet to restart play quickly. Everything was changing when analysed.

'Steve changed the shape, which worked well. That and just playing me every week,' Eustace laughs as he delivers the punchline, but he and his team-mates knew his importance. Hughes, without hesitation, declares, 'Jeff and Brys were similar to me but Eusty [John Eustace] was spot on. He'd been around the block for a long time but I just knew when he was speaking to me, telling me what to do, what a top player he was.'

Bryson's position had already been tweaked before McClaren, but it was built upon further. He says, 'My job basically was when Chris Martin got the ball at his feet, I had to be there. Fozzy [Craig Forsyth] would get the ball, I knew where Dawks [Simon Dawkins] would be, I knew what movement they would make, I knew what movement Chrissy [Chris Martin] would make, I knew Eusty would be in the middle and I knew I could take off and go into the space.

'Whether I got the ball or not, it moved their defence and stretched them. I would always pull people away from the ball, knowing I wasn't going to get the ball but it would create space for Chris or Simon. We'd then get it switched, get a cross in and because I'd already made that run, I'd be in the box. So I'd get a chance to score.'

Bryson went on to record a career-best 16 goals that year, many of which came in that exact way.

A three-year plan was how McClaren looked at the progression of his side, much like Billy Davies had seven years earlier. Unlike Davies though, he meant it. From the moment McClaren set foot in Moor Farm, he reiterated that it would take time to fully build a side capable of challenging for the automatic promotion spots. But what he didn't quite realise was the side he inherited was considerably better than they had shown in the early weeks of the season and that Clough's insistence on signing characters over players had more worth than expected.

Simpson, able to watch and learn from McClaren's methods early on, highlights the subtle changes that transformed the side instantly, 'Credit has to go to what Nigel did beforehand, because we basically only brought in a couple of loan players. There was no major change to it. But I think the players were geared towards being technical, to pass the ball and we could see the standard was really good. Even when we looked at old DVDs, they'd played well and played some good football under Nigel.

'Steve just changed the shape a little with how he wanted to play, he wanted to build from the back and play through the holding midfield and have pace in the wide players. The dressing room got a lift from having a change of manager for whatever reason and suddenly, everyone had a spring in their step and a smile on their face and they were enjoying training and producing it in games.'

McClaren's charges took care of Leeds for their first win on home soil, following it with a late victory at a strong Watford side. In search of a clinching goal at Vicarage Road, the final 15 minutes saw a tactical change that Derby would adopt countless times throughout the season. Martin was joined up front by Sammon, the wingers moved further forward and a 4-2-4 formation came into play as the side looked to overwhelm the opposition. On that day, and on many more throughout the course of the next two seasons, it paid off. 'Every change McClaren made worked. Everything he did that season worked. And the players were clinging on to his every word,' says Ward.

'You could see Sammo come on as sub that day, he scored. He changed Bennett against Ipswich; he made an impact. You look into little things like that and you think, "He knows what he's on about, he's quite good!" and you start buying into what he's doing.

For half a decade, Jim Smith was pointing the way towards Europe.

The Bald Eagle was not afraid of signing mavericks. From the sublime of Stefano to…Taribo.

Enter Fabrizio.
Exit Premier League.

Come 2006, enough was enough as fans turned on the board.

Thanks Inigo.

2007/08. The worst season in football history.

Seven thousand supporters travelled to Blackburn for the final 07/08 away day. Derby lost, again.

Nigel Clough would lead for almost five years.

But the club would soon embark upon a new era.

WeAreDerby.con

5-0. Bryson. Dreamland.

The Mel Morris era begins.

And, at least to begin with, mayhem would follow.

Frank Lampard would take Derby to Wembley, but he'd opt to stay in London.

What's it like to support Derby? This.

There were no excuses for us and everything was covered. We went out fully prepared and as long as we performed, we knew that the longer the season went on, no one would get near us.'

Ward's assurance of the quality of his team-mates was well founded and backed up game after game. A 2-1 loss on McClaren's return to Loftus Road was the only blemish on the record of the new regime as they made tracks through the division. Derby soon embarked on a seven-game winning streak that included victories at Bournemouth and Wigan. But it was at Pride Park where most of the excitement came, both on the pitch and in the boardroom. On the pitch, Chris Martin continued his fine form in front of goal, three goals at home to Blackpool in a 5-1 win showing the side playing at their free-flowing best. He'd made the number nine shirt his own and his ability to hold off defenders and bring others into play showed why Clough was so keen on bringing him in as his missing piece. It was also the second hat-trick of the season and with Simpson back at the club, it became a three-way conversation about what it was like to do so for Derby.

But in the stands, which were becoming more populated as fans returned, Pride Park had an update for the first time. Rush, brought in primarily to drive sponsorship across every area of the club, was able to secure naming rights for the stadium with energy drink company, iPro. A £7m deal that would last for ten years, it was tipped as one of the biggest independent deals in the Football League and after years without too much to be proud about, it felt almost right. The change didn't draw ire in the way St James' Park's reinvention as the Sports Direct Arena did, subtle enough to work and stylish enough to draw intrigue. It marked a pivotal step in the development of the club as a brand. The naming rights were the first step in major organisations like Just Eat and Avon Tyres becoming involved, which took Derby into avenues they'd never known before. Still, there were some downsides, with everything including substitutions having a sponsor's name put to them.

* * *

By the new year, Derby had produced scintillating football, electrified the league and taken themselves into second spot from the familiar comfort of lower mid-table. Just a single loss in McClaren's opening 13 matches saw 32 points picked up from a possible 39 and doubled with Clough's early away victories, the side had the best travelling record in the division. At home they weren't bad either.

Expectations grew quickly, and, in many ways, they never fell. No longer was a play-off push wished for, it became the least of demands. It was at this point though that the first signs of weakness seeped through and exposed some of the flaws in the system. A New Year's Day loss at home to a backs-to-the-wall Wigan was an insight into the sort of side McClaren's European brand of football would struggle to break down, not only that season but for years to come.

When coming up against more defensive-minded teams, Bryson's role was bypassed. He said, 'Fans wanted to see us attack, they want to see shots, they want to see us test the opposition goalkeeper but you can't go and do that against some teams, there has to be a way and a method of getting to that stage and then once you create space and chances, they become more frequent.

'It used to be good when we got an early goal and the opposition had to attack us, that's what we wanted. But it's why we always found it difficult playing a Millwall or a Wigan who would sit with ten men behind the ball. You struggle to break them down, the best teams in the world struggle. We were nowhere near being the best team in the world, but we played in a league where teams are very evenly matched. Your Millwall and Wigans have a game-plan to frustrate us and do us on the counter-attack because they know we'll have more of the ball. It makes it such a good league because there are so many styles of play within it.'

It's worth remembering at this stage that despite the style Wigan adopted, they were still one of the strongest teams in the division and finished inside the play-offs. If anything, their set-up was a show of respect. The next opponent was considerably better than the Latics though and it showed. The King Power Stadium hadn't been a welcoming location for the Rams but the manner in which they were torn apart in this 4-1 drubbing caused concern.

That defeat, inspired by David Nugent and Jamie Vardy, was no disaster. Leicester would go on to run away with the division and Derby's reaction was pleasing. As they had before, they reconvened and recovered with a seven-game unbeaten run which maintained the very realistic ambition of a top-two finish.

Patrick Bamford, today a figure of derision among Rams supporters, was captured on loan in January to add further strength on the wing. He contributed two spectacular winners and a late equaliser at Ewood Park to keep momentum going. Although often starting in his place, Ward bows down to the impact of the now Leeds man, 'Patrick scored some unbelievable and very important goals. He had so much ability if he could be bothered. A strike with his left was so sweet because he could make it do anything. If he wanted to make it swerve, he could do it. For a forward, he was just perfect because he'd got everything.'

McClaren's 4-2-4 came into full effect in the midst of the streak when staring at a two-goal deficit at home to Yeovil. Eustace was sacrificed at the break for Ward that evening and a 95th-minute winner from Martin earned a 3-2 triumph. The system worked and, in the process, Derby amassed 36 shots. The ability of the side to maintain their high-pressure game even into the dying embers of matches won 17 points throughout the course of McClaren's 36 games and in this seven-game spell alone, they rescued ten points. Two of the points came against Bournemouth, promoted the following season but by this point having all the makings of a Premier League side in waiting. Martin's beautifully curved late free kick felt huge, building on an even more important win from the unlikeliest of sources.

QPR and the Sky Sports cameras were the visitors on a bitterly cold Monday evening and they were treated to one of the worst goals of the season, a Eustace header from the edge of the box that evaded Joey Barton on the line. For QPR, second at the time, it was a bitter blow. Eustace knew the significance, 'It was a big turning point for us. I think it was a game where if we won, we'd really be in the mix and we'd had chances before where we lost or drew before that. It showed we were the real deal, gave the lads huge confidence and was such a good experience. But it showed the side of us where we could roll our sleeves up and win ugly. We had lots of good chances to win by more but that was a big turning point for sure.'

Having let that momentum slip at the start of the year, the team needed to back up this run again and just like when they faced Leicester in January, they had to do it against another side occupying a top two spot, Burnley. For the second time, Derby would come unstuck, although this was on a different level and in tougher circumstances to the Leicester defeat.

Already a goal behind and with Martin walking a tightrope after a soft yellow card early on, the Rams thought they'd equalised two minutes before the break when Hendrick struck. But Bobby Madley instead whistled for a dive by Martin – Bryson remembers, 'Chrissy was always good for a dive, still is,' despite contact on the forward – and brandished a flash of red. A second-half strike killed the contest and left Paul Simpson seething, not because of the result but because of the way it came about. 'We were robbed,' Simpson jumps on the question mid-flow. 'We knew we were going to have a problem because in the tunnel before the game, Madley actually said to Chris Martin, "You got away with one recently, you need to watch yourself today." That's not a good thing to be saying. For me, if that's not a referee going into a game with preconceived ideas of what's going to happen, I don't know what is.

'Looking back at it, and I've looked so many times at the video afterwards, nobody can tell me that he wasn't brought down. And it turned the game. I'm not saying we'd have beat Burnley, but that game turning around, and it was a six-point swing that, that really said we weren't going to get automatic, that's a play-off spot for us.'

The players knew what defeat meant. Johnny Russell remembers, 'The anger I had on a football pitch that day was insane. Not only does he not give us the goal, he sends off one of our main players.'

Realistically, it proved to be the end of a top-two push. Burnley from thereon maintained their form, losing just twice, while Leicester finished 17 points clear of their East Midlands neighbours in third. Speaking of East Midlands neighbours ...

* * *

Heading into a March home match with Forest on the back of four games without a goal, Derby needed to find a return to form to consolidate their place in the top six. Forest, although slipping down the table, remained a threat and as with any derby, it was destined to be a battle. And it was for the first five minutes or so.

As with the reverse fixture in September which had proved to be the final afternoon in charge for Clough, the axe fell on Billy Davies in the hours following.

He had a Jägermeister-drinking Scotsman to blame. 'For me, it's still the greatest day in my football career. It tops getting promoted,' said Craig Bryson. 'It's the only game people want to talk to me about and I'll never forget it. For me to do that and give something back to Derby fans and Derby as a club, considering how much they've given me over the years, it is truly amazing. We'd not even scored a goal in four and you're thinking,' Bryson lets out a puff of air, 'we've got Forest coming up here boys, it's massive.

'We started like a house on fire, got the early goal, scored not long after and then you feel we have a chance of going on and winning by a few. You could see their heads go down and then it's just a case of what do we do now? Shall we lay down a marker? Johnny scored a great goal, I got the penalty and we're 5-0 up and then for the last 20 minutes, we just kept the ball and the players were loving it. We got a big buzz out of it.

'My family were down for that game as well so for them to see that and be part of it, they'd have been gutted if they were just watching it on the TV. It all came together that day and I'm not sure I'll ever have a better one.'

The afternoon marked the first appearance of January loan signing George Thorne, who was made to wait for his first team bow due to the performances of Eustace in the midfield, and he added even more of an attacking intent to the side as he nailed the position down for himself all the way to Wembley.

* * *

Despite that goalless sequence prior to the Forest demolition, a play-off spot still looked likely from February onwards and after a strong end to the campaign, the Rams finished third. Top scorers in the division with 84 goals and having registered the highest points tally in their history (85), the turnaround under McClaren, Simpson and Steele was miraculous. A year before, Hull City finished second with six points fewer but the strength of the top two sides, with Burnley finishing on 93 and Leicester on 102, meant McClaren had picked the wrong season to decide to break club records.

It was Brighton who secured their spot in sixth after a final-minute winner against Forest on matchday 46, meaning they would have the task of trying to stop Martin from adding to his 23-goal tally. Having beaten the Seagulls twice already this season, Derby seemingly had Oscar Garcia's side's number.

Despite being the weakest of the four play-off teams on paper, Brighton remained a threat and started strongly. Jesse Lingard put the Seagulls ahead after 18 minutes of the first leg, only for a Martin penalty and a Tomasz Kuszczak own goal before the break to turn things around. Lee Grant was to thank for preserving the lead, tipping a Leonardo Ulloa header on to the post to leave Brighton's boss bemoaning 'a totally unfair result. We were better than them in all areas.' He had a fair argument but left to chase the tie back at Pride Park, they crumbled.

Will Hughes, in for the injured Bryson, flicked home in fine fashion to put the Rams 3-1 up on aggregate with a quarter of the tie to play. From there, they eased their way through.

It's often debated between fans as to the best performance at Pride Park. The victory over Arsenal in 1997 is spoken about, as is the 2007 play-off semi-final with Southampton. And the 5-0 against Forest earlier in this campaign. But considering the circumstances this fixture holds its place.

The second 45 at the iPro was the best of the season, goals from Martin, Hendrick and Thorne culminating in a 6-2 aggregate win and a place at Wembley. 'We still knew there was plenty to do,' remembers Ward, 'but we knew we were good enough. We were so confident in how good we were and we knew we could blow anyone off the park.

'Brighton were no mugs so to just wipe the floor with them the way we did, and it sounds bad, but it was so easy. When we got our first, they got deflated and we were relentless. We wanted to score as many as we could and to make them think they'd come across a proper team and we just finished them off big time. The Forest 2-1 was always a great day but to win a play-off semi-final, that tops it. The sheer emotion and feeling of what would come next means you have to take the Brighton one as second.'

It was another example of how easy football could be. 'Sometimes we'd watch the games back,' remarks Johnny Russell, 'or even during the game actually, I'd stand there and go, "How have we done that?" At times we were just playing around teams like it was training. The possession we were getting in games, and I know they're not won from that, but we were coming away with 70 per cent possession, which is just crazy. We were so free-flowing that nobody stuck to a position for the 90, you'd always see people roaming around and it was just incredible to play in at times.'

A pitch invasion ensued and a journey to the home of English football awaited. One hurdle to go.

ZAMORA

AS A HYPOTHETICAL ratio, if Steve McClaren had taken charge in the summer of 2013 and maintained the same form throughout those first ten games, Derby would have finished with a league record of 108 points. But he didn't, and they didn't, so it was destination London for 37,249 Rams fans.

The 6-2 aggregate destruction of Brighton was a statement, a display of the free-flowing football that McClaren had worked diligently on over the previous eight months. A side of lower-division players come good, built on a budget and with a manager desperate for a shot at redemption.

The opponents, Queens Park Rangers, were the opposite. Villains of English football for their overspending and FFP ignorance (they were later fined £42m for the 2013/14 season), they slotted seamlessly into the role of easy targets. Bankrolled by Air Asia chief Tony Fernandes, they'd already failed to pay their way to Premier League safety a season before and for the immediate future of the club, this final was critical. Victory would claim a bounty of £120m, defeat would leave them on the brink of collapse.

For supporters making the journey south, where the first train departed at 6.20am and had more than enough Rams on board for an already drunken rendition of 'Steve Bloomer's Watching', it was their first visit to the arch since the victory seven years previously;

a happy memory. For McClaren, it was his first working visit since *that* 2007 night under the umbrella; not a happy memory. 'I won't be taking a bloody brolly this time, I know that much,' he retorted after the second leg. Inevitably, it rained.

Paul Winstanley, having seen everything from Laurent Robert to a promotion tilt, lived for this occasion. It was the day that everything was set to pay off. He was one of the few survivors able to see the full transition over the seven years. He said, 'There was a genuine buzz and I certainly felt it. On the morning of the final me and Steve Haines, the fitness coach, we stayed in Brentford, and we were saying, "Phwoar, by 5pm today we'll be in the Premier League."'

There was little reason for them to think otherwise. In the last meeting between the two sides, John Eustace's header at Pride Park was enough for a 1-0 victory and in the months that followed, QPR had lost eight times. They'd only just reached the final too, scraping past Wigan after extra time thanks to Charlie Austin. 'We feared Wigan the most in the play-offs because they'd done a job on us,' recalls Jake Buxton. 'Uwe Rosler said he knew how to get a result against Derby so we feared them.'

The 1-0 defeat at home to Wigan at the turn of the year was a rarity under McClaren but outlined the one potential shortcoming of his style. Whether it be Wigan that day or Millwall in March, the solution to getting anything from a visit to Derby became blindingly clear. They just had to absorb the pressure and hit on the counter. QPR, while not the most adventurous of Championship sides that season, weren't a Wigan. Boasting quality in abundance, a side incorporating talent such as Niko Kranjcar were made to be more open and if anything, should have suited McClaren's style of play. It was the perfect opposition for his style of management.

Paul Simpson felt the belief too, 'We knew QPR were a good side but we just felt we had more energy. We knew we could cause them problems with our energy and pace going forward and were really confident. It wasn't arrogance but we just felt, since we'd come into the club, our record was as good as any team and we fancied ourselves.'

While the destination, the prize money, the support was all on a grander scale for the final game of the season, nothing else was. 'Nothing changed. We had suits and stuff like that but nothing else changed, it was just another game. We either go on to the Premier League or we stay down,' recalls Jamie Ward. Confidence or calmness?

There was just one dilemma for McClaren, Simpson and Steele when it came to personnel. Will Hughes v Craig Bryson. Bryson had 16 goals and a Jack Stamps Trophy to his name and with the prospect of a bigger Wembley pitch, his legs were sure to be crucial. Winstanley remembers a match that campaign where his total distance topped 14k, 'It hadn't been done since David Beckham against Greece.'

But he'd been injured for the second leg and in his place, Hughes had thrived. Could Derby's brightest young talent really be cut from the side? How could the player of the season be left out? McClaren should have known the answer himself but he turned it over to the squad.

'Before Wembley, Steve called me aside to have a chat about the selection,' said Buxton. 'He asked how I thought the team would feel if he was to make a big call about the line-up. Brys had been out injured before that and Will was tremendous in the play-offs, so going into that all the talk was about who would start. But Brys had been so important throughout the season for us. I said to Steve, "I hope you're not planning on leaving Brys out?" He just smiled.'

Bryson, already broken at missing out on the 11, added seething to his range of emotions, 'He spoke to some people beforehand which I think was terrible. He pulled me the morning of the game because I'm there thinking I'm starting like any other game and he just said he wouldn't be playing me today. I just said, "Well, that's kind of strange considering I've played nearly every other game."

'Yes, the boys were absolutely excellent against Brighton in the second leg but as soon as we scored the first goal, the game was over. Their heads went down, the lads expressed themselves and they were absolutely fantastic. But he was picking a team for a final based on one game and he didn't look at the other 46 games we had in the league. I was gutted.'

Bryson, six years later, still holds the anger of that day and later went on to mention it was the decision that ended his relationship with McClaren.

'Steve spent a lot of time in my office watching the games and I could see his pain because he didn't know which player to go with,' said Winstanley. His technical support played the deciding role. 'Steve didn't make his mind up until the morning of the game and on the morning, we went on an 11 o'clock walk around the hotel. I knew he would pull him because he told me before the walk he'd go with Will. So in we went for the team meeting at 11.30am and he named the team. I looked at Craig and you could see the pain on his face. But I could see what Steve went through in the build-up to that game and he was in a real dilemma, he was devastated by it himself.'

The decision was one that divided fans as much as it did players. Hughes had the potential to unlock any defence but Bryson was by now the ultimate fan favourite in a team of favourites. His energy, especially against the ageing Rangers midfield line of Gary O'Neil and Joey Barton, could have been telling. 'Bryson scored lots of goals but who do you drop from that second leg? Will and Jeff were brilliant, Craig had been carrying an injury the last couple of weeks. I think the manager made the right decision,' said Jamie Ward, who sided with McClaren. The players, like the staff and like the supporters, were split.

* * *

How were you feeling at 2.55pm on 24 May 2014? If the answer to that question is 'emotional', you've got an ally in Jake Buxton. Six years earlier, he was ready to quit the game having captained

Mansfield to relegation into non-league. He was now 90 minutes from sharing a Premier League stage with the world's best. 'I got emotional doing the national anthem before the game because I felt like I was representing my country even though I weren't, but singing it at Wembley … wow. I remember the noise was crazy, the horns and the support was all muffled. You couldn't really hear anybody on the pitch and I base my game around talking a lot on the pitch. Fozzy and Keezy [Richard Keogh] couldn't hear me. It was so weird.'

Nigel Clough had built a team of, without being disrespectful, nobodies. Steve McClaren had turned them into one of the greatest Derby County sides in two decades. Even matching them man to man against Harry Redknapp's Hoops was absurd. Chris Martin was let go for free by Norwich after a barren spell at Swindon Town. He was coming up against Richard Dunne, a man with 408 appearances in the Premier League. Jamie Ward had been plucked from obscurity at soon-to-be-relegated-to-the-third-tier Sheffield United. Against him, Niko Kranjcar, 81 Croatia caps lying about in his spare room and having played at the World Cup and European Championships. Even the managers differed in stature.

McClaren's reputation in England was in tatters when he took hold of Derby and he was back at Wembley, the scene of his greatest humiliation. Harry Redknapp had recently bowed out of the Champions League with Tottenham, where he'd beaten both Milan sides. Yet against all the back-stories and the history of each individual who walked the red carpet, this was supposed to be a final that belonged to the misfits. It should have been their final. It should have been promotion.

* * *

For 89 minutes, Derby ran the game in front of the biggest ever play-off crowd. Although chances remained at a premium, Lee Grant had a deckchair out in comparison to his counterpart Rob Green. Anchored by George Thorne, Derby were so dominant that they didn't allow QPR a single shot on goal. Charlie Austin had been nullified by Buxton and Keogh. Ward went closest for the Rams inside the first half, but after going in goalless, it was at the hour mark that the game turned.

Russell, 25 yards from goal, slipped the ball between the closing legs of Richard Dunne and could only be halted from a free effort on goal by Gary O'Neil, a red card waiting to happen. Thirty minutes left on the clock and with a man advantage. Peak McClaren-ball was rising. The man in the dugout, the architect, watched on in pride. Everything he had been working towards was coming together.

He remembers, 'All I wanted was for the team to play like they'd been playing all year. I know in a final that's the biggest let-down if your team doesn't play how they did to get there. I had that before and it's such a huge disappointment, more disappointing than losing. I just wanted them to showcase the football and what we were all about. I thought that it would take a lot of courage and we talked about courage a lot but we were superb that day.'

But for all the courage the former England manager witnessed from the technical area, he was growing in frustration as QPR couldn't be broken down. Buxton, by now a spectator, could only watch and wait. It was less a performance for him and more an early lesson on his road into coaching. 'We had to stick to the style, that's the only way we were set up to play and you couldn't just change it. We kept going and going but the problem was that we just couldn't get in behind. Johnny did a couple of times and then we changed him for Simon Dawkins and what happened is everything then became in front of QPR,' he says.

When Ward and Bryson did break the backline, they were met by Dunne, the bouncer at the back. 'When we did get in behind and get corners, Richard was immense,' says Buxton. 'He was like a better version of me and headed every ball away. We never hurt them like we had done other opposition where we'd get in behind and carve them open, we just couldn't do it.'

'Don't panic,' McClaren cried. 'We've got so much time to win this game, just stay calm.'

The ten men sat back, older heads content in biding their time, just waiting. For what, they didn't quite know. Redknapp admitted he didn't see how his side would ever score. Waiting for a reprieve? A hero?

'I don't think they'd been in our half and I didn't expect them to get in it because they brought Bobby Zamora on. I knew him well but he couldn't really run, they were just going to camp,' said McClaren. His words are the first omen. A flash of Ward's head 20 minutes from time was the second. 'Around the pitch the advertising boards had something like "Zamora 25/1. First Goalscorer",' he said. 'And I was looking at it thinking "no chance".'

* * *

Danny Simpson's throw midway into the Derby half fell to Junior Hoilett. He was faced with Craig Forsyth and Jake Buxton, with the former leaving it to the latter. Neither went for it. 'There were three or four things that we could have done better in the build-up,' says Ward.

'It started from the throw-in, we didn't get back into shape from it. We had a chance to clear it down the line,' recalls Derby's Paul Simpson, who at the time was stretching to see from his technical area at the other side of the pitch. Forsyth backed off, Hoilett nipped in. Buxton, half a second too late, hesitated before going to ground, where the ball slipped through him.

Buxton and Forsyth were out of the equation. Hoilett looked up and squared directly into the path of Derby's captain, Richard Keogh. He put out a foot. Simpson watched on.

The roar. The disbelief. The despair. Keogh and Buxton dropped to the ground. Simpson and McClaren had their heads in their hands. Winstanley, preparing for extra time and a future move to Brighton where he would lock horns with the destroyer of Derby, looked up to see the ball nestle past Lee Grant.

He recalls, 'I've since spoken to Bobby and he said he couldn't believe his luck. He just said, "I couldn't believe it when it dropped to me. It's the type of finish I do 50 times a day and it's the type of finish I love."'

There was no more time. QPR, with a solitary shot on target, were Premier League. Inevitably, producers panned to Keogh, who provided the money shot. A sobbing Buxton was next to be captured. 'It was just gut-wrenching,' he says. 'When people say it knocks the stuffing right out of you, I just fell to the floor. Keezy didn't deserve that and nobody blamed him at all. In the changing rooms after, even I didn't know what words to say. What do you say? Nothing got said. Steve said we'll go again next year and come stronger but even then, whatever anybody had said it wouldn't have made a difference. We were numb to whatever anybody said.'

If the trains back to Derby were a sorrowful place, imagine the atmosphere in the changing room. And on the team coach. Winstanley, in his final game as a Derby County employee, is the eyes inside.

He remembers, 'I could just see Richard Keogh with a towel over his head, head in his hands, hiding himself, just crying and shoulders going. You felt for him so much and felt his pain. He took the blame on his shoulders which he shouldn't have done. Steve gave a bit of a team talk about going next year but nobody was listening. It was so quiet, then slowly as things stopped there was a lengthy silence.'

The Wembley tunnel is one of the longest in football but the sound of Zamora and co. travelled all the way.

Just like the supporters on the way home, there was only one solution for Winstanley, 'There was a fridge in the corner that was full of champagne, beer, just in case your team won. After some silence, Davo the kitman walked over with a bin bag and just said, "Fuck it boys, we may as well have a drink. Let's empty this fridge," and started piling all the beers into a bin bag and put them on the bus.

'We all went up to see our families in the lounges upstairs after, some went straight on to the bus. I went to see my wife and kids and then the QPR families gave a big cheer from half the room when Bobby walked in. I was sat with Adam Legzdins and Steve Haines, Simmo and McClaren across. Everyone had a beer, but we were just whispering. I remember that song "Happy" was playing when they got the trophy.'

The stadium may have changed but for Simpson, the outcome was the same. He played the full 90 in 1994 when Steve Walsh broke Derby hearts. Twenty years later, the memories flooded back.

'It was worse as a coach. As a player, you're disappointed to lose but as a coach, you feel more responsible for everybody. The players, the supporters, and you're questioning everything you've done. As an assistant, you start thinking should I have said something else to Steve, should I have asked him to do this, should we have gone overnight. You question all the planning and it is really difficult to deal with as a coach. All we could do from then was send them away, regroup and go again the next year.'

The Rams would go again but somehow, things would never be quite the same. The reputations of those involved in the goal, particularly Keogh, were tarnished. The tag of bottlers had been unfairly pinned on to the club crest. It's a final that has gone down in folklore and it's one that every man, woman and child in a white shirt that afternoon wants to forget, even if Sky Sports remains intent on reliving it.

Jamie Ward's living room is a no-go zone, 'I still see it on telly from time to time. My little one wants to watch it when he sees it but I have to make him turn it off. I don't want to see that again!'

A STRONG DISLIKE OF
MIKE ASHLEY

A SCAN through the careers of many of the 2013/14 squad results in the same puzzling conclusion: how did that group of players get to the brink of the Premier League? Jake Buxton, Chris Martin and Jamie Ward were among those with a background that never suggested they could muster a promotion push.

But when they did, vultures soon began to circle around the carcass of Steve McClaren's beaten squad. Burnley, promoted under Sean Dyche, had their eyes on Craig Bryson and Richard Keogh. Will Hughes still had a legion of scouts fawning over him. Even the manager, reputation firmly rebuilt, was hot property again. There was only one thing for it, the Derby boardroom concluded. After a six-year rebuilding job, the bank vaults were to be opened and the queue for increased contracts could begin to form.

First to be given the pen was John Eustace, exercising a one-year extension. Craig Forsyth and Jeff Hendrick followed, Martin extending for four years once the season got under way. Money around the club began to appear in every corner but as the adage goes, money doesn't bring happiness. Take Bryson as an example, 'My relationship was basically broken with McClaren. He made a few comments that I didn't understand in pre-season. He wanted me to play a wee bit deeper for a bit more control and I'm just thinking, "Why the fuck would I want to do that when I've just had the best season of my life?" I've just scored 16 goals, 14 assists, why would I change the way I play?'

Sensing blood, Dyche chanced a series of bids for the Scot, coming up narrowly short. 'In the end, I just didn't want to leave. If we'd have got beat in the final 5-0 it might have been easier but the way we lost, it wasn't right for me to go,' Bryson said.

'I'm not going to sit here and say my head didn't get turned a wee bit and I did come very close to signing with them but in the end, Derby offered me a contract. People banded figures about what I was getting per week and I was only staying for money, but it was never the case. I stayed because I wanted to stay and I sacrificed myself a wee bit and thought that if I'm going to play in the Premier League, I want to play in the Premier League with Derby. Leaving Derby at that time wouldn't have been right. It would have been like me fucking off at the first opportunity. The way I see it is if you've got Derby and Burnley, you don't leave Derby to go to Burnley.'

Then there was Buxton, who had a batch of suitors for the first time in his career. While it was the news of Bryson's potential move that had Rams supporters worried, the situation for the cult hero was one which was kept under wraps. He remembers, 'Nigel came in for me and made an offer and honestly, it was actually a very difficult one for me. We'd just had this amazing season but Sheffield United had sold Harry Maguire and they had the money. If Derby had accepted the offer, I don't know what I'd have done.'

In the wake of Wembley, new investors were able to get involved. None was more notable than Mel Morris, the Derby businessman who had helped to save the club alongside Peter Gadsby. His acquisition of 22 per cent of the club gave Rush the financial might to throw funds around in the expectation of a repeat season, albeit one with a better finish.

Ward, one of the final signatures Rush collected, echoes Buxton's comments of 'if you're happy, it doesn't matter what the person beside you is on'. He continues, 'There were no contract problems for anyone. Everyone signs what they're happy with. It didn't matter if someone was on £50,000 and I was on £2,000. If I'm happy with my deal it shouldn't matter what others are on.'

Ward, seeing his colleagues offered long-term extensions, went into the meeting with a sense of optimism, expecting to secure financial security for his family, 'I was given a deal only until the rest of the season with a 50 per cent pay rise. It was frustrating for me because I was given a nine-month option but then you see people getting three-year deals or even five in Bryson's case.'

The winger didn't stay at the club beyond the end of that season, his deal not extended.

* * *

Incomings were few and far between as the side kept the identity that had served them so well in the months before. Andre Wisdom returned to Liverpool with Coventry City's Cyrus Christie slotting into his role of marauding right-back. Leon Best joined to offer a different attacking outlet (for different, read 'lack of'). But where Rush was made to really earn the figures on his soon-to-be announced five-year contract was in the pursuit of a permanent George Thorne deal.

West Brom knew the interest levels of Derby but after his show-stealing spell, they wanted to keep hold of their academy product, even if he didn't want to stay. 'I'm much happier now. I felt at home at Derby, I felt wanted at Derby, which I certainly didn't at West Brom,' was the line Thorne stuck to after Wembley but after a two-month pursuit and a series of failed bids, Rush finally had his man. Thorne's signing was the major statement, a show of intent and a warning to the rest of the division that the side of 2013/14 was only going to get better. But just four days and half of a pre-season encounter with Zenit St Petersburg later, physio Neil Sullivan had to break the bad news that he'd have £2.5m worth of talent stuck on his treatment table until mid-2015. Thorne's cruciate ligament was ruptured and Rush, barely with time to open the champagne, was forced back through the transfer window.

McClaren's scouts got to work on finding a replacement and naturally for a second-tier East Midlands club, they found their answer at the Bernabeu. 'Omar Mascarell came in and he was …' McClaren pauses momentarily. 'He was a bit Spanish, if you know what I mean. I remember his first session we did set plays. He runs up, all set, goal. The lads just clapped. Let's do it again. Other corner. Applause. Okay, come on, defend this one. Steeley, keeper all right? Top corner. I just blew the whistle. I'd seen enough.' With Eustace still a more than viable option, there was control again.

The final piece of the puzzle, Jordon Ibe, had the biggest short-term impact. Filling the void left by Patrick Bamford, the Liverpool loanee epitomised the changing of the guard at Pride Park and was a first inkling that the Clough era truly was over. He wasn't signed to replace Paul Coutts or Ben Davies and he certainly wouldn't have been collecting a weekly wage similar to them either. It was 2014 and Derby were now a serious player in the spending stakes.

In the three weeks the players were away from Moor Farm, little changed and by the time the side had reacquainted themselves with how to play together again, it was business as usual. A solitary defeat in the first 13 games of the campaign had Derby once again pushing the top two. A 5-1 hammering of recently relegated Fulham put the division on standby, a late 2-0 win at home to a strong Bournemouth and a 3-0 hammering of Reading on their own patch only raising the awareness of a side growing in self-confidence. Thirteen games in, top of the tree. Even a pair of defeats against Uwe Rosler's Wigan (who still had Derby's number) and Brentford couldn't halt momentum.

Five more past Wolves, three in 20 minutes against Brighton. Bryson, while not finding the net with the frequency he did the year before, continued to maraud forward, politely ignoring his earlier conversation with McClaren. Martin, the 2013/14 top scorer, didn't have such issues, registering 14 goals before the year was out including one in a Boxing Day battering of Birmingham as the snow descended on St Andrew's. By the time of 'Auld Lang Syne', the Rams were one point off the top two and it wouldn't be much longer before they returned to the helm. What happened over the course of the next five months had a lasting impact that is still felt today.

* * *

It's the hope that kills you and after months of running the division, hope had turned into expectation. Nothing aside from promotion would be enough for both the supporters and the players. With the addition of England international Darren Bent, it looked a certainty. The Aston Villa loanee, still aged just 30 and with 106 Premier League goals to his name, offered an altogether different alternative to Martin and replaced the departing Leon Best who returned to Blackburn having failed to find the net. Bent's first afternoon in the matchday squad finished with Derby in the automatic promotion spots and with more additions sure to come, it was where he would have expected to stay.

Victory on 10 January away at second-placed Ipswich elevated McClaren to the top of an English league for the first time in his career as a manager. Unknowingly though, this victory would go on to have serious repercussions for the make-up of his squad.

Buxton mentioned how at Wembley the side couldn't reformulate against the ten men of QPR because they only knew one way of playing and the holding midfielder was a key component of this. So when Eustace saw red and then subsequently the end of his career on that early kick-off at Portman Road, they would have to find another way.

'I think Ipswich were fancying their chances against a footballing team because Mick McCarthy had this hungry, aggressive team and it was important we could stand up to them. It was an ugly one.' It was Eustace at his best, biding his time until the 91st minute to collect a second yellow after an afternoon of harassing, pulling and generally irritating those in blue, all while keeping himself narrowly within the confines of the law. It was the last action for Eustace as a professional footballer, an injury picked up that day that he would never recover from.

He joined Thorne in the treatment room and Mascarell, who had by now shown ambitions of moving further forward, was the only remaining option to man the engine room. Unaware of the extent of Eustace's injury at the time, McClaren didn't opt to utilise the transfer window for that role. 'It was a big blow because George and then Eusty, they were our main players. I call that role the controller because he controls the game, he sees everything and sits in there. But when John had that injury, it left us weak,' he says.

Much was made of Derby's midfield quartet without Eustace. Possessing Hughes, Thorne, Hendrick and Bryson, McClaren had the finest set of young midfielders outside of the top flight. Eustace went under the radar though. 'I think Eusty is one of the most under-rated players that I've played with,' recalls Craig Forsyth. 'I was at Watford with him for two years and he was the same there, he just went about his business, didn't take any headlines but you could always rely on him. He was very underrated outside the team but inside, everybody knew how important he was to us and the way we played. It never quite worked as well as when he was there.'

A club at their peak, Derby were riding a wave by the middle of January and after the loan addition of Mascarell, it was time to go continental again. Raul Albentosa, a towering central defender from Eibar, was signed as the finishing touch that would assure promotion. Much like Mascarell, Albentosa was a hand-picked signing by trusted scout Chris Evans, the third component of what McClaren recalls as the 'perfect triangle with Sam Rush and Chris'.

Memories of Igor Stimac, the last great central defender plucked from abroad and still adorned on the walls of Pride Park/ iPro Stadium, rose to the surface of the supporters' minds and to mark the occasion, the club went Hollywood. 'The whole fanfare that went with that signing was over the top,' remembers Paul

Simpson. 'Steve was meant to go over and watch Raul play because we'd not actually seen him play live. I don't even know if Chris saw him live. Steve had a flight for one Saturday after a game to watch him play for Eibar and we found out at the last minute that he was suspended and not able to play, so the deal was rushed through without ever actually seeing him. Raul was flown in on a private jet, which is absolutely fine.

'But then if the player trains and is not very good, straight away players go, "What's that all about, why have you done that for him?" In his first training session, there was a top-up for players who weren't involved in the game. He got a kick in training and went down screaming as if he'd been shot. Straight away people were just thinking, "What have we got here?" This isn't what we're about.'

Without a word of English in Albentosa's vocabulary, Simpson was left perplexed by the giant of a figure traipsed across Moor Farm's training pitches. If he was confused, consider how physio Sullivan felt. 'One of the things I always look for is alignment issues so for me, it was refreshing to see the player had already been treated because he had a leg length difference,' he recalls.

The 6ft 4in Goliath had been dealt with by his médico in Spain and having already lined up against Messi and Ronaldo that season, the Championship should have been a breeze. And it might have been if he'd have just packed properly. Sullivan continues, 'He forgot to bring his insoles and rather than saying anything he just trained without them. From day one he would be in the treatment room. His English wasn't great but he'd say "pain, pain, pain" pointing to various parts of his body and ultimately, he was getting problems because he didn't have his orthotics. By the time they came it was too late, you already had the cycle of problems that it takes a long while to get over. Omar Mascarell would call him "Hombre Cristal", which basically meant man of glass.'

Buxton watched on, 'With the signing of Albentosa, Nigel had signed lower league or Scottish players where at previous times of success, they'd brought foreigners in. They'd brought Eranio,

Stimac and they knew the response of the fans and how much they liked foreign players. I understood where they were going and if Albentosa had took off he'd have become a cult hero. But he was just making excuses. He wasn't up to it.'

Albentosa's signing may have been plucked from a bad sitcom but it didn't impact the mid-season domination the club were poised to embark on. A blip (if defeat against Forest can ever be described in that way) in a 2-1 home defeat that saw Derby boy Ben Osborn strike in the 90th minute only rejuvenated performances. Bent, still a terroriser of defences at every division, quickly showed why McClaren had recruited him with a second-half brace at home to Blackburn. Martin struck next time out to end a personal drought in a win at Cardiff and when Tom Ince and Jesse Lingard joined up until the end of the season, they played their part in another victory at home to Bolton. The pair, signing from Hull and Manchester United respectively, were marquee additions. Both signings, equally impressive coups for a Championship club, were ultimately excessive. Though Ibe had been recalled by Brendan Rodgers, McClaren still had Ward, Dawkins and Russell at his disposal. Promising youngsters such as Ivan Calero, by now integrated into the squad and familiar with the set-up, remained viable options yet were instead tossed out on loan. Things were beginning to turn.

'When we saw Bent and Tom Ince come in on big money, it put a new marker down every time,' recalls Buxton. 'It can cause unrest. The first season Steve came in and what Nigel had created was a scenario where we all had a similar car, living in a similar sort of house, going on similar holidays. But it slowly started to get blown out of proportion. Things changed and people can start to get a little bit greedy.'

Cracks started to show off the field and one night in Bourne-mouth, a meeting of the top two no less, posed an even bigger problem for the coming months. 'Chrissy Martin was my glue,' McClaren sighs. 'To have the controller in Eustace out and then the nine being the glue and him being out, we couldn't do it without them. We didn't recruit properly for if they got injured.'

Fifteen minutes into the clash at Dean Court, Martin was forced off after an innocuous-looking injury. He wouldn't return for almost two months and with that, Bent was elevated to the role of lone striker. Buxton, by now staving off injury concerns of his own, remembers what the loss of Martin meant for the side, 'Chris was brought in to hold up the ball but when Steve came in, he saw a style of play where he could build him and then have Wardy and Russell around him, Jordon Ibe too. It was pivotal that it stuck at the number nine and allowed the Brysons and Hendricks to then get around him. McClaren got the style of play built around him and these new players coming in, they hadn't been embedded into the side and hadn't had those principles built in from the previous manager either.'

Bent, boasting an entirely different skillset and build to Martin that didn't include holding the ball up, couldn't do the same job as the man dubbed 'The Wardrobe' by fans. McClaren said, 'Darren had always been a player who played on the shoulder of the last man throughout his career, not someone who'd have a ball played into feet. The dynamics of the team had to change when Chris had come out the side. We spoke about it at the time because when we came up against Millwall and Wigan the previous season, they played with a deep block and stopped us, defensively were strong and we couldn't break them down.

'We needed a plan to revert to. Chris would come to feet, Darren would spin in behind. Two different aspects of the game but if Chrissy was injured, we didn't have a platform for anyone to hold the ball up.'

A 3-3 draw at Rotherham on a bizarre night in Yorkshire presented all the warning signs. Ince and Bent both scored to rescue a point but the loss of Martin was immediately felt through the core of the 11 and without that focal point to maintain possession, the tempo of the game plan changed. Defenders became isolated as runners bombed forward for balls that were not being retained and for the first time, this switch produced a mental fragility in the back line. Mascarell, by now looking more and more out of place each game, was at fault for one goal. Lee Grant was to blame for another, flapping from a cheap free kick.

The coaching staff were given the warnings yet oversaw a squad that remained top after successive home victories. Thirteen games remained and the Rams, despite injuries, were leading the Championship table. It was at this moment, the moment everything was due to pay off, that Derby County's bottle went AWOL.

* * *

'Are you committed to Derby County? Can you rule out the Newcastle rumours?' Every Saturday at around 5.15pm, BBC Radio Derby's Owen Bradley begged McClaren for an answer. When Alan Pardew left for Crystal Palace in late 2014, McClaren became one of the front-runners. When John Carver was installed on an interim basis, that should have been that.

'Me and Sam had many discussions on it, too many in fact and I'd say to him "just leave me to do my job and we'll see where we are",' said McClaren. Carver, quickly understanding that the role was too big for him, was unravelling and McClaren's name was flung through newspaper clippings on a daily basis. 'I was under contract, I said that, and I knew there was interest but I was here and doing my job. That was my line and that's what I reiterated. We had a good chance of going up, just everybody settle down! I just felt it was too much interference for me and I was focusing on doing my job and going up.' Five years after the rumours, McClaren reiterates the same line.

Rams supporters, seeing their team struggle for results, descended into panic. Anger replaced worry the longer they had to wait for a definitive answer. In one interview, McClaren said the speculation was 'disrespectful to Carver and to Newcastle'. When pressed for a yes or no, he simply said, 'I'm contracted for the next two years.' Radio Derby's *Sportscene Talk-In* went into overdrive.

If there was anyone who knew the situation as well as McClaren, it was Simpson. Having spent seven days a week together, he offers an alternative insight, 'When it first got mooted in December, I actually said to Steve, "What are you gonna do?" and he told me we had a job to do and we weren't going anywhere. So even at that point, it wasn't happening. Whether it was rumours or anything more I don't know, but at no point did I ever speak to Newcastle at least. I never asked him again because that was enough. Myself, Steeley and Steve never had a conversation about it at all and we were totally focused on what we wanted to do, I don't for one minute – and I spent more time with Steve in that season than I did with my own wife – and at no point did I think his head had been turned.'

For the players, Buxton included, they were as confused as supporters, 'We saw the speculation every week because it lingered for so long but it never got addressed. In all fairness, he obviously saw the Newcastle job as his dream job. He's from up that way, living that way and it was a massive club to manage. When asked about it I think he struggled to distance himself away from it because he wanted it.'

Bryson, already finished with McClaren on a personal level, was left frustrated, 'There's never smoke without fire. He was linked and he never came out and addressed it, he just avoided the question and that then grows arms and legs. From then, I expected him to leave.'

Another of the Clough old-timers, Ward was becoming a stranger to game time the longer the season drew on and was left with more time to analyse the situation, having seen Ince and Lingard steal his spot. He recalls, 'I think he took his eye off the ball. Not consciously and he probably didn't mean to but it did happen. I remember walking into the changing room when he first got linked with it and Jeff was in there. I said to him, "The worst thing that could happen is the manager leaving. We'd then have a new manager to work with his philosophy, but we've got him down to a tee." But for me, I think he thought he'd got the job to be honest. Even if he was taking the job, the best thing he could have done is squashed all the rumours and said he was here until the end of the season or whatever, at least nobody could say anything. But he didn't even say that.'

The situation was boiling over and events on the pitch only made the situation more volatile. First came the loss of Bent, injured in a 2-0 defeat at Fulham just four games after Martin limped off. Both strikers at the club were now ruled out for indefinite periods and there were no realistic solutions for replacements. Ward and Johnny Russell were both given opportunities but struggled to play in a role that, although their natural position, was alien to them in the system. The club toyed with the idea of another loanee but opted against it.

Defeat against Brighton followed before the first major sign of fan anger came in March, as from 2-0 up against Birmingham with just injury time to see out, goals in the 93rd and 96th minutes stopped Derby going two points clear at the top. The glass-half-full supporter pointed to the fact they remained joint first, the half-empty brigade at the fact they were joint fourth and only five points clear of seventh.

The unity of the first five months had been replaced by a team increasingly operating on an individual basis, Sullivan referring to how 'it was a totally different feel to the dressing room from January'. As Giles Barnes alluded to during the Premier League season, defeats breed selfishness and changing rooms become battlegrounds.

Whereas Ward had battled his way to becoming a Championship player from the lower divisions, the January additions were plucked from the top. Unwittingly, this provided another problem. Ward says, 'Ince, Benty and Lingard are all really good individuals but the thing that got the club to where we were was sheer hard work and determination. I remember someone, maybe Bucko in the *Telegraph* saying we want warriors. At that point he was playing wizards and he lost his warriors. Individually they were all brilliant. But as a three they just weren't right for us. They should have had someone doing their dirty work. I think if you sat back and looked at where and when the downfall was, people could clearly see. They all scored important goals for us but at that point it became more about individuals rather than the team. Unfortunately, the wizards were out there because that is where I think our downfall was.'

Birmingham was the catalyst and with just two points out of the next 12, even a returning Bent couldn't keep the top two dream alive. Within the space of a month, a two-point lead ahead of the chasing pack had turned into a six-point deficit and attention had turned towards just staying within the top six.

* * *

Flash forward to the final day of the season. A slight resurgence and no defeat in six had kept play-off ambitions alive and within Derby hands. By now the new-look front line had contributed 11 goals in just three games and McClaren's free-flowing football was at its very best. Defensively though, they were a shambles. Grant picked the ball out of his net on seven occasions on visits to Huddersfield and Millwall. Major issues needed to be ironed out but with no time for an overhaul, McClaren was left to pray for a point on the final day.

The curtain-closer was a visit from Reading, Steve Clarke's men already guaranteed a spot in the bottom six. McClaren had done the task Rush most wanted and got a city back invested in their club. From barely 21,000 under Clough to 30,806 supporters now (with a season average of over 29,000), the city had fallen back in love with their club. Before the echo of 'Steve Bloomer's Watching' had cleared the air, they were preparing for separation.

'It was horrendous,' said Paul Simpson. Having only just let him recover from the recollection of Wembley, Simpson is presented with more trauma. 'Going into the game we actually knew Reading were good and it was going to be tough. We'd limped towards the end of the season and we just hoped we'd be able to produce because we knew we were capable of it, we knew we had enough ability to be able to do it but we just weren't sure how much was left in them. It really was a case of just getting through this match, dusting ourselves down for the play-offs and get us going again. But we were battered, our players went to pieces and unfortunately the rest is history.'

Within 90 seconds, Will Hughes's slack pass caught Albentosa napping, Keogh went to ground and Reading took the lead. McClaren, already forced into a position of such desperation that he had moved Stephen Warnock into the holding role and recalled Conor Sammon, could only watch on in disbelief. Bent's penalty miss late in the first half was pivotal, Michael Hector's strike clinched it. A late penalty was added for good measure and a season that offered so much was reduced to a shambles.

When Eustace saw red at Ipswich, the least the side expected was a play-off place. The consensus, given the previous year, was top two was the ultimate ambition for the squad. Watching on from the West Stand on 2 May 2015, he could barely believe the state his team-mates had descended to, 'You can't use the McClaren and Newcastle link as an excuse and if any of the lads have said that, it's not right. The lads should take responsibility.'

As the dust settled, the inquest began. Was it down to the injury to Martin? 'The club hid behind that,' admits Buxton, another missing on final day. 'When Chris got injured, we hid behind it as a club. A little bit of an excuse because they'd spent the money on players in the squad which was strong enough.'

Was it down to the speculation over McClaren? Hughes struggles to work it out, 'It's difficult to say. I can't remember the day to day but it's normal, even if you don't think it is, that it might consciously affect you when he's been linked. He didn't act any differently with us. Whether it affected us on the pitch, I'm not sure.'

The loanees? The downturn in form suggests they certainly didn't benefit the team in the way most expected them to. McClaren himself continued the inquest on a personal level and after four exhausting months of repeat questions, he finally got definitive, saying at the time, 'My intention is to sort this out. No one has told me otherwise and until they do, that is my determination.'

* * *

Derby may have missed out on the play-offs but somehow, the management team were still on schedule for their three-year plan. It wasn't the three-year plan that worked out for Billy Davies eight years earlier and, if promotion ever did happen, it would need to be within that final season. But as Simpson remembers it, they wouldn't be given the chance. Derby's hand had been forced and with the turning of the supporters, McClaren was sacked. He says, 'The way it all ended was horrible really. Steve said when the dust was starting to settle, "There's an opportunity and we could go to Newcastle" but I told him I didn't want to go. He asked for my opinion and I said, "You have to turn it down. This is where we need to stay." He thought about it for a while and said, "I'm going to turn it down, as long as we're able to commit ourselves for the next three years to finish this job." I was willing to sign another contact.

'I know for a fact that Steve turned Newcastle down. I said to Steve, "Look, I'm absolutely knackered. I want to go away with my wife for a couple of days, can I do it?" and he said, "Yeah, go and have some days in Spain." So, he rang me on the Wednesday night and asked me when I was coming back, which was the next day. "Right, I think I'm getting the sack. I need you to come back." He turned Newcastle down and then he got the sack.

'We were left in a situation with nothing. Even when it got to the point that I was still employed, he said to me that Newcastle had come in for him again. When he got the job, he wanted me to come as his assistant and I said, "No. I'm not coming." I told him I would only go if I got the sack at Derby. I wasn't leaving Derby.'

Simpson wasn't made to wait long before returning McClaren's call.

'I ended up ringing him one night and said, "Right, I think I'm going in to get the sack tomorrow morning." And he said, "If they do that, come to Newcastle straight away." It was all really disappointing though because we felt as though we were going in the right direction even though we had a massive disappointment at the end. We just felt as though we were still going to try and achieve what we wanted with Derby. We all tried everything to make that team a success and make it a successful season but whatever we did, it didn't work, and we lost our jobs.'

The last word on 2014/15 goes to Buxton. From the emotions of losing Clough in 2013 and being disrespected by the new management team, he had won them around and transformed himself into one of the best central defenders outside of the Premier League. But more than that, he had seamlessly transitioned from unfancied hoofer of the football to leader of men. He says, 'I expected him to go. I think at the end of the year we all expected it. I even think it came out at the end of April he was leaving. We then had the end of season awards and it got announced he was definitely staying. We had meetings where he told us the same. He asked me if I wanted to stay, I asked him if he wanted me, and then he was Newcastle manager. I don't know how true it is but I think it was maybe already agreed when we were flying at the top.'

THE DERBY WAY

IN MAY 2015, Paul Clement was working with Cristiano Ronaldo and Gareth Bale at Real Madrid. In July 2015, he was working with Jake Buxton.

The decision for Clement to begin his managerial duties in quiet old Derbyshire was a significant indication of the draw the club had at this time. Carlo Ancelotti's go-to man had suitors across the world game after signalling an interest in branching out on his own. No longer would he be perceived as the other guy.

'He is the perfect appointment at the next stage of Derby County's development and we are looking forward to the coming season with a great deal of optimism,' Sam Rush told the waiting press. Excitement grew.

Steve McClaren had already successfully used his contact book, acquiring Omar Mascarell from Real Madrid and Jordon Ibe from Liverpool. Clement, though, had closer connections to clubs of that magnitude across Europe. Where would Derby's next captures arrive from? Speculation began on the contacts Clement would be able to seek a favour from. Derby would never get a Cristiano Ronaldo but was there someone in Real Madrid's Castilla squad who fancied a go at British football?

We, and Clement, would never find out. What he was presented with upon arrival was a selection of names, names already sounded out and contacted before he even started discussions to take over. Tom Ince and Darren Bent made sense considering their run in the second half of 2014/15, but they were as good as confirmed without prior agreement. It became the theme of the summer. When tracing back to the moment Derby lost their identity, it's somewhere within these few months. Players, good players admittedly, were added on an almost daily basis.

But it was the deconstruction of the style built by Nigel Clough and mastered by McClaren. There would be no scouting in the SPL, no endless weeks of perusing League Two for the next Buxton or John Brayford. What would be unfurled was a list of players delivered directly to Clement. Eager to get his teeth stuck into the big boy chair, this list hinted at early warning signs and a lack of freedom when it came to decision-making. Bent and Ince arrived on astronomical Championship wages, as did the rest of those highlighted and pre-arranged.

One of those men who was first approached to join in the summer was Andreas Weimann. Often overlooked at Aston Villa, Weimann was a coup and joined Bent in forming a dangerous trio of attacking options. 'Steve McClaren was still the manager when I first knew they were interested. I did go in the summer before I signed in June just after the season finished with Villa. I went to the stadium to meet Chris Evans and Sam Rush before Paul Clement was announced,' he says.

'They told me he'd be coming in as the manager but it hadn't been announced yet so they showed me their plans for Derby and the stadium and a week later, Paul Clement was announced and that's when I agreed to everything. I wanted to know I'd be in his plans before signing.'

Days later, Jason Shackell returned for £3m. One of those whose attitude didn't fit the mould of a Clough team, his post-Derby years saw him skipper Burnley to the top flight. Now he was to return, the hope being his pairing with Keogh would solidify a back line who crumbled in the second half of 2014/15.

With Alex Pearce, Chris Baird and Scott Carson joining, Derby had a new look.

Having never done so to this level before, Derby were spending significant sums of money and it all came from the pocket of one man. Enter Mel Morris.

One of the League of Gentlemen of 2006 and a lifelong Ram, Morris had acquired 22 per cent of the club after the Wembley defeat but always did so with the intent of absorbing control from the Americans. The full takeover wasn't completed until September, but he was already bankrolling from the early months of 2015, highlighted by the loan captures.

Weimann's signing came as a relief and a slight concern for the manager. The pleasing aspect was he was presented with Premier League-calibre additions by the recruitment team. The worry was that it began to represent interference. Before being allowed to deliver a wish list of players, Clement was presented with a selection pre-arranged, and all he had to do was sign on the dotted line. Admittedly it wasn't the first example of signings confirmed before a manager was. The two-day gap between Clough's sacking and McClaren's hiring saw Zak Whitbread added to the squad, despite no manager being in place. He was a loanee though and Derby had a defensive crisis, one which Clough was looking to fill with John Eustace.

There was one slight concern – the squad was starting to bloat. Jamie Ward, Eustace and Whitbread were the only first-teamers to depart in the summer. Raul Albentosa would be quietly moved out on loan to Malaga in pursuit of those darn insoles. Aside from that there was little in the way of outgoings.

With a new squad in place, all Clement had to do was find the right balancing act between coaching Cristiano and Chris Martin. There were hints of nervousness from a man who had won it all in the game. Physio Neil Sullivan recalls one his first encounters being somewhat peculiar, 'On the Sunday night before pre-season started, I'm in the building having to sweep up because Paul was having some work done around Moor Farm and it wouldn't be ready for the players and it was apparently all about this perception. It seemed to me that he was too worried about the frilly stuff.'

Playing-wise though, whatever he did worked. 'We were massively impressed,' Buxton remembers. 'We went to Holland for a pre-season and he did a PowerPoint and a video analysis presentation on what he expected from us as a group and over the season, I was blown away with him. He looked very comfortable for first appointment and you could tell he had been around top players.'

Buxton found himself a spectator under Clement, but through pre-season it was clear that Craig Bryson was always in the plans. He says, 'I really enjoyed working with Paul. It was kind of a different pre-season. It wasn't so much about running, it was technical where you'd be doing everything with the ball. Obviously, it was still really tough but it was a different method of getting you fit and maybe a bit more of a football specific method. He'd won the Champions League and came with a lot of respect, everybody liked him and it was a clean slate again for every player.'

Then, in Clement's first game as a manager, it all fell apart. He had George Thorne back fit, Martin leading the line and a strong core running throughout the team. But 21 minutes in, Bryson went down, returning only intermittently until February after knee ligament damage. A blow but at least he still had Hughes, right?

Hughes recalls, 'Being injured under Clement was one of my biggest regrets I think, although obviously I couldn't do anything about it. Bryson's turned out to be as bad as mine and I'd have loved to have played that season. I think Clement's ethos, he had the right style of playing and then when I think about it, it could have all turned out differently.'

Hughes would never return under Clement and only featured towards the end of the season. From being fresh with the options of 2013/14 to losing two key components, it was Bolton away that was the catalyst for years of financial freedom that led the club all the way to the courts.

Absent of the duo, Rush delved into his Wasserman contacts. At this stage, there were still midfield options to call upon. Baird and Jamie Hanson were both midfielders in a former life, with Jeff Hendrick and Thorne fully fit. Instead, Derby spent £10m in a day, a move that would expand the squad beyond a healthy number.

'I was blown away,' admits Bradley Johnson. The £6m man was captured seconds before the closure of the August transfer window. 'By the facilities, Mel's aim, his ambition, his plans and it was him who made my mind up and sold the club to me. He spoke about his three-year plan to get to the Premier League, told me what he'd done for the club, showed me around and it was something that I thought was another good challenge.'

Why Johnson never got settled into Derby within his first two seasons is a mystery, but the moment he took to Sky Sports News certainly didn't help. 'I was stuck in front of a camera doing an interview and my head was all over the place. It was only when I came off, went back and sat down that I got a text from my brother saying, "Oh you've just signed for Derby City then?" and I'm like "Oh yeah, all a rush mate." He said, "Derby City?" I said, "Yeah Derby, why do you keep on saying the name?" and he said, "Derby City?" and I went "Yes Dean, Derby." And he just replied "City?" I went, "Oh my God." Looked at my phone, Chrissy Martin messaged me saying "welcome to the city, mate."'

Following Johnson into Moor Farm was Jacob Butterfield. He'd just had the season of his life at Huddersfield but even with that, a fee rising to £6m raised concerns. Rush's first offer was one sixth of that but as clubs began to see the financial might of Morris, the fees being charged were on the rise as clubs knew that Derby would pay them. Huddersfield had paid £500,000 for him a season previously.

Unsurprisingly, this new group struggled early on. Clement, favouring a slower style of play that trod a fine line between astute and boring, struggled to find the balance. Without a win in his first four, the home defeat to Leeds began to cause pockets of worry.

Fans, still seething at the collapse under McClaren, found patience to be wearing thin. In the opening weeks, new captain Baird reacted angrily to the east stand after an audible groan when he opted to pass backwards. It's a moment Buxton remembers, 'Bairdy killed himself by doing that. It didn't go down well.'

The realisation that this new style would be slower than McClaren's took some time for players and supporters to understand but when the squad began to click, results came. In the 19 games following that defeat, Derby lost only once. The style may have been slower but the results spoke for themselves. At Hull they eased to a 2-0 win in a Butterfield masterclass, with a focus on solidifying the back line meaning Scott Carson conceded only ten times.

Things were going right. So right in fact that Morris's appearance on *Sportscene Talk-In* during November saw him begin to talk of Clement as being Derby's answer to Sir Alex Ferguson, 'If you look at what we are trying to build at Derby, I think Alex Ferguson defined the culture and the philosophy at Manchester United because he had that long-term tenure. In a similar way, here Paul has an opportunity to help shape how we run this club.'

By new year, it was top two again. A loss in the first game of 2016 wasn't disastrous, particularly as it came at leaders Middlesbrough. There was still little sign of trouble for Clement, with even acceptance of the new style of play. So used to the fluid build-up of McClaren's game, the slower pace favoured by Clement and his coaching team has earlier frustrated home crowds. With results came acceptance. Pockets of disapproval remained in the playing staff, however.

So used to the style implemented by McClaren that certain aspects of training became a drag the longer the season went on. 'I think if you think about the way they trained, it was all very slow and one-paced and maybe that reflected his results very early on with draw after draw,' Neil Sullivan recalls. 'They got fit from playing the games rather than training, so it was all a bit different. The gym had all of the weight racks that Mel had bought to put in to make the gym as fancy as can be, they were put in storage because they didn't agree with lifting weights and it goes against everything done in the past. Sometimes I think when you are new to a building you should ask questions of the staff who are there: what do you do well, what can we improve on, but you don't get asked them. It was just a case of this is how things are gonna go and this is how we roll.'

Much had been made of the decision to take the captaincy away from Richard Keogh. Even more had been made by supporters of what they perceived to be a close relationship between the then skipper and the chairman. Allegations two years later from Sam Rush claimed Morris had instructed Clement not to hand the armband to Keogh, despite the fact the relationship between the two over the years was stronger than any other. Sullivan remembers that relationship up close, 'I remember Keogh coming off the pitch at one point in training and I was stood next to Mel. Keogh is shaking his head and says to me, "Can't the chairman see how bad that is?"'

It wasn't the only showing of discontent. Darren Bent, who scored just once under Clement and was starved of game time, recalls, 'As players in the dressing room, we knew it was inevitable that it was going to crumble. Training had changed, the intensity had changed, his philosophies that he had brought in at the start of the season and in pre-season started going out of the window, because we weren't getting the right results. Ultimately, he didn't really like confrontation, so when certain players who were not in the team were going to see him, they weren't really getting answers.'

Bent was one of those, only getting an answer via Twitter in the years after, Clement labelling him overweight and lazy.

Considering the substantial fees paid in the summer and the bloated squad, nothing aside from top two would do and come the new year, that looked unlikely. A 1-1 home draw with Reading left Clement six points behind Middlesbrough at the top of the table and the chasing pack were closing in. It's a game that Clement described at the time as his worst as head coach, the side booed off after limping their way to a point. Fans were worried, no doubt Clement was too. One man was more worried than most.

Morris was still new to chairmanship come January 2016. He was staring at a business that wasn't meeting his demands, uncharted territory for one of the most successful businessmen in the country. As he would do in his other interests, Morris wanted answers. There felt like no better time to get them than in the changing room, immediately after the match, in front of the head coach and the players. Unsurprisingly, the news leaked to the press.

Johnson looks back, 'It's not the case that we were doing badly so he felt he had to come down, he was in the changing room when we won games as well, so it wasn't weird him being in there that night. It was more of a shock for players that he was going a bit crazy at us. Mel is the most positive guy that you could meet. He's always happy and always smiling and I get on with him really well, so it was more that nobody could really say anything back to him because everything he said was right.

'He was just coming in to say, "Lads, what's going on?" Because it wasn't effing and blinding, it was him as he is to us. Okay he's not a mate, but he's got that side to him where he cares about everyone at the club. He come in and was just like "lads, what's happening?" and it got blown out of proportion with everything as it does in the press, who said he was in and giving us a bollocking but it was more just passion which you can accept. He's a fan, he owns the club, he spent a lot of money and he put together a team who should on paper have been winning.

'It's the first time that I've experienced that with the chairman coming in, but it would have been different. For instance, now I'm at Blackburn and I don't know the Venkys, they're in India so we have no contact with them. If they came in, it would be like, "What you doing? You've not been here for so many months, you come in and go crazy?" But Mel was always around the club so it wasn't a real surprise for many of us.'

Morris's journey down through the west stand was with the best of intentions. Even Buxton didn't take objection to the chairman's entrance, 'How it got received wasn't as well as he wanted it to do but I can understand why he did it. It's only because he's passionate and he wants to get the club promoted. There's a fine line with being too involved and making rash decisions and not being involved at all. Maybe coming into the dressing room wasn't the right thing to do but I understand and if I had invested that amount of money, I'd want to know why people weren't doing their job. If you build cars and they're not being built right, you come down and expect higher demands.'

The issue was not in Morris's actions, it was more it was an indication of the lack of power Clement had over his squad. Having worked at the Bernabeu, he knew all about pressure and demand. After all, he'd just been sacked despite winning the Champions League the season before. But now as a head coach, Morris's closeness to the players fell on him.

The changing room was just one instance of this. 'Paul would turn up late for staff meetings sometimes because he'd been summoned by Mel in the mornings to explain the formation or the line-up or something like that,' recalls Sullivan. A constant figure on the training ground, the chairman was more involved than most.

Clement's arrival also meant the hiring of goalkeeping coach Pascal Zuberbuhler. His experience with Morris was strong over his two years at the club, but he admits the training ground was a place like none he had been in before, 'Mel Morris is a very interesting guy. I've never seen a chairman so close to the players, so close to the training and so interested in the training. He had all the cameras and so sometimes he'd come in and say "why did you do this this morning?" He wants to know. Normally a chairman is not interested in the training but he was so interested in the situation.'

The cameras and the presence on the field started to grow on Clement. The man Morris claimed could be his Ferguson was under constant scrutiny and had he not been so new to the management game, it's a situation he may have spoken out against. As wins and draws became draws and losses early into the new year, Morris cancelled the pre-planned trip to Dubai in favour of more training. The move was greeted favourably by players and the staff but there was a clear motive behind it. Still pushing top two, the cancellation was a warning shot in Clement's direction. A 'buck up your ideas' sort of move.

Again, Morris opened his cheque book. Nick Blackman arrived for £3m after the best six months of his career with Reading. Abdoul Camara, an unknown quantity from Angers in Ligue 1 came in for just over £1m and Marcus Olsson joined from Blackburn. No side in Championship history had ever spent as much as the £25m shelled out in the pursuit of promotion.

The identity of the club was lost. So desperate were they for promotion, all that came before had been forgotten. The fees rocketed, the squad grew, the wages became eye-watering. At the time, fans didn't worry. For the players who had been through the mill at the club already, they did. Bryson was one of those left wondering what direction the club was heading in, 'I think money does change that community. You sign different players and maybe a different kind of ego, essentially. When Nigel was signing players, Derby would be the best club they had been at. We're then signing players who would maybe say Derby is a step down from clubs they've been at. You don't know if they have the same motivation and the same burning desire to get promoted. The team doesn't have the same spirit as it first did, but we have better players. But I did wonder what would happen if Nigel had that money to spend.'

What was a strong core had been ripped apart. While trying to remove the scars of previous seasons, what had instead been stripped back was the aspects that saw the squad develop so quickly under McClaren. 'We had a lot of change at the club at that time, a lot of players coming in,' Johnny Russell says. 'It was difficult to be honest. You're always going to miss the characters who leave, Wardy was a big one for us and the boys loved him, same with Bucko. It was difficult losing guys like that and players you had been with.'

And when it came to the money, what was on offer surprised even Zuberbuhler, 'The players had amazing contracts and even though you're talking about a Championship club, from the first day it was Premier League. Salary wise, training, work wise. I think this time Sam Rush was also at the club and he gave a little bit too much for new players – it was a lot of money for me, the amount spent. I was in Leverkusen in Germany where they spent a lot of money to buy the BayArena but still, the money Derby spent was impressive.'

With the club lower than they had been at the same point in the previous two seasons, Morris acted. His statement on the club website included the following quote, 'It was clear in this plan, which was briefed to supporters, players, sponsors and all our stakeholders last summer that promotion this season was not the primary target.

'The priorities were building on the Derby way and style of football enjoyed in the past two seasons; adding depth and strength to our playing squad; and, developing and improving player and team performance.'

Five points adrift of the top two, Clement had turned into a Moyes rather than a Ferguson. 'We went on another Derby-esque run,' admits Bryson, 'and we didn't win in five or so, dropped to fourth and he got the sack. I found it to be harsh. I don't know what goes on behind closed doors but from a players' point of view, we liked him and got on.'

Inevitably, there was fall-out. Neil Clement, retired footballer and brother of Paul, tweeted and hastily deleted, 'Good club derby with good players good fans and a mug of a chairman.' To the outsider, the spending of £25m on a Championship team meant promotion was a must. When Clement first took the role, he spoke of a 'same desire and ambition to make Derby a Premier League club'. With two years of near misses, there was no other aim and if they failed to make it, significant financial pressure would rise.

At least that's what you might have expected. Three months before the sacking, Mel had candidly told the *Football League Paper*, 'If we don't get promotion this season, we won't get rid of Paul.'

Upon getting rid of Paul, he cleared comments such as that up. Speaking with BBC *East Midlands Today*, he expressed that promotion wasn't necessarily a target, 'Paul's horizon was shorter-term than ours. He was the one who wanted promotion this season. We wanted to build on the squad, develop them, get on a rising tide of performance and let that carry us through into the Premier League – whether that was this season, next season or beyond. I think, for Paul, that was too long a view.

'Every player he has wanted, he has had. All the signings were all signed off by Paul. We put a lot of money behind him, even up to the last couple of weeks. At any point in time, Paul could have embraced the plan we had.'

To continue the mayhem, the captaincy went back to Richard Keogh. Just to round things off, Morris had one final comment, 'Put it this way, if I was picking the team, he wouldn't have been playing some of the players in some of those games.' The situation was bizarre and would only get stranger over the coming year.

* * *

There would be no big-name replacement. Supporting Morris's assurance that promotion wasn't a necessity, he launched Darren Wassall into the hot seat. Wassall, his only management experience being that 45 minutes against Ipswich two years earlier, was handed the keys until the end of the campaign, regardless of what happened. The reception was mixed.

On the positive side of the decision was Johnson, 'We all knew and got on well with Wass, he was always around and we knew he was an ex-player at the club there as well. He knew what this club wanted and the ambition. Mel could have gone and signed another manager who didn't really know much about the club but when you've got someone who has been there for so many years and seen the transition, it was a no-brainer for Mel to take over.' Johnson quickly corrects himself, 'For Wass to take over*.'

Zuberbuhler, one of the few kept on after Clement's sacking, saw first-hand the change in style, 'The players received a big wake-up call from Darren, there was nothing I can remember negative though. He said he wanted players running and fighting and showing heart, otherwise they had nothing to do with this club anymore.'

It wasn't universal delight though. Weimann describes the situation as 'a bit strange' while Sullivan recalls, 'Not everybody took to him.'

He continued, 'Under Clement you'd maybe get away with a couple of things while training was going on. If you were a bit sulky then nobody would say anything to you but Darren wouldn't accept that. One of the first training sessions he sent Nick Blackman in because of him sulking and he set his stall out straight away. That didn't go down well.'

Wassall's first task of instilling a smile back into the squad slowly began to reach completion. Two wins in his first three further solidified a top-six spot that had never really looked out of reach. His first win at Brentford was Derby's first in eight games and despite the wretched form in the back end of Clement's run, they were still only five points from second spot.

The new man was naïve. Inexperienced in senior management, the gulf between that knowhow and academy football was no more apparent than one afternoon in Rotherham. From leading 3-0 with ten left to play, Leon Best scored twice as part of a 3-3 draw. 'For the first 80 minutes of that game, I remember thinking, "Wow, we're actually playing unbelievably here." It was one of the best performances I've ever been involved in,' said Bryson. And when you consider the amount of games he had played in by this point, it's quite the claim. Then it all went to pot.

'I just remember after the game trying to work out what happened, walking up to the Derby fans and just getting the "fuck off, you're a wanker" and the V-sign and all that. It's merited though because it was embarrassing. You can imagine what the changing room was like, arguments everywhere. There were even some fans waiting outside just for a bit more abuse.'

Outside the ground, the same level of unrest was apparent. Scuffles broke out, anti-Morris chants began to be roared by solo individuals. The anger was only matched by Jason Shackell, who on the pitch launched a tirade at Wassall in full view of the travelling support. Promotion might not have been the aim for Morris but for the fans, it was the only acceptable end.

To counter Wassall's mismanagement in that final 25 minutes, Morris hurried his pursuit of someone to guide him. That someone would be Harry Redknapp. 'It was a little bit all over the place,' Buxton remembers. 'At the start it was a good appointment of Darren but then we had Rotherham away and there was a commotion from then on – is Wass staying in charge or is it Harry Redknapp? What's happening here? Harry was coming in with his entourage and then on his own.'

The future *I'm a Celebrity* winner would be there strictly for when Wassall required him. As it turns out, that wasn't too much according to Johnny Russell, 'He was a good guy, Harry. There was a few of us who would ask him a lot of questions about his career and about players and jobs he'd done, so he always had a good story. He didn't really get involved in the training side, he was at games overlooking there, but I think it was a weird position for him to be in. He didn't overstep or seem like he was trying to take over, so he was always there if you needed him.'

His presence was vital though. Still at slight risk of dropping out of the top six, the final month of the season saw Derby take 14 points from 21, including a brilliant 4-0 win over Hull. With Bryson and Hughes now back, options for those midfield spots grew, though the broken leg of Thorne on the final day drew criticism for many who believed it was an unnecessary risk.

The last crack at the play-offs had fallen apart at the hands of Redknapp, the mastermind of the QPR smash-and-grab at

Wembley. This time around, it was hoped that he'd be able to aid Wassall all the way. And coming up against a Hull side they had already beaten twice over the course of the season, what could go wrong?

Answer: everything. 'That Hull game is just the biggest frustration for me,' a downbeat Hughes says. 'If you look at that first leg we got battered and conceded goals late on and little moments like that, things change in those instances. That was one of my biggest frustrations.'

Two first-half strikes knocked the wind out of Wassall's side but that naivety again came into play in the 90th minute with a goal that ultimately sealed the tie. Russell says, 'It's one of them days where even to this day I can't put my finger on what went wrong. Just soft goals that we gave away, especially the last one because he's ran the length of the park, where one of us just had to take one for the team and hit him. But we'd poured numbers forward quite naively trying to get a goal back, because we didn't want to go there with a two-goal deficit. And that just backfired massively on us.'

Away, Derby played like Derby should play. If Morris was looking for a 90-minute example of the 'Derby Way', this was it to a tee. Rampant from the off, Russell cut the gap to two before an own goal before the break meant they were back within touching distance of a comeback that would have been described as IstanHull.

Weimann hadn't even made the squad for the first leg but starred in the second, an evening that hadn't been seen from him since signing in the summer. He recalls, 'We went out there and the first 20 minutes we sprinted around and tried everything possible to get a goal and we got the 2-0 lead. Bryson had the chance five minutes into the second half to make it 3-0 and then we would have gone on and won it. But because we put so much effort in for the first 60 minutes, that last half an hour Hull saw the game out well and we didn't really create any more chances. But it was just a frustration because of how we played in that first leg.'

Ultimately, Morris's first full season as chairman had failed. To his tally he had two managers, countless negative headlines, £25m spent and a club in worse shape than when he took over. With Wassall not returning for a full-time stint, he had to make sure the squad was right for the continuation of that Derby Way.

FOUR IN ONE

IN SERIES one of *I'm Alan Partridge*, there's a particularly perfect scene where the title character sacks his entire staff, his reasons for doing so worsening as he works his way around the office. The first employee is sacked for leaving a coffee mug on his desk overnight, the next for tutting. The third because she's 'a rotten shit'. It's Alan's way of getting rid of his skeleton staff as quickly as possible. The scene in the corridors of Moor Farm throughout 2016 and 2017 was probably quite similar.

Over the course of 2016 and in the pursuit of promotion, five different managers sat in the dugout. It's a year incomparable to anything that came before or after. Off the field, Derby had been significantly backed in a way they had never been previously. But on it, they would fare no better, devolving into a circus. After Paul Clement and Darren Wassall had both tried their hand, it was time for another refresh.

Come the summer, Derby were desperate and on a collision course with becoming what supporters had despised only two years earlier. The financial splurge had gone a long way to crushing the bond between supporters and players that was built so well by Steve McClaren and Nigel Clough, the philosophy had been lost and having almost sold their soul, the club bordered on becoming the new (and less successful) QPR.

Three successive seasons of near misses and what many perceived to be two straight years of 'bottlings' had left the support turning from hope to disdain, with a new consensus that the players were running the club. 'Many supporters felt that the players needed a good kick up the arse,' one fan simply put it. 'They had too much power and the standards had slipped, rumours were circling around about some of their behaviour and all of that, certain players they thought were running the dressing room.'

It was a fair assessment. McClaren and Clement, two quieter characters, had both lost their roles after results waned and it was painfully obvious at times that certain members of the squad had issues with Wassall. Rotherham away was evidence enough of that.

That's why Mel Morris's next move was, on paper at least, the most logical he could have made. Clement was seen to many as a soft touch and Wassall hadn't the necessary managerial experience, hence the addition of Harry Redknapp. Even McClaren had risked losing the respect of the changing room in the manner of the 2014/15 capitulation. The club needed authority off the field and a leader to guide them through to the next stage.

Nigel Pearson was the man for the role. 'He is a proven winner, a highly experienced manager who has a track record of success in the Championship and has also coached successfully in the Premier League,' was the line Morris delivered on the appointment. That final line was the most crucial. He'd already seen McClaren, Clement and Wassall fail to deliver promotion, so his attentions turned to someone who had done it all before at Derby's expense. Upon the sacking of Clement, Morris spoke of how it wasn't 'all about promotion, rather about the philosophy'. Pearson's appointment was all about promotion.

As with the appointment of McClaren, Pearson came with added bonuses. Once again, the manager would be supported by two individuals who had Derby County running through their system. Chris Powell was a major coup. The former England international was a mainstay of the mid-1990s side under Jim Smith and a top-class manager in his own right. He had worked under Pearson at Leicester in his playing days and just the mention of his name drew respect across the game.

Joining the duo would be Inigo Idiakez, ten years after being forced out of the club under Billy Davies. 'We had a couple of offers because Nigel always wanted me as a first-team coach wherever he went,' Idiakez says. Part of Leicester's academy staff when Pearson was at the club, he was just waiting for the opportunity to follow him somewhere new and try his hand at working with the seniors. 'He rang me the day before he was appointed and said, "You're going to be happy with this, Inigo. It's Derby County." I didn't believe him but it was just a wow moment. Signing the contract was very easy.'

Having tried and failed with Clement, Rush and Morris returned to a formula that came so close to working, as they brought familiarity back to the club. Idiakez and Powell were both club legends in their own right, so much so that pre-match videos on the Pride Park screen still show Powell singing the original 'Steve Bloomer's Watching'. Both men were ingrained into the club's recent history in the same manner that Simpson and Steele were.

In a footballing sense, the decision to hire Pearson was correct. His pedigree and CV spoke for itself and Derby themselves knew how well-oiled his Leicester side was. Six times he had come up against Derby since 2011 and five times he emerged victorious, often heavily. His promotion campaign in 2014 saw the assembly of one of the finest Championship sides in recent memory and his ability to steer them to Premier League safety paved the way for the most unlikely title in football history.

It was away from football that the doubts hung. A steely, fearsome character during his Leicester days, his singular top-flight campaign had led him down a dangerous path. It first began in December of 2014 when, late into a 3-1 home defeat to Liverpool, he told a supporter to 'fuck off and die'.

Then there was the incident where he pinned Crystal Palace's James McArthur to the ground by the neck. Two months later came bullying accusations when he delivered his infamous 'ostrich' belittlement of a local journalist. A day later came another row with a journalist and that summer, he was sacked after the leaking of a sex tape involving his son (not Pearson himself, Derby had already been through that saga years earlier).

How would he have changed in his year hiatus from football? In his first press conference he stated, 'It was important for me to start at a club where I felt excited about being back in management.' In many ways, the move didn't differ from when he took over from Sven-Goran Eriksson at Leicester. At the time, the Foxes had spent millions under Sven without finishing the job, so it's little wonder the task at Derby piqued Pearson's interest.

The appointment was a risk considering his recent past but, with other clubs also interested in his signature, Derby were hardly alone in their pursuit. And after all, maybe he was what the club needed? A general to put the players back in line and finally get past the underperforming of previous seasons.

Goalkeeping coach Pascal Zuberbuhler had played under Pearson back in his West Brom days and knew that the man he would work under was nothing like the one put in front of the media. He recalls, 'When I signed for West Brom he was the assistant coach under Bryan Robson. He took the team for five games and it was fantastic for me. He pushed negativity out and gave me a chance, so it was nice to see his face again. But Nigel's a completely different guy from the playing style and football. He has his direction and he looks very hard and strict but his personality is actually very nice and he makes a lot of jokes internally and it was brilliant to have him as a gaffer.'

Whether a hard reset was what the club needed at the time is questionable, but with the incoming Pearson it was inevitable. His Leicester side was built around hard work rather than the intricacy seen under McClaren and even at times under Wassall. His squad, focused more around individual talent than drive, would have to adapt to the new methods and the 'Derby Way' would be thrown out of the window.

'I thought Nigel Pearson was brilliant,' says physio Neil Sullivan, now under his fifth manager. 'He would have been a star for the club for years to come. Nigel realised things needed to change, he identified what he wanted to make different and that involved some players who would be surplus to requirements, even though they were maybe popular or a voice in the dressing room. But if you're hiring somebody to make those changes you have to back them and stick with it.'

The summer was difficult. Fans wanted change without knowing exactly where that needed to come. First out was Jake Buxton, who had been benched throughout the previous season. He says, 'Nigel was the only manager who was honest enough to tell me I wouldn't play every week and be in the first two or three centre-backs. Him, Chris Powell and Idiakez had bottle. When I spoke to previous managers nobody had an answer because every summer I had an opportunity to leave and it was only him who said it would be for the best if I did go.'

Without knowing where else change was needed, that uncertainty and frustration stemmed through to Pearson. Struggling to ship players out, it took until 27 August for any permanent additions to be made and by then, his position was already in jeopardy.

Five points from the first four games wasn't a total disaster, particularly as the two home draws were against strong outfits in Brighton and Aston Villa. But a day before adding to his squad came a humiliating evening.

In the first competitive meeting between the two sides, Pearson's feeble outfit lost 1-0 away to Nigel Clough's Burton Albion. When Clough left Burton for Derby, there was a three-league difference, the closest the two sides had ever been to each other. Yet now, the irritating smaller brother had humiliated the older sibling.

The only plus-point came with the return of Shaun Barker to competitive football, four-and-a-half years after his injury. Barker looks back, 'Even though it was for a different club, he gave me that moment for Derby. For me, for him, for everyone involved. That was the pivotal, monumental moment of my entire career, the five seconds' worth of football that Nigel allowed me to have. It felt like it was for more than just me. It would have been nicer to do it at Pride Park and for Derby, but it was a special meaning.'

Barker, whose first and only impact was to nod clear from a corner, would make five more appearances before retiring from the game.

* * *

Missing on the night was Jeff Hendrick. After an attention-catching Euro 2016 with Ireland, Burnley came calling and paid £10.5m on deadline day for the academy product. It was good business for both parties, with Hendrick's Derby career threatening stagnation after years of under-achievement. The money supported the addition of Matej Vydra days before, a new club record signing at £8m. The hope was that he would provide the spark to reignite Chris Martin back to life. Derby's number nine had long struggled for goals at the back end of 2015/16 and another dry evening at the Brewers took his wait for a goal to 14 games. He wasn't alone by this point, with Derby scoring just once in Pearson's first five games.

Deadline day saw the incomings of his Watford colleague Ikechi Anya on a £4m deal and the 11pm announcement of 34-year-old free-agent goalkeeper Chris Weale. It wasn't anywhere near enough to provide a flash of hope that things would begin to change and the decision to allow Martin out on loan to Fulham was, to paraphrase Pearson in an earlier life, 'very, very silly or absolutely stupid'. Martin went on to rediscover his form at Craven Cottage in the first half of the campaign while Vydra and loanee James Wilson struggled from the off.

The Burton defeat was followed by 15 days without a fixture and in that time, the coaching staff got to work on rebuilding. With one goal in five games, it wasn't difficult to figure out that the side had struggled to gel to a more compact system. 4-4-2 wasn't working and the expectation was that a new look would be worked upon. Quite what happened in those weeks is a mystery, because Derby lost their next two games on home soil and sat three points off the bottom.

'The mistake Nigel made was that he based his teams on a 4-4-2 and he got success playing it at Leicester, they battered teams in the Championship with Vardy and Mahrez and whoever else,' said Craig Bryson. The Scot was on the receiving end of most of those batterings and knew that if Pearson could get the side to mould to his methods, they'd be the ones handing them out.

'We would get battered 4-0 every time. But you know, with Derby we'd been through a stage of playing a different formation so maybe if he bit the bullet and played a 4-3-3 and got used to that, had a couple of windows, brought in the type of players that he wanted and that he thought could play a 4-4-2 in the way he played at Leicester, I think he'd have got on a lot better.'

Bryson, however, had no bad words to say about those who came before and after Pearson. He didn't even hesitate to say, 'I really liked Nigel.' There were plenty who didn't though according to Idiakez, 'From the beginning Nigel tried to implement his ideas and the players didn't buy into it. As staff there were too many of us doing the same things, which I spoke to Nigel about. Me and Kevin Phillips were just doing the same job. It was a dream because it was Derby but I just didn't enjoy my time. I didn't enjoy watching them play, it wasn't our way of playing or what we wanted. The players were all right, but I always felt that they weren't happy with us.'

Already, discontent was growing. It seems laughable today but there was almost an inevitability about when Morris would be organising another pay-off. He would have at least hoped for a reprieve when Vydra struck the opener at home to Blackburn 69 minutes in. Yet the squad displayed their fragility and conceded twice within the next four minutes to lose 2-1. Nine games into the season, a non-compliant group were ten points adrift of the play-off spots and dumped firmly in the bottom three.

That afternoon was where the support revolted. Three goals in nine games and just six points was an abysmal return for all involved, not least Bryson, 'We didn't play well on the pitch obviously and I think one or two players were pissed off a wee bit because they weren't in their preferred position and he had a different opinion on a few players as well. But I think he knew exactly what was wrong with the club straight away, what was wrong with a couple of players. I won't say who, but he knew what was wrong and I think if he had a couple of transfer windows, he would have sorted it.'

Bryson's words are pivotal. Pearson felt he knew what, or maybe even who, was wrong at the club. Martin was moved on, Johnny Russell found it difficult to be favoured by the manager, Lee Grant left on loan. 'Fans will have a different opinion because they only see what happens on a Saturday, they don't see the Monday to Friday, the work leading up to a Saturday and all of the other stuff that comes with a football club, they're just seeing a Saturday,' continues Bryson.

'I'll hold my hands up, we didn't play well, we were near the bottom three and I remember that hostility because people expected promotion. If he kept on going we might have ended up in a relegation battle, you never know, but for me, I'd been there for a good period of time and a lot of the things that he was saying were hitting the nail on the head.

'If you were shite, he'd tell you that you were shite, if you were good, he'd tell you. He was very much like Nigel Clough, old-school and when he spoke you listened to him. You can see what he's done now, I liked his style, I liked what he was saying. I think he probably wanted to say more but he had to keep players on side, try and get to the windows and whatever happened, happened.'

* * *

Less than a year before, Morris entered the changing room to berate the squad in front of a startled Paul Clement. To an extent, and with years now to reflect, it is perhaps less surprising than it was at the time. Still early into his days as chairman and with millions of pounds of his own money pumped into the club, he wanted to understand why his investment hadn't produced results. After all, Morris is a businessman to his core. He was still learning that football is different though and it's presumably a moment he now looks back on with some regret. Perhaps not as much as how things unravelled with Pearson.

'The chairman was involved in everything,' said Idiakez, whose dream return was already a nightmare. On 27 September, it all came to an abrupt finish. The Spaniard continued, 'The relationship between the players and the chairman was good, so it was very difficult for us. You had the manager and his staff in between and it was difficult. For me it was okay because it was just training and the players were amazing with me, but the problem was more with Nigel because he was the one who was making the decisions. The chairman had TVs and everything there and sometimes there was more management with players than the team.'

The mention of TVs by Idiakez is pivotal to provide context to the situation at Moor Farm at this point. The reports days later began to emerge of drones being used to allow individuals to keep an eye on training methods. It's easy to imagine this may not have sat well with the traditional Pearson, nor the alleged questions over team selection.

Having travelled for the away trip to Cardiff, news broke at 5pm that Pearson and Idiakez had been suspended by the club. It was passed to the coaching staff, including Sullivan, hours earlier. The physio said, 'Nigel said to us that he had a conversation with Mel, who was unhappy about selection or tactical stuff and Nigel wasn't used to reporting in that fashion like every other manager has had to do. He allowed some statistics to go out and tried to appease Mel's need to know what was going on I think. So we get to Cardiff and have an evening there, train the next morning and then lunchtime comes and then he tells us he's just been relieved of his duties.'

It's a far cry to the events of the previous Friday, when Morris reaffirmed his commitment to Pearson and so, with another episode unravelling, the media frenzy returned. Once more, with rumours of matters turning physical, Derby's dirty laundry was inspected nationally. Reportedly due to an incident on the Monday, Morris's final decision wasn't made until arrival in Wales.

Idiakez remembers, 'I have no idea what this incident was because Nigel never told me anything about that. We drove to Cardiff to play and then before a meeting with the players, they just said we were out. And after five minutes, they had taxis on the door, we got in them and that was it. Chris and Kevin stayed and they were asked to take the team. I tried to get an explanation, but nobody got in touch with me.'

Did things turn physical? According to Sullivan, there was no chance, 'Everyone speculated on a to do but we were in the building and if anything like that had happened, we'd have known about it because people work at desks right outside of the office so I can't believe that really happened. I think ultimately he's a very demanding chairman and not everybody can be able to deal with it.'

One man not sacked was Zuberbuhler. He had been in the role for just 14 months and already was preparing for life under his fourth boss. Unlike with Clement's shock dismissal though, he had already been making plans for life after Pearson. 'There were two hard minds punching together with the chairman and with the head coach. It was a clear explosive direction. I realised very early on. It was a "boom" and everybody was just waiting for it to happen.'

Idiakez, with such a storied past already with Derby, drew this particular chapter to an unhappy close, 'I deserved more but I just got a phone call [to say he was sacked]. The CEO phoned Nigel first and said he was sacked because of an incident on the Monday with the chairman. And then he phoned me after five minutes, told me I was sacked in a 30-second conversation. I really felt I deserved more.

'Another club would have been okay for me but not Derby. The chairman and the CEO didn't do well and they treated me badly. I felt quite bad and then I had a year that wasn't depressing but hard to swallow because it was a special club for me. It's not a family anymore. It's a different club to the one I joined.'

'It was doomed to failure,' said one source. 'I equated it to Brian Clough at Leeds. You've got a massive personality and ego walking into a dressing room of personalities and egos, you'll only ever get one winner there. His style immediately turned the players off, there was anarchy and somebody had to pay the price.'

Pearson and Idiakez were officially removed from the club within the coming days and that evening in Wales, with Powell taking temporary charge, Derby picked up their second victory of the season.

* * *

Steve McClaren's Newcastle tenure was a disaster. Having worked so hard to rebuild his reputation in his homeland with Derby, over the course of nine months in the north-east it was lower than it had ever been. With six wins in 28 games and the side in 19th, Mike Ashley finally bit the bullet and looked elsewhere. He appointed Rafa Benitez, who could not avoid relegation.

Yet, despite his time with Newcastle and particularly after the collapse of 2014/15, McClaren immediately emerged as a front-runner to take over from Pearson. The two other contenders, Powell and Steve Bruce, were cast aside quickly and soon after confirmation of Pearson's sacking, McClaren was installed.

'Did McClaren come back? I completely forgot that!' It's no surprise Will Hughes lost track of his later years at the club. The damning final three months of McClaren's first reign saw supporters turn, before an ultimately inevitable split. At the time, there was little prospect of ever seeing him within Derby County employment again, yet here we were, barely a year later.

With Clement, Wassall and Pearson all in and out, it seemed longer than a year. So long that by now, fan resentment to McClaren had decreased as nobody had been able to build on the work he had done.

McClaren recalls, 'How did it happen? You'd have to ask Mel how that came about and why. Like I said, yes there was speculation and interest from Newcastle. Yes, at the end of the season I committed to Derby. Yes, I then got sacked. Yes, I was very lucky Newcastle came back in otherwise I wouldn't have had a job. But I just felt that I'd not really done anything wrong as such, I still felt it was a bit harsh. And yeah, that was as much my fault. The grass is always greener.' Yes, yes, yes from McClaren.

'Mel wanted his own manager and me, Sam Rush and Chris Evans had this great relationship so maybe he just wanted a fresh start. But on reaching out, me and Mel had a frank discussion, shook hands and he said "come back". The team was bottom three I think, I looked at them and felt we could do something with them, so I did.'

McClaren had to win over the fans again and was sent out on a leash to apologise in front of the media for the events of the first spell. He told BBC Radio Derby – the organisation that had long pushed for him to do so – 'My mistake was not quashing the rumours and not committing. That's my fault and I apologise for that. By the time I committed to the club, the club had every right to sack me.'

He didn't need to win over the players though. Johnny Russell had heard the rumours but, much like supporters did, he would have to wait until seeing McClaren in the flesh before welcoming him back. He recalls, 'It was gutting for us to lose him that first time because of the way we played with him and the seasons that we had under him. But everyone was excited to get him back because that was still fresh in the memory. I remember being sat with Thorney and a few other boys when he came back in. Nothing was really said but we seen him, he seen us and we all just started laughing. It was like "'here we go again".'

'It was just like normal for me,' McClaren reflects today. 'It was just the same enthusiasm as going in the first time, there were good players signed but I felt we'd just gone away from the football we wanted to play so we just went back to that. Footballers are fickle people, we're all fickle people. When you're winning, they pick up and we started winning and playing football.' Was the 'Derby Way', as mentioned by Mel Morris after sacking Paul Clement in 2016, back? Did it even exist? If it did, it was seemingly just McClaren-ball.

He would be the only one to return but joined up with Powell, the two renewing their relationship from the 1990s. And it was a duo that worked brilliantly. Still with a large chunk of the squad from his previous residence, the switch back to a more familiar formation paid off immediately. Just like in 2013, the tenure started with a home victory over Leeds. In front of over 31,000, the dishevelment of Pearson's days was replaced by the warm, open arms of 2013/14-style football. 'I went in, looked at it and the job was just to get us out of trouble, stabilise and plan for next year. That was it. I said, "Fair enough, I can do that." The football was roughly the same and in the first three or four months I don't think we lost a game. We went back to enjoying it and being in control.

'So, I got them out of trouble, we were stable and we were never going down. We got into the play-off positions and that was a big mistake. If I look back it was a mistake because expectations went through the roof.'

* * *

The first 13 games were almost perfect and produced 30 points. It was nearly a replication of McClaren's original impact as a head coach, in which 32 points were amassed from the same number of fixtures. The expectations grew in exactly the same way as they did in 2013. The battle for a seat at Pride Park returned and talk turned from surviving to thriving. Zuberbuhler remembers, 'I liked Steve's international experience and as a manager, how he talked to the people and his intensity, if he made a meeting it was like a cinema. He was running around like a tiger, left right, left right. It was fantastic. I liked him very much and especially his positivity.'

Instantly club records were being set again. But eight consecutive clean sheets at home, including a 3-0 victory against Forest, provided a false dawn. McClaren had got everything he could out of the side and with victories now very much expected rather than hoped for, he would be made to pay for his initial success. A new year meant a familiar tale as the bottle again went missing.

McClaren says, 'I said to Mel that the team was not good enough. "I'm telling you it's not good enough to go up. It's not as good as the other one. It can be, but we'll plan for next year." But we got ourselves into the play-offs and all expectations meant we should be winning every game now and we should be up there. We over-achieved and I couldn't believe we went from there to there with what we had, with that squad. I did what was asked.'

He'd actually done more. Come 2017, only a point kept them outside of the top six. But McClaren was to fall victim to his own success and unlike 2013/14, he wouldn't be afforded time to correct it.

'I think he had a completely different squad to what he had before,' Will Hughes says. 'We'd brought quite a few new players in so it was a new squad, completely different. A lot more of a different ability but also very different characters, and I don't know if that helped or not. Before we had all the old pros who worked hard and everybody got along and clicked. But when you bring that many players in it's hard for all the new signings to play well together. His approach is fantastic, and I played my best football under him and I enjoyed my football the most underneath him. But it was difficult for him to come back after his success the first time, to replicate that.'

Results started to slide in January and to counter this, the club got their hands dirty. Martin, who had struck nine times for Fulham in the first half of the campaign, became the focus of McClaren's attentions and he wanted the man who he built his squad around back at the club. Conversations between both parties were kept under wraps but when Martin made himself unavailable for Fulham and took a day off from training, the news leaked. 'We're not a train station, you can't come in and out when you want,' said Fulham's boss, Slavisa Jokanovic. 'I don't know if he'll play for Fulham, but I'm sure he's not going to play for Derby.'

It's little wonder McClaren went to Mel with his demand for the forward to be dragged home. Martin had scored 40 goals in 78 Derby appearances, far and away his best return, and it was no secret that he didn't want to leave the club in the first place.

McClaren continued, 'Chris was the only thing we were missing and I said that to Mel. We had Benty, Nick Blackman was injured and didn't know what his best position was, so we had no number nine. I said, "If we get Chris Martin, we might have a chance of going up" because it's all we were missing. Well, that and someone who can protect.' For that role he brought in Julien de Sart but, as Omar Mascarell had done in 2014/15, the young loanee from the mainland (via Middlesbrough) struggled immensely.

Fulham's assurance only made McClaren, Martin and Morris more determined and in a last-ditch attempt to humiliate the Cottagers, Derby announced a new three-year deal for their number nine. Martin said at the time, 'I am very happy that the club and the manager see me as part of the long-term future. I am committed to being as successful as I possibly can be with Derby County. I enjoyed playing under Steve McClaren in the past and I feel that he got the best out of me, so I look forward to doing so as soon as possible.'

Martin was in an impossible situation and his comments only worsened proceedings. Fulham, understandably acting out of spite by this point, refused to cancel the loan and instead referenced in a statement that they had an option to purchase the forward. There was no budging and to his credit, Martin went on to appear 13 more times for the Londoners. But, with most of his touches now being booed by his own supporters, he added only one more goal.

The distraction and the obsession with Martin only harmed Derby. After a narrow loss at Newcastle, three home games in ten days was a welcome opportunity to make a top six claim. It was a catch-22. Win all three, McClaren's stock would be high and he would be adored by supporters with a side he didn't feel was good enough. Fail to take at least seven points and he'd be at the mercy of Mel, with talk of bottling only getting louder.

Two points were claimed from Bristol City, Cardiff and Burton. The rot was setting in. Defeats at Aston Villa and Blackburn worsened the play-off push and a Friday night in Brighton was one setback too many for Morris, who had spent the days before sharpening his knife once more.

McClaren says, 'We went into that Brighton game and I always remember Mel saying to me,' "You will know if you're going to get sacked. It won't be sudden; it'll be a gradual thing." So not a gradual sacking but I would know it was coming. Before that game he gave me a "you need to start perking up now" and I just thought "okay, appreciate that".'

A pre-sacking would be unheard of in any job aside from football management, probably at any other club too.

The Seagulls wiped the floor with Derby, a 3-0 win that could have been more. 'We had Bairdy at centre-back with Alex Pearce, and I was dreading it because Brighton were a bloody good team. We just couldn't cope with their intensity and front three, so I was really disappointed,' said McClaren.

'I know the game wasn't good, I know it was on TV but that's why you have to stay calm. You have to have leadership. We stayed calm; we were okay. I knew the next season we could build a bloody good team because we had that nucleus still. We were having a blip, that's it. But we'd have been all right.'

McClaren hadn't been given a second warning and instead, it was on the team bus back that he first got wind that his time may be up, 'I remember getting on the coach and someone got asked a question from a reporter about speculation that I'd be losing my job on Monday. I just went, "Eh?" We'd just lost to Brighton who were top of the league, with a team who is depleted. I said, "We're in the top half, we've done the job and it's the first I've heard of it." I spoke to my agent and I remember I was going to watch Burton I think the next day. I told Mel and said I wanted to go and watch them because they had Forest and we were playing them the next week. But I never got a phone call back.'

Though Paul Simpson hadn't returned to the club with McClaren, the two remained close. That weekend, prior to any decision being made, Simpson and his old boss shared a text conversation. 'Steve would ring to get things off his chest sometimes, ask my opinion on different things. He briefly mentioned that he'd want to speak to me in the summer to get me back in as well. They had a heavy Brighton defeat and I sent him a message on the Sunday morning, "Do you want to have a chat?" and he said, "Yeah, I do." So I said we'd meet for a coffee face to face, and then that night he texts me and says "I've been sacked" and that was the end again. We did meet but it wasn't to get things off his chest.'

McClaren was sacked – again. He'd been given just 26 games and, in the process, had taken the side from the bottom three to top-six contenders. But it wasn't enough for Morris. 'The only man who has all the answers over everything that season is Mel,' McClaren says. 'I was baffled by it then, I'm baffled by it now. The Sunday afternoon I got a call from Sam saying, "You're sacked." Wow. I was not happy. I still don't know to this day why. I just don't know why. I guess I just raised expectations too far. If it had been a slower, gradual move up and we got to halfway, I would have been fine. But we went on such a run and we got to the play-offs. It leaves a sour taste for me but that's football. I don't hold grudges but I do still feel like there is … unfinished business.'

* * *

Steve McClaren. Inigo Idiakez. Chris Powell. Paul Simpson and
Eric Steele. Even back to John Gregory and Colin Todd. And Roy
McFarland. For most, their time in the coaching team ended badly
and had a negative impact on their statuses. It would be enough to
ward any former player off making a return to Pride Park, but once
more things came full circle with the appointment of Gary Rowett.

Another member of Jim Smith's glorious side of the 1990s
and having made a name for himself at Burton and Birmingham –
where he was unfairly dismissed earlier that season – Rowett took
the poisoned chalice. 'Gary was the best coach I've worked with
or seen on a training pitch,' says Paul Peschisolido, who having
been outcasted by Phil Brown in 2005, was back then given the
opportunity to work with the then academy coach and saw early on
his pathway to senior management.

'He was relatable, he felt like one of the lads and his sessions were
so fluid and sharp. For me, he could be the future England manager
because of his attention to detail, his passion, his relationship with
players. I can't say enough good things about Gary.'

The appointment of Rowett was another step away from that
'Derby Way'. Similar to Pearson in the manner of his football,
Rowett's Birmingham side were compact and focused around
battlers as opposed to individuals. Early on in his Derby tenure,
that became clear. Will Hughes, still the most gifted youngster
produced in years, found himself out of the picture in favour of
a more solid, structured midfield of Bradley Johnson and Jacob
Butterfield. Matej Vydra too struggled for game time, with the
January addition of David Nugent in his spot.

By the confirmation of Rowett's appointment, play-off hopes
had been eradicated by all but the most optimistic supporter.
Instead of building for a push, his nine games in charge were
merely an opportunity to look towards building the side how he
would want to and familiarising himself with where things may
need tweaking.

This is Derby County though and that's not how things work. What would unfold next would transform the club and yet again drag their name through the mud. Over the course of the season there were drones, physical altercations, sackings, humiliations and some pretty filthy tactics. To round it off, boardroom implosion and allegations of serious financial misconduct.

* * *

Sam Rush and Mel Morris had the perfect working relationship to the outside eye. It was Morris who handed Rush a five-year contract in 2015. It was Rush who approached Morris about even getting involved with the club again. Each had the other's best interests at heart and under them, the Rams thrived.

Off the field, a stream of new partners got involved. Rush was vital in the iPro deal, the sponsorship from Just Eat too. Prior to Morris's involvement, he'd been the one who had seen the pathway to drag the club forward on the field from the lethargy of the Clough days. Through this, he had managed to bring an extra 10,000 into the stadium on a weekly basis.

One was rarely seen without the other when it came to public engagements. Supporter communication was at an all-time high after Rush's introduction of the fan forums multiple times through a season. It allowed supporters to hear from the decision-makers, providing a greater clarity behind the direction of the club. On the flip-side it also allowed some supporters to use the space as an opportunity to complain about the catering.

At the first forum with Clement as manager in October 2015, Morris introduced Rush in glowing terms. 'I think there was a misquote in the press. He said it was five years, I said I thought it was 20,' Morris gushed. 'He's the reason why I joined the club in the first place.'

Quite how things went so catastrophically wrong between the two is one of the only underlying mysteries during the recent history of the club and one that will probably never be revealed. The inquest began on 30 April 2017, when a club statement confirmed Rush was 'taking time off'. Within three days, time off became a sacking. 'Derby County Football Club has today dismissed with immediate effect, President and Chief Executive Officer Sam Rush on the grounds of gross misconduct and breach of fiduciary duty,' read a statement.

Rush released a statement of his own, speaking of his shock, Morris countering it with an intriguing interview in *The Ram*. He wrote, 'The decision came at the back end of a process that went on for about two and a half to three weeks. Often, in my businesses, I form a review. This one was a review of our financial and contract records in the business to reconcile pretty much everything that we had seen from a financial perspective, tying it back to the contracts relating to them.

'We've had a tremendous relationship, no question in my view. Characterised, it's a friendship. A strong friendship. I anticipate this will end up in the courts and we're relishing that opportunity.' Morris closed by saying, 'I say the season has been a disaster in many ways. I take responsibility along with the execs and indeed the footballing side of the house for that failure.'

The situation, as Morris predicted, would end in the courts. Morris sued one way; Rush sued back. Prior to this, Rush won his case for unfair dismissal. But with the release of a hefty document, the sheer delirium surrounding the situation reached epic new heights. In the document used by the club to formulate their case, it's difficult to pick out the most bizarre accusations. Here are some highlights:

- An allegation that Tom Ince's mum was paid £700,000 for scouting. Nope, not Paul Ince, the notorious former England footballer. Claire Ince.
- A £1m scouting report that recommended Derby sign Kylian Mbappe and Ousmane Dembele.

- The claim of ten sham transactions being made without prior approval of the board.
- A reported £100,000 ambassadorial role for Craig Bryson and £12,500 paid to West Brom for each George Thorne appearance.

Rush fired back, alleging all dealings were approved by the executive board and that Morris had even sat in on talks with Paul Ince in 2015. He spoke of not having the power to sign off on deals, these instead being done solely by Stephen Pearce, who sat ten metres away in the Pride Park executive offices. His defence spoke of Morris's perceived 'hands on' management of the club and what he recalled as the ordering of Paul Clement to take the captaincy away from Keogh.

The situation was messy and neither party is at liberty to discuss what came of the final agreements. Requests were made as part of the process of writing this book. A club statement in October 2018, 17 months after the dismissal, read 'The Club and Mr Rush have settled their respective differences on agreed terms, they are now moving on with their lives and no further comment will be made.'

So that clears that up then.

GARY'S TRAINERS

GARY ROWETT isn't from Derby. He's never supported the club, never had any affiliation towards them before signing as a player and yet, in 2017, he became a Ram for the third time, deeming Derby County as his club.

Rowett's love-in with the peaceful surroundings of Derbyshire began more than two decades earlier. From struggling to make the grade at Everton, his three years under Jim Smith were the best of his career. Compared to individuals like Igor Stimac and Stefano Eranio, Rowett went under the radar, but he was as pivotal to the promotion side and the European-pursuit squad as anybody else.

He recalls, 'We were a bit of a renegade bunch of free transfers to start with and I just remember every season we just seemed to bring another top player in, but they were top people too. Igor and Ace [Aljoša Asanović] came in first and then you had Eranio and [Francesco] Baiano, [Paulo] Wanchope and Jacob Laursen. We socialised together, we all lived in a very similar area. Everyone lived over on Heatherton Village because I think Peter Gadsby got everyone in his houses, but it was great because it built such a good team spirit up.

'When you actually look back, I remember beating Arsenal 3-0 at Pride Park, Chelsea 3-2 at the Baseball Ground. I look back at Dean Sturridge and just think, how much would he be worth now? You under-value it at the time, but he'd be a top, top striker. You don't get many of those periods in your career, where you look back and you have such a good group of people and players, and also the staff of Jim and Steve [McClaren]. A lot has been said about Jim but he was just binding it all together really with his humour and his character and his charisma. It's hard to say exactly what he did because he just made everyone feel so good. It was a really nice time.'

Seven years after leaving, he was back for phase two. A run coaching the youth team was Rowett's first venture into the post-playing side, an experience he describes as, 'Massive. I didn't just want to be one who jumped into a job on the basis of being a good footballer. I wanted to be someone who would learn the ropes and actually go into it knowing if I learnt it properly and made a statement, I could be a success.'

Even at that point, the signs were there. Terry Westley, at the time forced into the main role, simply said upon Rowett's decision to depart, 'Why are you leaving? You could be the manager here.'

So, just like the man he had replaced, the cycle continued. Player, to coach, to manager. 'I always felt it was a role I could achieve but it almost felt in some ways, in a strange way, that it was one of my targets. It's such a huge job,' he said.

Come March 2017, Rowett was one of the most in-demand British managers in the game. His role at Birmingham, only magnified further after Gianfranco Zola's horrendous spell in succession, had him in that curious corridor between top-six Championship and bottom-six Premier League roles. Norwich were in for him, Nottingham Forest and Aston Villa at differing times too.

He says, 'I was sat in the Joiners Arms in Quarndon having a meal with my family and I think there was a lot of speculation around me and the Norwich job. Derby had just been beaten 3-0 at Brighton and I got a phone call just asking if I'd be interested from my agent and it kind of developed fairly quickly. It was never going to come down to money or anything like that, it was almost like if I was offered it, I would never turn that opportunity down.'

The Brighton fiasco spelt doom for McClaren but allowed a pathway back into management for Rowett, three months on from his Blues departure. Still in the area and familiar with Morris, Rowett's name first became linked prior to McClaren's return and with an air of unease still sitting around that second spell in charge, Rowett's unveiling was some time in the making.

Allowing Rowett nine games of relative nothingness to assess his new squad, it was on this basis that he was forced into some difficult decisions. He continues, 'We were transitioning away from some of the players who had been there and were so highly rated. The reason I came in was that the club felt it needed to go down a slightly more pragmatic route. They tried the 4-3-3 and the free-flowing football but they hadn't managed to get up into the Premier League, so the whole point of me was to be more pragmatic and see if we could bring some of the elements of the Birmingham team I had to Derby.'

That he did. Rowett's Blues were steady. Built on a budget and with a side unfit for the play-offs, Derby had experienced Rowett's philosophy first-hand. Their 2-2 draw in 2015 was the first warning, a 3-0 victory at Pride Park a season later offering further proof of the clinical style he looked to adopt. If Derby, with a squad who only a season earlier had shown no capability of embracing Pearson's resolute style of play, were to succeed, they'd need a new look.

The first cut was the deepest, as Will Hughes made way. Already shown a glimpse into the lack of a role he would have under his latest new manager, it was Watford, not Barcelona, who made the bid. In that same portacabin-turned-media suite that he was unveiled in by the M25, he can't stop the smirk breaking across his face. 'Every manager is different,' he begins.

He was right of course. Besides Clough and McClaren, no manager had got the best from Hughes. Asked to play deeper at times, out for Clement's tenure and without enough to judge him on under Pearson, the once boy wonder had lost his way. He continued, 'You're not going to be everyone's cup of tea and he was honest with me and said I wasn't his sort of player. I had to accept that. It was best for both parties at the time to move on because having played the majority of games, I didn't want to be one of those players sitting on the bench and picking up a wage. It was the right decision.' Will he ever return? Hughes laughs. 'I'm still young.'

Right decision for Hughes, but questions began to be asked of the club when £8m was the reported fee. At a time when Britt Assombalonga fetched £15m, it felt an insultingly low sale. Jacob Murphy, two months Hughes's senior and with 119 fewer appearances at Championship level, cost Newcastle £12m. The £8m (if it even was that high) was the same as Kevin Stewart's transfer from Liverpool to Hull. Stewart had 11 goalless Premier League appearances to warrant that move.

It was an indication as to where things were going. Tom Ince, another player who boasted on his day the best individual quality in the division, swiftly followed. His sale to promoted Huddersfield for £10m paved the way for Tom Lawrence's arrival. Hughes and Ince's sales rubbed much of the quality associated with McClaren-ball from the squad. The Derby Way, no matter how many times it was fed to the fans, wasn't working and in its place came an era known to many as the era of the shithouse. No longer would there be a focus on match domination, because it hadn't got the club into the Premier League. The summer signings began to show how different things would begin to look.

First came Andre Wisdom. A career stalled after his role in 2013/14, he added steel without attacking intent to the right side. To his left, Curtis Davies joined. More associated with stopping than playing, his signing came with a knowledge of how to get out of the division. After all, two years earlier he'd led Hull City there with victory against Derby. The third incision of power to the squad came with a face almost forgotten from the Pride Park corridors.

Since being sold in a desperate chase for finance in 2005, Tom Huddlestone had almost reached his full potential. He'd played for England, appeared in the Champions League with Tottenham and progressed to a position where his right foot was one of the most sought-after prizes in English football. A thing of majesty and with an overall technique likened to that of Glenn Hoddle, his signing was another coup. Where Hughes was more likely to roam, there was no doubt about where Huddlestone could be found for 90 minutes on a Saturday afternoon; right within the centre circle.

Here began a theme though. Huddlestone and Davies were both past 30. Scott Carson, Chris Baird, Bradley Johnson, David Nugent and Richard Keogh were all already there. Craig Bryson, Jason Shackell and Darren Bent too. Derby, who reached Wembley with an average age of 24, were getting old. Or rather, they were getting experienced.

'Signing older players was based on the fact we had to get a net spend that season to help the finances,' Rowett begins. 'We made about three or four million in transfer fees that season and how do you get players in, inexpensively on that? Curtis was £500k because we found a clause in his contract. Do you go and sign a young player for £6m or sign someone who has been in there, done it and been promoted before? You had Joe Ledley [free transfer] who only came in because the Kieftenbeld deal got messed up.'

Almost overnight, Johnson had become one of the senior heads in the midfield. Mainstays Hughes and Hendrick were gone, Jacob Butterfield found himself loaned out. Johnson said, 'The lads that Gary brought in weren't a case of "they're old", it was lads who had been there and done it and they knew what it took to get out of the league. Hudds and Curtis beat us in the play-offs. It was a case of just knowing we had a good squad when he came in, but different managers have a different way of playing. His philosophy was around experience and having a knowhow of games because coming in from Birmingham, he just said, "Look, everyone talks about this Derby Way but it's not got you anywhere." He was a realist.'

* * *

A resolute beginning of the season, with seven points from four games, provided a glimpse into the make-up of Rowett's philosophy. Abandoned was the need to keep the ball for the sake of it. A 1-0 home victory against Preston finished with just 41 per cent possession. Weeks later, in a draw at Brentford, they had 24 per cent. This wasn't the Derby Way and those on the field resembled that. Come one Saturday afternoon in Sheffield, two of those who had been at the heart of that motto endured afternoons of similar emotions.

First to Johnny Russell. To Derby fans, the perception of Russell was that he was the heart of the team, the joker behind the scenes and just a chap you'd want a beer with. For the first three years, that was accurate. Things changed though and the Russell emerging into 2017/18 was a shadow of the one even he recognised. He says, 'There was some behind-the-scenes stuff the year before and I never felt the need to come and speak out because the club had been so good to me. I didn't really want to go back to that place that I was in the season before feeling-wise because it's the worst season I've had in my career, my head and my heart weren't in it and it was a difficult time to come through. But I just felt I needed something different to try and rejuvenate me.'

What he certainly didn't need was one of the toughest weeks in his career. It started with a contract saga. With his existing deal up at the end of the season, he turned down his first offer. 'They came back right before the Sheffield United game and the way they had worked it, it was slightly worse than the first, so I was just like, "Oh for fuck's sake!" I said no to that one but still wanted to negotiate, and I think this was by the Thursday. They released it to the press that I had turned down a new contract and then I scored an own goal at Sheffield United two days later.'

Over the mid-2010s, there were some special own goals. Lee Grant's double-fisted effort at Wolves and Darren Bent's aggressive swipe against Leicester in the FA Cup come to mind. But for sheer technique, Russell tops the list. 'I came all the way across and it shouldn't have been my guy. I worked so hard to get back into the position and I've read his touch, tried to hook it away but I've caught it so clean on my right foot, and I have never hit a ball like that, I just drilled it bottom corner.'

The other man that day who was set to experience similar emotions was Craig Bryson. There had been murmurs of interest for the Scottish international and with the side beginning to transform from any semblance of that built by Clough and mastered by McClaren, the need for him at the club fell into question. 'There's a picture I always look at of me after scoring against Sheffield United and I look gutted,' he says.

Rowett's system incorporated two holding midfielders and no box-to-box man. Bryson continues, 'You're not going to get the best out of me playing deeper but if that's where he wanted me to play, I'd have tried to adapt. But he maybe had better options in there with Tom and Bradley at the time, which you kind of understand if you're not playing. I wanted to fight for my place and stay and we both agreed on that, but I think he had an idea of a couple of players he wanted to bring in, Kieftenbeld could play that position. But then another conversation we had, he said he couldn't get the players out that he wanted to get out.'

Bryson departed for a season-long loan to Cardiff on deadline day. It was here that his promotion dream would come true. In his place came the experienced Joe Ledley, another player past 30 but one who had considerable top-flight experience on his CV.

The Welshman, who had starred in Wales's run to the final four of Euro 2016, was joining a side still struggling with an identity crisis. True, they had dealt far better with the new focus than they had under Pearson, but there were still significant issues to iron out. Rowett remembers, 'After one game we had a meeting with the players where you could still just feel the disappointment from the previous few seasons because we had quite a few who had been there over that period of time. We had a sort of "wow, this is a harder job than even I could imagine" because things didn't seem to go our way. I remember the United game and things didn't go that badly but as often is the case in management, it can turn against you.'

Matej Vydra's first season in a Derby shirt was a horrendous one. Within a month of arriving, the man who paid a record fee for him had been sacked and McClaren returned with the sole ambition of bringing back a striker he already knew. Vydra looked and felt unwanted, with his two goals under Rowett the highest return of any of the four managers throughout the campaign. Averaging a goal every seven games over the course of his past two Championship seasons, he'd retreated into his shell by the time Rowett had even arrived.

But at home to Hull, signs of why Pearson spent £8m began to appear. That night, in a 5-0 hammering, he scored twice. His tally was already just one below his entire 2016/17 total. Surrounded by experience and paired with David Nugent, he had a purpose. 'We went into a 4-3-2-1 which we partly put in because of Vydra,' Rowett begins. 'We'd watched his games previously where he was having to play out wide in a 4-3-3 but most of his goals came as a second striker and he was one I just felt that, you know, he'd scored 20 goals in the division and had been promoted with Watford, I felt there was such a talent there.

'We saw him in training and he was so talented and so technical and so quick. Yet there were some obvious flaws psychologically where you needed to get him in a good place and for him to feel like you really trusted him. I did an awful lot of work with him of showing him clips of previous goals he'd scored, building him up with the other players which was just as important. It wasn't just about him feeling good, it was about the other players valuing him as a player and realising how good he actually was.'

One of those who noticed was Bradley Johnson, who says, 'Gary knew he wouldn't have to come and put his arm around me and see how I was doing; he knew what sort of character I was. But someone like Vyds he had to look after and make him feel loved and he did that. He was always talking and joking around with Vyds and if he ever needed anything, he'd give it to him. When the manager does that for you, he gets the best out of you.'

The words and the meetings with Vydra were one thing; the psychological work was another. To many, being told how good you are would feed into a delusion of grandeur. But such was the fragility of Vydra, damaged almost beyond repair after two horrendous years, Rowett's methods simply brought him to the level of any other young, budding goalscorer.

'We put a highlights reel of him on all the TVs that Mel had put up in the training ground and people would come up to him and just say "wow Vyds, what a goal that was." Little things would build his confidence and his self-esteem. We did a lot of work with him and I had a lot of one-to-one meetings with him in my office. People would speak and say we were lucky because Vydra had a great season. Well yeah, but he wasn't in the team before. When we went in, he was with the 23s, so we had to do a lot of work with him. Once you get him in a good place, he wins games single-handedly,' said Rowett.

The initial signs of life stemmed back to Vydra's first outing under Rowett the season before, with a goal at Forest. Now, a man rejuvenated, he did it again in October 2017. It took the Czech marksman just 24 seconds to open the scoring against the Rams' big rivals, Nugent sealing victory in the second half. Three more wins immediately followed, two of those impressive results on the road at Norwich and Leeds.

As well as Vydra, the influence of Sam Winnall was crucial. His quick-fire brace at Elland Road came in a rare start alongside Chris Martin, who was soon to be loaned out again. 'Sam was another one who was just a goalscorer,' Rowett says. 'He's one of those players where if he doesn't score in training he'd be annoyed, if he doesn't win games he's annoyed and I think he came from a position in Sheffield [Wednesday, who he had joined on loan from] where he wasn't playing and he just grew into the role.'

Nights like Leeds saw new ways adapt in Rowett's managerial style. When compared to McClaren's football, it was ugly. But as he told the squad upon arrival, that football had taken them nowhere. A squad of promise had become one filled with end results. Of the 18 at Elland Road, 12 had played in the top division.

The steeliness displayed in the squad allowed them to go to places like Middlesbrough and Ipswich and win games. The Riverside saw Vydra strike thrice in a 3-0 victory, Winnall two in a three-pointer at Portman Road. Even at home, teams like Burton and Aston Villa were being seen off. The move from McClaren's total football was difficult to adapt to with fans and players used to controlling the ball, but 33 per cent of possession against Villa resulted in a 2-0 success. Derby were stifling their way to the top of the league.

By new year, it was the familiar feeling of top two for the Rams. Wolves, possessing a squad bankrolled by a relationship with super-agent Jorge Mendes, were uncatchable. But that second spot was there for the taking. Two points behind them were Cardiff and Bristol City, two sides who really possessed no more than Rowett had at his disposal. Cardiff may have had the knowhow of Neil Warnock but their squad (Bryson aside) had few stand-out individuals. Bristol City were a team with a work ethic but a tendency to fall away. And with Rowett now boasting a fuller squad of wise old heads, it should have only taken that knowledge to maintain the push.

* * *

So quite why Derby only won six of their final 20 matches is a mystery. The 2014/15 collapse was understandable. The rumours of McClaren had the club on edge, the loss of Martin and Eustace tore the side apart. In 2015/16, Clement's sacking and a January of questionable signings disrupted the structure of the changing room. A season later, McClaren's steam had run out, Derby returning to a more suitable mid-table position. Yet this time around, there was a new squad. Only Keogh, Russell, Thorne and Forsyth remained from that first capitulation, and one of those was about to depart.

When Russell rejected his second contract offer in August, the news was fed to the media. The fans had begun to see an individual who they perceived to have ambitions elsewhere and come January, the ambitions would be realised. He said, 'People started to take notice of the MLS when Beckham went over and that's when I started to watch it at night on Sky. I loved America, always went there for my summers so it was just a place I'd always wanted to go to and I thought it would just be a dream. We actually played Sunderland on the first Friday night and there were a couple of rumours that came out, clubs were sniffing about and they were asking if it was something I'd be interested in. I wasn't saying no to the idea.

'Although I'd got back to my old self in the way I was playing, it was just something that was constantly niggling at me and I just felt it came back up again. My daughter had just been born so I felt at the time that it was something we always wanted to try, and it just felt like the timing was right. Ideally I'd have liked to have seen out the season but the decision was made, Kansas wanted me in to start their season, Derby didn't want me about knowing that I wasn't going to be there which I can understand.'

In his place came Kasey Palmer, a Chelsea loanee with bags of potential and an unusual amount of individuality for a Rowett side. Palmer, whose Derby career never truly got going after finding himself stuck behind the coaching staff in the dugout, should have been joined by another youngster.

The January window is a hellish one. It's an opportunity for the wealthier to derail seasons by snatching players who have impressed thus far, while for those with promotion ambitions, clubs can name their price for those in desperation at getting over the line. Come deadline day 2018, the situation was being experienced first-hand by Rowett who, after days of negotiation, thought he'd landed one of the Premier League's hottest prospects. He remembers, 'You end up sitting on deadline day wondering who's going to sign because there are so many names thrown at you. We'd done a deal for Ademola Lookman at Everton. It got to seven o'clock and we were waiting for him to come down and then we were watching Sky and he signed for a club in Germany.

'We'd actually agreed the deal and then suddenly you've got four hours to get another player in and it's how difficult it is. You've got your list but you're looking at then doing deals that can be done. It's a notoriously difficult window and you can make mistakes in it, down to reasons beyond your control. We ended up letting Craig Bryson go in the summer to sign Kieftenbeld because we knew that deal was done, and in the end it fell through. We would never have let Bryson go if we couldn't bring him in, so there's so many things that can happen and that always seem to happen. But some of those windows can be crucial in defining your season.'

He had managed to get one more deal over the line in the month though. In August 2007, Cameron Jerome struck his first Premier League goals against Derby in a 2-1 win for Birmingham City. Just over a decade later, he was called upon to try and fire the Rams back there. Jerome recalls, 'It was a move that was really planned since the summer. Gary got in touch with my agent to find out if I'd be interested in going over to Derby and I was keen on doing it in the summer, so I went for it in January.' A cut-price option at £1m, Jerome's capture was simply to solidify the striking options and soon after moving from Norwich, his importance grew with Sam Winnall ruled out for the campaign.

Jerome was another of those who had the experience Rowett craved. His direct replacement of the outgoing Martin centred more around how the manager looked for his strikers to work. Rowett said, 'Chris was coming in and out of the side but the team wasn't suited around his strengths. He didn't have those midfield runners in that system, there was another main striker behind rather than having the two athletic midfielders that Chris played so well with. Cammy just fitted the bill of a player who wouldn't cost us a massive amount and would be a good deal.'

Jerome's issue didn't come from his goalscoring, it came from the timing that he put pen to paper. February was right around the corner and once again, it was to cause meltdown. A 2-0 loss at Sheffield Wednesday was not a disaster. It proved monumental though. Petrified at the prospect of yet another collapse, every section of the club became on edge from one result and fear engulfed Pride Park.

'Don't you think Derby's a weird club?' Jerome asks. 'If you look at it from the outside, the squad was up there with the best in the division – if not the best – but at that time, a couple of rocky results and everyone just starts to question things and the manager starts to question his tactics.

'The fans would get restless and Derby have obviously got history of being in strong positions in prior seasons and not getting over the line, so that then has a negative effect on the whole club. It just felt like a "oh they're doing it again" sort of thing, that sort of mentality. The boys might have believed in the changing rooms that we're good enough, but it was just like the atmosphere in the club was sucking everything down. That played a major part in us continuing that bad run for so long, I think. I know obviously the fans want the best and everyone does, and it's hard to say the fans wanted us to lose a game, but when we played at home it was away fans giving the banter and it just creates that negative atmosphere.'

Jerome, within three weeks of his switch, hit the nail on the head. He'd played at Pride Park in previous years when the fear had begun to become noticeable. Being inside the club though was when the magnitude of the fear factor struck him. The fans felt it and almost expected it. There was no avoiding it for the players, or for Rowett.

He continued, 'It's amazing because at a club like Derby, everything is magnified. I remember us going on that unbelievable run and I think we maybe went to somewhere like Blackburn and lost, we lost one game and it was the first in a while, and I can just remember the feeling. It was weird, it just felt like our chance of promotion was over, even though we were second in the league. There was so much talk about the wobble and it was so hard to change and turn it around.

'Derby is such a fragile place that if one thing went wrong, everybody would jump on it. National press, local press, everyone. It was no fault of their own but it's just such a great narrative for everyone to look at.'

The fear emanating from the stands to the pitch only made the situation worse. From being second at the turn of February, the club, not just the players, collapsed again. Eight games without a victory had taken them 17 points off the top two.

This capitulation was the most extreme yet. In the three previous campaigns, there was reasoning behind it, but this was without explanation. A new squad, a new playing style and yet the same fragility as seen so many times before. It was most on show on another Friday evening, this time against Sunderland.

The visitors, bottom of the division and 'diabolical' as Jerome remembers them to be, were a wreck of a football club. The Netflix series following that campaign showed them to be in a shambolic state. But they came to Pride Park and won 4-1.

'Sunderland is a prime example,' Jerome says. 'We managed to get played off the park by them and 4-1 flattered us. It's at that stage where you're just looking around and thinking, "How are we getting this so wrong?" Like many have probably said before me, it was an all-round factor. I wouldn't put it down to one thing, I think the players got anxious and not as relaxed on the pitch, the management team and everyone felt the pressure and the stress. But it all relates to each other. The fans relate to the players, the players to the fans, the management team to the players, visa-versa, and it's a knock-on effect and something which had a real bad effect on the players at the time.'

It was this defeat that again had pockets of fans calling for change. Some, still longing for more possession-based football, had reached their limit with Rowett. The style was acceptable when it got results but the minute it stopped working, the atmosphere turned. What they were to get instead of more upheaval was even more limitation in the side.

It began at Preston where, off the back of that catastrophic evening, they stole a 1-0 victory with their only shot on target. Tom Lawrence's winner that day was followed by a 3-0 beating of Bolton, where Vydra scored his first goal in just over two months. With the loss of confidence in the side, it had affected the forward once again.

Another loss of form was on the cards though. Defeat at Wolves can be swept to the side, particularly when Ruben Neves's ridiculous volley is considered. Defeat for the second time in a row at the Pirelli Stadium can't though. 3-1 to Burton, just a notch below the 4-1 to Sunderland in the season review of most damaging results. Something had to change if Derby had any sniff of a play-off spot and change it did. There would be no return to the Derby Way though and instead, Rowett shut the doors.

Johnson, one of those to come in for maintained fan disgruntlement, was asked to sit even deeper. Around him, Weimann and Lawrence would retreat. Two left-backs would come into play and Rowett's plan B became simply to contain. 'What we were doing wasn't working,' Johnson admits, 'and credit to him for realising that and actually going "forget that, go back to basics and this is how we're doing it".

'The quality wasn't coming through, so sometimes you then have to strip back and just say "listen, we're going back to basics. Defend like your life is on the line and then you'll get confidence off that and build off it. You win one game doing it that way and then you slowly start getting back to how you were." Credit to him because he recognised that, asked us to defend from the front and let teams have the ball. Whereas normally fans at the club were used to us controlling it, we'd always been a possession-based side and we'd always batter teams with the ball. He said, "I don't care, just let the other team have the ball."'

It started at home to Cardiff on an evening that was weeks in the making. When a smattering of snow fell on Pride Park in March, it shouldn't have counted for much. The stadium had only ever had one match postponed for adverse weather conditions and by Sunday morning, the sun was shining. But the decision to postpone the midday kick-off enraged Cardiff, their squad and particularly their manager, Neil Warnock.

Derby had an injury crisis at this point and Rowett had told the press as much in the run-up. Upon postponement, fans still reached the ground which, by that point, showed few traces of heavy snowfall. The club shop also tweeted that it would be remaining open that day. Cardiff and their supporters' groups contacted the EFL, furious at what they saw as underhand tactics. Warnock, a master of that particular skill, branded the cancellation a 'stitch-up' and a 'disgrace'. Rowett, having already drawn the ire of Nottingham for his choice of matchday footwear, turned his attention to Warnock. A simple comment of 'I didn't actually realise he's a qualified health and safety inspector' was enough to claim victory in the duel.

Cardiff's squad were equally angry. Defender Greg Halford tweeted as much on the day from outside the stadium, Curtis Davies simply replying with the eyes emoji. Things would only get more bizarre though courtesy of Sean Morrison, the Cardiff skipper. A leaked video only escalated the hilarity in the build-up to the rearrangement, calling out Richard Keogh and his central defensive partners Alex Pearce and Jason Shackell. The reasons for the abuse ranged from Keogh's trait of cutting the ball back to his defensive partners right through to the fact Shackell 'doesn't show his dick'.

You had to spare a thought for Craig Bryson in all of this. He said, 'I was actually in Edinburgh with my missus when I saw it, I just saw it on social media like everybody else. I think it was heading into an international break so the lads were all away on holiday and we had a few days off, so I have no idea why it happened or what it was about, I think it was a just a good bit of banter … I say good, maybe not.'

By this point, Keogh had not only been the victim of Morrison's viral embarrassment, he'd relinquished his grip on the captaincy and, temporarily, his place in the side for the first time since signing in 2012. In the armband was Davies, the more vocal of the two and for Rowett, offering additional wisdom where defence grew in importance, 'Curtis was the perfect captain for me. I always look for someone you can build a bit of a relationship with, speak to a lot about certain things and really be your sort of manager on the pitch. That's what you want, someone who will extol your characteristics and virtues, and it's why we brought the likes of Curtis in. The team had fell short, had not quite made it and I just felt that there were certain elements that might give us a chance moving forward.'

Rowett's new look had first been trialled against Middlesbrough to no effect, but with practice it would come a step closer to perfection. The back five were bolstered by Weimann and Lawrence, both tucking in front of Andre Wisdom and Marcus Olsson. Johnson and Huddlestone were the solid base without attacking privileges and Jerome, well, he was asked to do everything else.

To his credit, he did. Despite falling behind to Cardiff in the rearranged game, it was Jerome who was the victor in one of the worst moves ever crafted in English football. In the 20 seconds before his scuffed finish, the ball touched the ground once and was an apt goal for the new Derby. The second, from more slack Cardiff defending, was powered in by Vydra before the perfect finale. 'That season we got promoted with Norwich, Cameron was always moaning because he'd start every game, run his socks off for 60-odd minutes and then Gary Hooper would come on and score two goals and he'd get all the credit. But he'd tire out the defence and it was a running joke,' says Johnson.

Johnson's memory of Jerome always seemed to end around the hour mark but at Derby, Jerome was in it for the long haul. With the clock running down, the striker's engine saw him nudge Morrison off the ball, place him well out of danger and slip it through the legs of the onrushing Neil Etheridge.

The victory saved the season and gave Rowett faith in his new system, which now revolved around their star forward. 'Gary just wanted me to go out there and be strong, be aggressive and work the defenders. He found a formula that seemed to work and it got us to where it got us,' says Jerome.

A 1-1 draw at Villa Park the following weekend kept play-off hopes in Derby's hands and a final-day victory over Barnsley ensured the familiarity of the top six for two more ties. To come were Slavisa Jokanovic's Fulham, hurting at missing out on the top two. In their ranks they boasted the creative control of Tom Cairney, the terrifying pace of Ryan Sessegnon and Aleksandar Mitrovic's brute strength.

The home leg was almost perfect. Jerome was again the man to rise, thundering a header 34 minutes in for Derby to take a one-goal lead to Craven Cottage. It was the Rams' only shot on target and with 26 per cent possession during the evening, Johnson had to simply watch for the most part. He recalls, 'We would just let them pass from side to side. Fulham could pass anyone off the pitch so it wasn't a surprise that they had all of the ball at our place. They'd have 40 passes but they weren't going anywhere. Gary knew the focus wouldn't go down well with a few fans but he could see that bigger picture and where we were going with it.'

It also saw a mammoth effort from the back line, particularly Davies. His role of centre-back was relinquished, the task simply shadowing Mitrovic all evening. The Serb's goalscoring record for the half season was better than one in two but Rowett's ploy of squeezing his ability to find an inch of space paid off, remembering how Davies 'absolutely nullified him'.

The question was on repetition and although Derby had delivered solid showings on the road in the final few weeks, there was to be no repeat. The Rams, who increased the defensive focus with Ikechi Anya's first start since March, looked more vulnerable from minute one. 'I made a couple of decisions where we left Vydra out from the start, feeling that their passing ability meant he'd be better coming off the bench like he did against Cardiff,' Rowett says. 'Maybe I should have started him looking back. We ended up playing Ikechi as well who had been injured and ultimately, Fulham were just a little bit better than us and they rightly got promoted.'

Two goals after half-time were the killer blows. Rowett adds, 'Fulham were probably the best team in the division since Christmas and were such a good team at home. We actually started quite well but it was one of those nights. Mitrovic was absolutely brilliant on the night and we didn't deal with him in quite the same way, which was no surprise because he was a Premier League striker, and they just performed really well. It was just a night where you had to take your hat off and say you were outperformed, outplayed. It summed our season up I'd say. We just didn't have what Fulham and Wolves had, so therefore we fell short.

'I still felt that the season was something of a success though. And at that point, we were only two or three players away from being a side who would get promoted the season after and I think that was my thoughts after that one.'

* * *

Rowett was, even after the collapse, a man in demand. From January onwards, rumours had begun to circle about the Stoke City job. Not with the same severity as those which derailed McClaren's first tenure, but they were noticeable. It was hoped that the signing of a new contract in January would stop the interest and seemingly it did, with City selecting Paul Lambert to relegate them instead. But following his sacking in May, it came full circle.

Six days after the season was cut short, Rowett asked Morris for permission and a day later, he was installed as the new manager. Immediately, the outcry began. 'Snake' was the word of the moment and Rowett, who had told the media that Derby was his dream job, was hounded. A season later and with his new side struggling, thousands of supporters made the journey to Stoke to wave inflatable reptiles at Rowett, many more taking glee in his dismissal as the Potters flew to the wrong end of the table.

It was, under Morris's chairmanship, another summer to search for a new manager. Rowett, who was hugely criticised for what many perceived to be a financial move, has the opportunity to open up about how that week really went between he and his boss, starting with some backstory on their relationship: 'I had a great one with Mel. I went in and heard all these stories about him that would put you on edge, but I found him to be absolutely brilliant.

'He's a guy that massively cares about the club, he desperately wants to do the right thing and desperately wants success. He was very driven by wanting to know that you were maximising your resources and you were doing everything you could do to win games, which I'm sure is the way he's built his businesses up. He'd always come in for a beer after games and bring his family into the manager's office and he and his family were absolutely a pleasure to work with. At the end people think that split is acrimonious, and people think this and that but people make decisions, that's that.

'I sat down at the end of the season with him and we were just talking about what we needed to do to get promoted. I felt we were two or three players away, but it was clear to me at that point that the club were wanting to go down a different route which I felt was going to be very, very difficult to achieve and very hard to achieve in one season. It was a case of slashing the wage bill and just getting it right down.'

Going into the Pride Park role, Rowett was aware of the financial tightrope he would have to walk and managed it excellently the previous summer with over £12m generated and a significant net gain on transfers. This time around though, he felt the situation would be more severe.

He continues, 'I was just honest with Mel. You have to believe in the plan to be able to take it forward and feel like you could make the team better and it felt a bit like a different approach for me, so it was just hard to imagine it being successful.

'It was more the speed of which the changes were going to happen that got me. The financial constraints were one thing, but it was the speed of how quick it would have to be. It was almost going to be a massive clear-out and lots more youngsters coming through, which is hard because when you work with a load of players and you've built a relationship with a lot of them, to suddenly have to just part with a lot of them is difficult. It is difficult to start again because in my mind, we've just had the play-offs where we've won the first leg, lost the second leg and so therefore if you can just add two players to it, you won't be far off.

'I just think it was a role that suited another coach than me, that was just me being honest. I'd always wanted to manage Derby and you have to understand, it was a really difficult decision to leave but I just felt it would be hard for me to be able to believe in the plan moving forward and therefore I chose to go to Stoke. People make decisions in life and it's one I had to, at the time I felt it was the right decision for me. That was it, really. It was disappointing that I made that decision to go but it was mine to make, at the time there were those circumstances around it and it is what it is.'

Simply, Rowett left because he didn't believe he was the right man for the job. Little different to any other role but in a position where in excess of 40,000 follow your every move, scrutiny was inevitable. He was a snake, a traitor, his trainers were now terrible. With that one decision, Rowett became public enemy number one.

Following my first approach for this book, he opted not to speak as every time he does, it ends in abuse. Months down the line however, he hopes the situation has calmed. 'Unless people know the circumstance and are sat in your shoes, they're always going to judge it on "you've left the club therefore you're a traitor" and I understand that. Derby County has been a big part of my life and I understand how important it is to people, I get that, so when you take the decision to leave you know the criticism is going to come.

But ultimately for me, I didn't leave for money or on bad terms. I left because I felt I desperately wanted to get promoted out of that division and I just wasn't sure how we were going to do that and I felt as though it wasn't the plan we were looking at now, it was more to rebuild.

'So yeah, I look back on my time with fondness because we did a decent job from ninth to sixth, but I get the criticism because as a manager, you get it every time you lose a game. It's ironic though because I still live in the area and I speak to a lot of people now about it and they're all brilliant with me. We talk about my time there and I have a massive fondness still for the club, but it will move forward with me just being a small speck on the history of it, but nobody can take that away though. If you could lose February from Derby's season though, they'd have probably been promoted about six or seven times by now.'

HI, SPY, CRY, BYE

IF YOU were Mel Morris, what choice would you have made in the summer of 2018? Cursing at the loss of another manager and with costs needing to be cut again, you've got two options. Do you a) hire Mick McCarthy, a man who will solidify your club and build on the foundations Rowett had forged, albeit without much excitement and likely without your crucial players. Or do you b) give the job to an unproven, recently retired footballer with minimal coaching experience and no connections to the club. All praise to the chairman because when that second option turns out to be one of the greatest English footballers of all time, the choice becomes a little simpler.

Experience hadn't worked in Morris's appointments so far and although Paul Clement didn't have a track record in management, his coaching background spoke for itself. So when Frank Lampard came on to the market, it was a risk-free decision. His résumé as a manager was empty, but it wasn't required.

'I turned to my wife and said, "Fucking hell, that's Frank Lampard calling me!" Craig Bryson laughs. There was no bigger appointment Derby could have made. For any club, it would be an enormous coup. A record goalscorer, Premier League and Champions League winner, one of the few members of Sven's golden generation who kept his nose clean. Lampard's signature was a victory for the club on so many levels. Commercially, sponsors wanted to be associated with the Lampard brand. Internationally, the media wanted to cover his every move as a manager.

Playing wise, people wanted to be inspired by him. So many greats before him had found management a different beast but they were able to at least provide momentary gains for the clubs they wore the tracksuit of. Whether Lampard worked out or not, there would be benefits for Derby.

After all, who wouldn't want to share a training pitch with him? His new squad, all in different corners of the earth at the time of the announcement, slowly gathered themselves. For Bradley Johnson, he was one of the many who had come up against Lampard on the pitch. He recalls, 'I was buzzing when he got the job because he was someone I've looked up to throughout my whole life as a midfielder. You know, he's one of the best midfielders in this country, if not the world. What he's done in the game is just unbelievable. So, for him to come here and for me to get the chance to work underneath him and him being your manager, I was very much looking forward to working with him.'

A year earlier, Bryson was cast aside. Now, he found himself wanted by a man who had mastered his position on the pitch, 'If I couldn't learn from him, I wouldn't learn from anybody. I remember him phoning me and saying to my wife, "That's Frank Lampard on the phone!" I was in a wee bit of awe. Then I was in the gym with my mate up in Glasgow and he text me. I was just showing my mate like "ooh, Frank's texting me". Everybody was like that for a wee bit, it was surreal. These are people you only see on TV and you watch for years, he's then phoning and texting you and wanting you to be a big part of his team.'

The impact of Lampard on the squad he would be joining was monumental, but then there was the draw he would present for potential signings. Inevitable rumours around former team-mates began to circle and Salomon Kalou's name was bandied about. But the task from Morris was to reduce the age of the side and to do that, Frank's connections would be pivotal.

Inevitably, all eyes turned to Chelsea. Lampard's capture meant that Jody Morris, the mastermind of seven trophies for the Blues' youth team, would be joining. Morris entered with considerably more experience as a coach than Lampard, but the manager had the bigger reputation. Together, they concocted the perfect hybrid.

Mason Mount was known by the pair. Trained and successful under Morris, idolising Lampard, he was tipped for major things having had a successful season at Vitesse Arnhem in the Eredivisie. Why he would jump at the opportunity to work under his idol and the man who provided him with youth team glory is no long story. On the same day as Mount, Lampard would greet Harry Wilson.

Fresh from his successful loan spell at Hull City, Wilson had signed a five-year contract with Liverpool just a week earlier. He'd never met the manager, yet when the opportunity arose to link, it was too good to turn down. 'I think there were 11 or 12 teams in total which were enquiring about taking me,' begins the Welshman. 'Derby were one and since speaking in that first phone call with Frank, I just felt everything he was saying. I felt like he was the one who had watched my game the most and he told me how he'd seen me at Hull, he'd been over my games and liked the way I played, told me how he saw me fitting into the way he wanted to play.'

What may surprise is that the name Frank Lampard meant nothing to Wilson. Not in a disrespectful way, but he had no interest in joining a club purely for the name of a manager. Instead, the draw was the ideology and extent of Lampard's knowledge. He continues, 'A lot of people ask me what he was like but I think, even if he wasn't who he is, I just felt the way he was on the phone I could have been speaking to anyone. He was the one who had analysed my game the most and that was the massive incentive for me; it was just a bonus that it did happen to be Frank Lampard.'

Wilson and Mount may have joined on the same day but aside from coming up against one another in youth football, they had no relationship. Still, they were soon to be forced into one. It began when paired together to live in a hotel, before searching for a place to crash for the season. Their pad would be Lee Grant's old house, now vacant after his move to Manchester United. Equipped with a gym and surrounded by team-mates, the duo would settle into Derby life together.

Wilson said, 'I felt we were similar people, both hard working and don't really like to go out off the pitch, so we just got on well. And that helped our relationship on the pitch because we understood each other and each other's game. Fik I knew as well having been with him at Hull the year before.'

Lampard's scavenge of promising young loanees continued with the addition of Fikayo Tomori. Like Mount, he had been at the heart of Morris's Chelsea side and despite a rawness to his game, was seen as one to grow under the tutelage of Keogh and Curtis Davies.

The loanees were one thing but the decision by Mel Morris to rescind his conversation with Rowett and inject more funds into the transfer budget began to raise eyebrows. Rowett's talks with Mel post-Fulham had centred around the need to strip the squad and build on a budget, the key reason he opted for Stoke. Instead Lampard was handed millions to assemble a squad of youth and established Championship players. Florian Jozefzoon came first for around £3m, later followed by Martyn Waghorn in a deal believed to be more than double that. Paired with the captures of Jack Marriott, George Evans, Scott Malone and Duane Holmes, it's little wonder Rowett describes that business as 'surprising'.

The captures were at least aided by monies received. Matej Vydra's 2017/18 goalscoring exploits attracted Burnley for £11m, Andreas Weimann departing for Bristol City for £2m. And with the wage bill significantly cut having lost Darren Bent, Chris Baird, Jason Shackell and later Cameron Jerome, Lampard's first squad in management took shape.

* * *

When it came to management, Lampard had a lesson to learn. His first evening may have been close to perfect with a last-minute Tom Lawrence winner at Reading, but what followed wasn't; a heavy defeat in his home bow against Leeds and a loss at Millwall. A trio of wins were then followed by a defeat and a personal red card at Rotherham. That afternoon at the New York Stadium told the tale of the difficulty he would first have in management. Simply put, Lampard wasn't used to losing football matches.

Johnson concedes that the Lampard he got to know, particularly after defeats, wasn't one he ever expected to encounter, 'I didn't expect him to come in and be a manager who would shout at anyone but when he had to, he would. Both he and Jody are passionate and when we needed a rollicking – and he gave that a few times – he wasn't shy to do it. It's something that I was surprised about because I didn't expect it from him. But as a player, his standards meant he was a born winner. When we did lose a game, it would affect him as much as it would us because I think he still had that player head on where he was just gutted every time we lost a game. It affected him probably more than us because he is a born winner, he's used to winning so when he loses, he takes it really hard and gives a bollocking.'

Lampard's red at Rotherham, issued after hunting the linesman towards the corner flag, showed a different side to the man. Day to day at the training ground, things weren't so frantic. With less on the line within Moor Farm, it was a more serene Lampard that Bryson saw, 'Jody would take the bulk of the sessions, but Lampard would then come in and do team shape, how we'll play and then a few drills. Lampard was the nice guy; he was the good cop and Jody was sort of the bad cop. If we needed a rocket up our arse, it would come from Jody. He was more aggressive with it than the gaffer.'

Where Lampard brought the persona and the international attention, Morris brought the eyes and the tactical mind. He knew what to look for in a young player and as the likes of Jayden Bogle and Mason Bennett grew into the fabric of the first team, his impact began to be felt. 'They both knew what it was like,' Johnson says. 'When managers come into a club, they've got a job to do, and they think "I can't bed in the young lads because we need immediate results" so they never look at the young lads. But Jody had been there and done it with Chelsea and knew that we needed to give these young players a chance to get the best out of them.

'They had to be put in situations that were uncomfortable, training with the first team and having the intensity which is a lot different to what they're used to when they train with the 23s. It's not throwing them in at the deep end, it's just breaking them in slowly and then the thing with Mason [Bennett] was that he'd been unlucky during his career with injuries. The only way you get over it is by working hard and where Mason had managers before who wouldn't give him a chance, he knew that he would get a chance so he worked extra hard. He got given a chance, every young lad knew they'd get a chance underneath them and it pushed them on to do well.'

Bogle and Bennett grew in importance as the season matured, with the likes of Max Bird, Jason Knight and Jayden Mitchell-Lawson all appearing or being involved in squads.

Lampard's introduction to the hot seat had been tough. Comparisons began to be drawn against Steven Gerrard's time at Rangers, throwing conversations back a decade. But he would grow and come September, it clicked in style. At home to Brentford, Wilson opened his account after being slipped through by Bryson. That same day, Mount beautifully curled a free kick inside the post.

These two in particular started to grow, almost in tandem. It's little wonder, considering they spent every waking moment together. Wilson said, 'When we'd get home, we had hours to ourselves. Both of us are quite big gamers so there was a lot of PlayStation getting played and then we'd take it in turns cooking, families would come over if we had a home game, they'd come down on the Friday so we'd have them there on the weekend. Time went by quite quickly.'

The role of Richard Keogh in the changing room over the years has been much spoken about.

When Clement took over, rumours began to emerge that he had been specifically instructed not to hand Keogh the armband. Yet everyone knew that he and Mel were close, almost like a father and son. Regardless of his influence for better or worse, he's a man who went out of his way for others, neighbours included. 'He'd be coming around and making sure we were all right,' Wilson laughs. 'Then there were a couple of lads living nearby as well, so we passed the time quite quickly but I think having Richard next door was a big help because he was fantastic with the both of us on and off the pitch.'

From that Brentford afternoon, the side propelled. The longer the season continued, the clearer one thing became: Lampard could motivate for the big occasions. One League Cup evening at Manchester United was telling. 'You're expected to lose so you can play with as much freedom and as much confidence as you want because you're not expected to win the game,' Bryson admits. 'Lampard was like, "Look, you're playing against a Premier League club and this is where you all want to play. Go out and show you can do it." Premier League clubs show you that bit more respect. They give you a wee bit longer on the ball when you're trying to build the play so you can play out from the back. The bigger the tie, the better the team would play.'

In the dugouts that night, it was master v apprentice – Jose Mourinho v Frank Lampard. The Portuguese had won two Premier League titles at Chelsea over a decade previously, with Lampard arguably the star man.

But on the pitch was where the magic happened. Derby went behind early but kept themselves in the game and on the hour, got their reward in spectacular style through Wilson's long-range free kick. The Welshman relives the moment, 'I had a little chat with Mase [Mason Mount] who was debating whether to cross it but I felt it was a bit too central to whip it into the box, so I just thought

I'd try the technique. I knew straight away that I'd caught it sweet and to see it fly in, unbelievable.'

Late on came Jack Marriott's first goal for Derby, nodded past former Ram Lee Grant who was on to make his United debut following the dismissal of Sergio Romero.

After Marriott gave the Rams the lead, the tie looked like being sealed in the 90. 'When Jack scored,' remembers Craig Forsyth, 'I was running back past the halfway line and Anthony Martial said to me "you boys deserved that". It was at that point you think, "Hmm, if they're saying that, we must have taken them aback."'

A stoppage-time equaliser sent the match to penalties, where all eight Derby kicks found the back of the net before Scott Carson saved from Phil Jones to send Lampard's side through.

That result was followed up by a loss at Bolton, but the stakes were lowered, and the exhaustion was still wearing on the legs from a few nights previously. A 4-1 win at West Brom was ticked off weeks later, leaving then Baggies manager Darren Moore at a loss, 'Derby were so much more clinical on the night and we couldn't recover. I said to Frank and Jody in the room how good and energetic they were, and it gave them confidence because coming to an almost Premier League team, it was incredible.'

Later came the journey to Chelsea in the League Cup, a coming-home party for Lampard, Morris, Mount and Tomori. The 3-2 defeat was a further example of the way the side could rise to the big nights and, sadly, an early audition for all four.

Three days after West Brom, the best 30 minutes of the season arrived at the Riverside. Middlesbrough, a promotion pushing side, were overrun with Derby's possession past 80 per cent within the opening 20 before Bogle's late own goal narrowed the takeaway to a point. There would be setbacks, not least the loss at Gary Rowett's ten-manned Stoke, but they were almost always overlooked by inexplicable victories elsewhere.

Take Norwich in the final game of 2018. Three days before, a lacklustre loss at Bramall Lane put the Rams on the brink of dropping out of the play-offs. At Carrow Road, with Derby 3-2 down and ten minutes to play, a light flickered in the side as it went out in the stadium. Two goals after the restart snatched the unlikeliest of victories.

'The floodlights going out was the best thing that could have happened to us because we had to go off and have another half-time,' recalls Wilson. 'We gathered our thoughts and the manager was able to get messages into us and the last 15 minutes of that, we were a different team. It's definitely one of my highlights for the year.'

It was almost like Lampard had a switch that he was able to press at these biggest moments to inject a bit of himself further into his squad.

* * *

For a man who is hailed as being the inspiration behind Pep Guardiola, the actions Marcelo Bielsa took in his first months at Leeds United were somewhat silly. Two games into the season, his immediate effect on his team saw them devour Frank Lampard's new side in his first outing at Pride Park. Guardiola himself had months earlier stuck his colour to the mast, hailing Bielsa as the best coach in the world. He was, tactically at least, levels above most other managers in Europe, supposedly. The impact of his introduction into English football had been immediate and by January his Leeds sat at the top, eight points clear of Derby. They were almost certainties for promotion.

So quite why, in 2019, a year where all of the information you could possibly require on other teams (as well as countless angles of every match played in previous months) is a couple of mouse clicks away, he chose to send a spy to every training ground in the Championship is a puzzle. For four months, he later told the press, he had done the same. But it was only one Thursday afternoon on the grounds of Moor Farm that the grisly truth behind Bielsa's ingenious coaching methods first came to light.

It should have been an uneventful day, no different to any other pre-match routine. Lampard and Morris were finalising their plans for the visit to West Yorkshire the following evening, the squad being put through some of the standard team drills they were by now well accustomed to. As Thursday sessions go, it was nothing extraordinary.

'The day before a game we don't really do much, just some boxes, circles and some five-a-sides,' says Bradley Johnson. 'At the training ground the pitch is downhill and then uphill is where the car park is. We can see the driveway so we can see who comes in and then we just saw two police vans coming into the training ground. Everyone has a look up but we just carry on doing our bit and then they just stop at the top of our pitch. Four police officers get out of the van and one of our security are stood with them and by this point, our security guard was pointing down and we don't know what he's pointing down at.'

'Everybody was turning around at the players like, "Fuck's sake, what have you done now?"' laughs Craig Bryson. Over the decades, visits from the Derbyshire constabulary have never been too unusual and wouldn't be in the months after. This was more unexpected than any before though and with a heightened sense of urgency. The two police vans, packed inside with Derbyshire's finest, hinted at a crime far beyond what had ever come before. Players and coaches, by now fixated with the potential of the conversation Lampard was sharing with security and police, froze. Which of the squad would be leaving in handcuffs?

'Jody got us going and playing again,' recalls Johnson, 'and Frank comes down, the police get back in their vans and all of a sudden the manager says, "They've seen someone in our bushes" and we were just like, "You what?"'

What looked at first like a major police incident descended into bewilderment. Johnson continues, 'The vans put their sirens on and just sped to the exit, training stops again and so we're all looking and then they jump out of the van and start shouting and screaming. Then we see they've got a man outside our ground.'

A singular individual, later reports claiming them to be a 20-year-old intern, was found brandishing a backpack with wire cutters, ogling into the sanctuary of Moor Farm's training pitches. 'We went in to eat and the gaffer just said it was someone with a wire cutter. About ten minutes later, he got the news and just told us "apparently it's someone from Leeds watching us train" and we could not believe it. He was fuming,' recalled Johnson.

The news immediately leaked into the public domain, sparked by tweets from the Derbyshire Police account. Confusion, a fair share of hilarity and the most posts in a week to contain the words 'public footpath' ensued. One night later, with preparations ruined and the match now developing into an *Emmerdale* side-plot, Leeds eased to a 2-0 win. Speaking through his translator before the match, Bielsa admitted the individual captured was sent to Derby on his orders. The admittance was a major development and took the story beyond just a Derby vs Leeds tale. Bielsa had now involved the rest of the division, sparking a multi-club letter demanding an EFL investigation.

The saga only got more bizarre into the following week. Come the next Tuesday, the story rumbled on, but Derby had their eyes elsewhere. A Wednesday night FA Cup replay at Southampton was the priority for Lampard, but still the talk was on events six days earlier. As the team coach arrived at St Mary's, Bielsa began a press conference. Though speculation mounted about a resignation in the wake of his confession, what followed was the extension of a now personal vendetta.

For 70 minutes, Bielsa turned into a university lecturer, albeit one with an unusually strong understanding of how to work PowerPoint presentations. The admission that he had spied on 23 other teams was bad enough, but at least it was a universal insult. But as Derby were the ones who made the discovery, it was they and particularly Lampard who took the brunt of his wrath. Spreadsheet after spreadsheet of his tactical analysis on Lampard's squad was presented to a press room lapping up the words of the messiah. All of his findings were delivered to not only the press but to every side in the division, Derby bared for all to see. Bielsa, the tactician of a generation, had attempted, and succeeded, in publicly humiliating the rookie Lampard. 'We do analysis too,' Lampard winced after victory that night. Leeds were fined £200,000, and the EFL swiftly changed its rules to prevent anything similar happening again.

By this point in his Derby career, Bryson had seen it all. Even for him, the saga was a new development, 'I don't know if it's a form of cheating but it's not morally correct to crawl through bushes and watch someone train. It was weird and to watch his PowerPoint presentation, I don't know if he was trying to justify it but I saw it on Twitter and the lads were just like, "Fucking hell, did you see that?"'

* * *

The impact of Bielsa's actions affected Lampard personally and that hurt was passed on to his squad. In the next seven games, Derby collected just eight points and slipped out of the top six. Leeds on the other hand propelled, destined for promotion.

But sometimes, it takes a drop of magic from an unlikely source. The prospect of a fourth consecutive loss was growing the longer Wigan held the lead at Pride Park. As they had against Bolton, Rotherham and Ipswich, Derby couldn't break down relegation fodder. Then Bennett decided to flick an 18-yard overhead kick with his weak foot home and all was well again. Lampard compared Bennett to Gareth Bale in the aftermath.

The drop in form coincided with Mason Mount's injury but upon his return – a 6-1 victory over Rotherham – the midfield began to click. Wilson had found himself thriving centrally, Johnson embarked on his best spell in a Derby shirt and Mount just went about doing Mount things. Martyn Waghorn struck a hat-trick, then Mount did the same against Bolton. A draw a week later at Birmingham was a setback but fate was in the hands of Derby still, with Bristol City still to come away.

Before then was the visit of QPR, now managed by John Eustace. As he had done to such aplomb in a Derby shirt, his Hoops sat deep and absorbed, grinding the threat of creativity down and minimising the time of actual football played. 'I remember looking at the clock and it was late 70s and I just got a little bit anxious because I knew we had to win it,' says Wilson. Fail to win and it would effectively be all over, so the nine minutes of added time were a blessing. A foul on Bogle allowed the Liverpool loanee to grab his 13th of the season from the spot, and he followed that with a late second.

Then to Ashton Gate, where Derby ended Bristol City's realistic hopes of a top-six finish with a smash-and-grab 2-0 win. A draw at Swansea left sixth place still in Derby hands for the final-day visit of West Brom, where an early Waghorn header was cancelled out at the start of the second half and with Middlesbrough winning at relegated Rotherham, the Rams' hopes were on a knife-edge. Bennett put Derby back in front with 20 to play and Wilson's penalty quickly eased the nerves. Lampard, with a fresh-looking squad, had maintained the same level of performance as Rowett had.

The late-season upturn coincided with Leeds's collapse at the top. With four games remaining and a three-point gap over Sheffield United in third place, they did a Derby. Wigan, playing with ten men for 75 minutes, left Elland Road with their only away victory of the season. Defeat at Brentford and an ill-tempered draw against Aston Villa completed the collapse, with a final-day defeat at relegated Ipswich ensuring their regular season ended in capitulation.

Would that actually matter going into the play-offs though? After all, not only had they destroyed Lampard's men twice, they'd humiliated them. They'd spied on sessions, exposed tactics and turned the manager into their own personal meme. To borrow a modern term, Leeds were living in the head of Lampard rent-free.

The first leg was too familiar. Although the Rams had put up more of a fight than in the previous two meetings, a 1-0 home defeat was still disastrous. Kemar Roofe's goal ten minutes into the second half was followed by an overruled penalty after Craig Pawson reversed his decision. At this point, no side had ever overturned a home defeat in the history of the Championship play-offs and with a journey to one of the most hostile grounds in English football, there was nothing to suggest Derby would buck the trend.

And Leeds's players knew it, according to Johnson, 'When they came to our place and beat us 1-0, I remember a few of their players who weren't involved were on our pitch after clapping their fans and you got that feeling of arrogance. "We've done it already" is the feel I got from them. You'd see some of their players and they'd say, "Good luck next season." We were like, "Well we're playing you again in three days." "Yeah but good luck next year." They had arrogance about them, and you could tell they had it and it worked for them.'

There were just four days to wait before the return leg. That meant four days of enduring a ditty formed in the afternoons before the Pride Park meeting. With spygate still very much in the mind of supporters and particularly Lampard, the adaption of Oasis's 'Stop Crying Your Heart Out' was designed to make a further mockery of the Rams manager's handling of the situation in January. Echoing around Pride Park in the wake of the Saturday defeat, it became the theme to the overall saga. Even upon arrival outside Elland Road, it was all that could be heard from passing cars.

'I've played in big games at Elland Road against Liverpool and Arsenal,' says former Leeds man, Johnson. 'When it's a full house, it gets rocking and I remember speaking to Fik, H [Harry Wilson] and Mounty before the game and just said, "You won't have played in a game or a stadium with the noise you will hear tonight." They just said, "Yeah, yeah" and I was like, "Seriously, it's going to be electric."

'We went up to Leeds the night before and then we had all their fans at the hotel, they were there singing Leeds songs because everyone, even those who worked at the hotel, were all giving it to the lads. We felt the buzz as soon as we got into Leeds. I knew a lot of people at the club and I could just feel the confidence they had around the place. I remember walking out and trying to call Mounty after the line-up and they've sung their song. We get together in a huddle and Mounty's just looked at me and gone "wow".'

Wilson, facing what looked increasingly like being his final game in a white shirt, saw the occasion as 'one final opportunity to get our own back'. How Derby would do so was a mystery, considering they'd been well beaten on three separate occasions already. Add Stuart Dallas's opener on the night after 24 minutes to an atmosphere now like no other in English football and it almost looked like becoming a damage limitation evening. Johnson admits, 'For the first five minutes, you couldn't even hear each other. You had to shout at them and then they went 1-0 up and it just erupted.'

But Leeds had a certain fragility about them, particularly at home. When presented with opportunities to push towards automatic promotion, they had fallen apart. Wigan was the notable example, but defeats against Sheffield United and Norwich – the only two to finish above them – hinted at a frailness under pressure.

Goalkeeper Kiko Casilla had been signed by Leeds from Real Madrid in January 2019. Noted for being good with the ball at his feet, he'd so far flattered to deceive in a Leeds shirt. But even when Jack Marriott was hunting down Bennett's flick over the top, there should have been no issue. Marriott, 20 seconds on to the field, caused a problem. Casilla flapped, Liam Cooper misjudged his challenge, and Marriott tapped in on the brink of half-time.

Derby began to believe. Wilson says, 'I felt that it was happening when I was out on the pitch. Before that we were pushing and Bennett hit the post from a corner, so I felt their goal had lifted us. Jack comes on and gets that good fortune. That goal took the wind out of their sails and gave us a bit of belief heading into half-time.'

The next 45 minutes were quite simply the best 45 in the recent history of Derby County and the unthinkable was achieved. Within a minute, the tie as a whole was level. Wilson said, 'I didn't realise Mase's goal was so soon after half-time. I think when it happens, you're not sure of the timings and that but it was the first 90 seconds or whatever that he got the goal and we kicked on from there.'

Wilson was the first to mount Mount, but his own moment came next. Bennett, developing into a forward in his own right in the season's closing weeks, drew a tug of the shirt from Cooper. The Welsh wonderkid, already with nine set piece goals in all competitions, duly slotted past Casilla. It was at this point that the first white scarf – handed free to every Leeds supporter as an early Wembley present – fluttered from the stands and on to the pitch.

Johnson's nous was crucial in preparing his young squad for the hostility they would experience. But for the man who knows all too well what it's liked to be booed by his own fans (Johnson experienced it on the opening day of 2016/17), he knew how the cauldron of Elland Road could turn on their own. He remembers, 'Goals change games and if you could write a perfect script for a game, we scored at the exact right times. I said this in the changing room to everyone. "Look, if we get their fans turned on them it will be hard because when they go, 40,000 turn and I don't think many of these have the character to get through that." We turned the fans and as soon as we had that second goal we just thought "right, we can go here".'

Though Dallas levelled the tie overall, it never really felt like it mattered. Especially so when the walking danger that is Gaetano Berardi, now Leeds' most red-carded player of all time, launched into Johnson for a second yellow with 12 minutes left.

And that's why from the moment Keogh shrugged Patrick Bamford off the ball on halfway, what came next was somehow an expectation. Just over 12 months earlier, Sean Morrison's video mocked Derby's skipper for feigning runs before cutting back. But under Lampard, he had developed into a defender with attacking midfielder instincts.

Exchanging passes with Mount and finding himself 25 yards out, he could have gone for the ultimate redemption for 2014 and struck for goal. Luckily, he didn't, feeding Marriott to dink his shot over Casilla and into the corner to give Derby an aggregate lead they would not relinquish again.

Still sore at how the entire Leeds squad had celebrated regardless of being involved or not on the Saturday, the city of Derby descended on to Elland Road. 'We didn't necessarily want to rub it in,' begins Wilson, 'but we wanted to show them that we could celebrate as well. I remember looking around and seeing Keezy on his own so just jumped on him. We had all the emotions in the air and we couldn't quite believe what had just happened.'

Even Johnson, the first of the squad to meet an already bouncing Lampard on the pitch, couldn't contain himself, 'I've still got ties to Leeds, so I didn't want to celebrate in front of their face and rub it in because I have a lot of respect for any club I play for. But after the way they celebrated and giving it all of the spy glasses, it was a good night celebrating there and then back in Derby.

'We got the gaffer singing the Lampard song in the changing room and we had the door open so we made sure they could hear us singing it. It was a good night to rub it into them. But we'd do it again. We'd let them beat us three times during the year and then win that game, we did it when it was most important. They thought they'd do it again but we did it when it mattered the most and the gaffer and Jody really enjoyed that, so we did rub it into their faces a bit.'

To celebrate, it was back to the Kings Head in Duffield, where a bar tab of £2,802.30 was picked up by the manager, continues Johnson, 'I don't know if that actual photo was true because there's a J20 and I can't recall anyone drinking that! But we came back to a pub and had a few together and enjoyed the night. You've got to celebrate those sorts of things; they don't come around very often.'

* * *

Derby would never be able to match what happened on that night in Leeds. The fact that the celebrations were on par with what a promotion party would look like is a stick now used to beat the club with. The pitch invasion of everyone from kitman Jon Davidson through to chairman and owner Mel Morris was understandable at the time, but they only served to heighten hysteria. As hype grew over the performance in the days after the 4-2 victory, a slow realisation dawned that such a high level of performance may be unmatchable come the big day at Wembley.

Perhaps that should have come as no surprise because after the biggest away wins of the season would regularly follow a comedown. After Manchester United was defeat at Bolton, Norwich and then a laboured draw against Middlesbrough. The euphoria too of Lawrence's opening-day winner at Reading came before the 4-1 loss to Leeds. Because of the magnitude of what had come before, Lampard's Derby consistently had an issue with maintaining the level they had achieved on their biggest nights.

Wilson contemplates whether the timescale between the semi and the final made a difference to the overall conclusion of the season, 'We just felt that with the final two weeks after the season, it just felt a disadvantage to us because we were off a high in the semi and if we could have gone straight into the final, it would have helped us a bit.'

It had been five years since the last trip down Wembley Way. In that time, so much had changed at Derby and yet, it was all still the same. Having never come any closer to reaching the Premier League, the want for top-flight football was as strong as it was in 2014. Not just in the stands and from owner Morris, but for some of those still aiming to heal the wounds of Zamora. Keogh, Bryson, Bennett and Forsyth all remained at the club; Wisdom had returned. The want for redemption remained.

As Bryson would find out in advance, that desire was still as strong as ever across the fanbase too. Having wished he was at Elland Road for the comeback, injuries curtailed any chance of what would have been a final bash at achieving an eight-year goal. Instead of wallowing, the Scot and David Nugent went to Covent Garden, too polite to reveal to supporters his disdain for

Jägermeister. He says, 'Me and Dave were in the same boat, we went down the day before and met a couple of Derby fans on the train, had a couple of drinks and then you see the videos that appeared on social media the next day. It was an unbelievable experience for me though just to see how the fans are and how they approach a game and approach a big game and to see how they turn up and how it's a big weekend away for everybody. It's so big for them, I tried to treat it like that but during the game I was like everybody else, kicking every ball, running after everything.'

To go personal, I still recall the moment the team line-up was announced. Having emerged from the flat-lager haven that was the Crystal Club below the arch (side note – Marcus Tudgay was in there and I considered approaching him about this book but quickly realised I was in no fit state having now moved to the Diet Cokes), blurry eyes tried to make sense of the 11 selected by Lampard. With two weeks to formulate his game plan, he left Marriott out. Instead it would be Bennett leading the line, with the injured Holmes replaced by Tom Huddlestone. Disappointment had already set in. Without Marriott and Waghorn in the 11, the two holding midfielders of Johnson and Huddlestone hinted at a move away from the focus on attack seen before. It's the move that would go down as Lampard's worst as a manager and the choice which many say cost promotion.

Huddlestone and Johnson may have been a negative decision but it's not difficult to read into Lampard's thinking. In the years since Derby failed, both had succeeded in gaining promotion via Wembley. Although they'd failed to reach the arch with Derby, success at Hull and Norwich meant they were able to provide that level of calmness. Even more so did Ashley Cole. In for the suspended Scott Malone, the January signing would play his final professional match at a place he and Lampard knew so well.

Johnson provided the warnings before Leeds and come Wembley, he would do the same again. He says, 'For a lot of the young lads like Boges [Jayden Bogle], I just said it was just another one for us. There's a lot riding on it but you can't go out there thinking about that or you go into your shell. You just have to relax, treat it like a normal game and if we win, we win, but if we don't, it's not the end of the world, is it? I tried to bleed that into the young lads. But most of the team had been there before so we knew what the atmosphere would be like and obviously the gaffer had played in many big games. so it wasn't anything new to him. He had that relaxed feeling about the game.'

Anyone expecting to see a side still bouncing from the second half in Leeds quickly realised that wouldn't be the case. It was 37 minutes before Mount fired Derby's first shot on target, into the arms of Jed Steer, and soon after came Villa's eighth unanswered goal of the campaign against the Rams. Anwar El-Ghazi's header put them into a half-time lead but still, it was no disaster.

What followed was a disaster, however. Unchanged at the break, Derby emerged slowly. Five years earlier, it was Keogh's botched clearance that conceded the game. Taking to the field that day, the scene of those tears, he knew first-hand what it was like to make a mistake at this level. Now, so did Kelle Roos. The Dutchman had done okay since replacing Scott Carson after the new year. Handpicked by Eric Steele in years previous, he'd never quite made it. Loaned out to five clubs at Championship, League One and League Two level, he'd even achieved play-off success on loan at AFC Wimbledon. But he'd never made it at Derby.

'It was just sloppy play and mistakes from players that cost us,' remembers Johnson. When a shot from distance ballooned into the six-yard box, Johnson was stood ten feet away from his goalkeeper. As the cry of 'Roos' bellowed, Johnson waited for him to collect the ball at height. Instead, having waited for it to cushion into his chest, Roos was beaten to it by John McGinn, almost a full foot shorter than him.

Finally, it prompted the introduction of Marriott, then Waghorn. Bogle hit the side-netting; Marriott went inches wide on the turn. It was the Derby that everybody expected to see, but they'd waited 70 minutes before getting off the bus. When they did halve the deficit through Marriott, it was an infuriating reminder of what should have been. Lampard's two-week plan had been ripped up. Perhaps it was his naivety and freshness to management that meant he favoured a more assured approach, but Marriott's appearance had been cried out for and assumed in the days in advance.

Now, he and Waghorn were dictating, with the final ten minutes an onslaught. 'Nothing clicked until the 80th minute,' Wilson sighs. Those last ten, plus an additional seven, were dictated 30 yards from Steer's goal. No closer would they get. A fourth season of play-off pain in six years was in the bag.

Johnson's Norwich had controlled their victory in 2015, a day he puts at the top of his career. Now, he was nursing the wounds of his most painful defeat, 'If you get played off the park by the better team, then you just weren't good enough. But I didn't feel Villa were better than us. They didn't create many chances, they just scored from our mistakes. Towards the end, they'd blown up and if we had another five minutes, we'd have got that equaliser. If we'd have got that, we'd have gone on to win it. I'd rather get battered and played off the park because they weren't better than us.'

Inside the changing room, the personnel had changed but the pain remained. As the side convened, those who didn't make the squad embraced their broken team-mates. After defeat in 2014, Bryson was taken for a drugs test. The chance to enter the changing room this time around was a first for him. He says, 'The changing room after the game was horrific, we had everybody sitting there gutted. There's a lot of emotions running through you, you've just lost one of the biggest games and even down to a wee thing like financially, for players that's a massive game.

'Everybody knew that team would get broken up. The loan players would go back, there would be a few moving on, it wouldn't be the same. We'd heard the rumours about the gaffer going to Chelsea and then you're starting to wonder if it's his last game. After the game Didier Drogba came in and just had a wee bit of a chat with us, but it wasn't a nice place to be in. You then go and see your families, everyone is gutted for the next couple of weeks, you go away and you regroup. The uncertainty over my future at that time as well, I had to focus on that but it's not nice. I don't know how fans take it.'

* * *

Uncertainty would spread through the entire squad. Contracts of first-team players were running out, loans were ending and the impending sacking of Maurizio Sarri left Lampard right at the centre of the confusion. For Derby, although the stakes weren't quite so high as they were for Villa, defeat guaranteed an almost complete rebuilding job.

First to the loanees. Tomori, Mount and Wilson all laid stakes for being crowned with the Jack Stamps Trophy and it was the defender who walked away with it. The least-hyped signing of the three, Tomori's capture was more expected to be as a back-up behind Keogh and Curtis Davies. A mixture of calmness, aerial ability and blistering pace saw him grow into a necessity of the side, becoming more important to the make-up of the back line than even Keogh.

Mount's injury away at Accrington led the club to struggle for two months in his absence and it was only upon his return that the play-off push restarted. Wilson had developed from a slow beginning to top the scoring charts. More than that though, all three developed a matureness as footballers and people that meant they were ready for more than this division could handle. Tomori and Mount returned to Chelsea, the former speaking on full time about a season he felt he may never match in the game. Mount, already called up for England, was never likely to return. Wilson was the only question mark.

He says, 'I wasn't really thinking about my future at that point. I was gutted because I wanted promotion at Derby because of the hard work I, the players and the staff had put in, all of the emotions the fans had been through that season. When it didn't happen, on the day I didn't think about it but when you get a couple of weeks off in the summer, I was thinking about it on the sun lounger and yeah, I knew it was my last game. I wanted to be playing Premier League and I was hoping it would be with Liverpool but if not, it would be someone else.'

Loanees would leave. So would stalwarts. Johnson departed, Efe Ambrose (the only man ever to have a chant about him without playing a match) as well. But then there was the big one. Bryson was signed under Clough as a sort of replacement for Robbie Savage. An unknown £350,000 quantity from Kilmarnock, nobody knew those funds would be the best money spent in the recent history of Derby County. For eight seasons, Bryson was the one constant. Managers had passed, so many of them. But Bryson always remained, even after his loan to Cardiff. With a heavy heart, it was time for him to move on from a city he had called home for so long.

He says, 'I don't want to say I was semi-offered a contract but there was some chat there. But for me I just wanted to go back home. I'm not going to say it was an easy decision because it wasn't. My mum had a heart attack, and so me and my wife needed to go back home because I'd been away for eight years. It was time to go home and with my son being born as well, it just felt right.

'But Derby means everything to me. I'm looking forward to the days I can just come back as a fan and experience an East Midlands derby in the crowd, do the things that a fan does. And I hope the club knows that if ever they need me, I'm absolutely here for them. I love the club. I joined as a boy and I became a man while I was there. The fans were fantastic to me, took me to their heart and I just hope that I was able to make them proud. Obviously the one big regret is missing out on promotion. I had it with Cardiff but I just wish that it was with Derby.'

Bryson's departure was quick and as painless as it could be. Johnson too, leaving for Blackburn in July upon the conclusion of his contract. The loss of Lampard and Morris though would have ramifications long into the following campaign.

With a legacy like Lampard's at Chelsea, it was only a matter of time before he would have ended up back at Stamford Bridge. Mel Morris said as much himself early into Lampard's reign at Pride Park and days after the final as speculation intensified, he told TalkSport as much, 'One day maybe Frank will manage Chelsea, I don't doubt that will happen at some point in the future. But I just hope when that does happen, he can pick up Chelsea at a time where he can go on to be successful. We've got two years left on his contract and would obviously love to retain Frank's services, and I've had no indication that's not going to be the case.'

That was 28 May, the morning after the events of Wembley. It was a situation we all saw coming and yet it took 37 days before he was finally confirmed at Chelsea, with Jody Morris and fitness coach Chris Jones following. In that time, he went on a summer holiday, infuriated supporters with radio silence, had a video emerge of The Clash's 'Should I Stay or Should I Go?' playing at a social event, and opened talks about a contract extension. It was a sad ending to a relationship that offered so much and having been stung a year earlier by Rowett, those familiar feelings of rejection returned. Once again, Derby weren't enough.

Upon confirmation of Lampard's departure, he and Jody both took to social media to put the record straight. The split, firmly amicable in the end, saw videos shared across Derby's social timelines, a far cry from the average corner flag club statement. Morris's heartfelt Instagram post offered some explanation if one was needed. 'The silence of late which some of you took as disrespect was the complete opposite. We had no choice but to keep quiet while negotiations were ongoing and would never want to mislead anybody. I hope you can see we have nothing but love and respect for this football club. @dcfcofficial will be the first results I look out for.'

Another era over and with five months of the 25 years this book focuses on left, the finale should be calm. Should.

THE END

SO WE reach the final five months of this long, exhausting 25-year journey through Derby County. There have been highs (not many), there have been lows (very many). On a personal level, when I began the writing of this book in 2019, I felt there would be nothing left after Wembley heartache.

The plan was always to conclude the prose on 31 December 2019, providing the full 25 years and not a day more. Wrongfully I assumed that this chapter would be more about how Phillip Cocu was acclimatising to management in England. Maybe he'd been able to formulate another play-off push, rebuild a squad, enjoy a nice quiet few months. A couple of thousand words and we're done.

I failed to consider the prospect that within these four months, Derby would sign England's record goalscorer, have three players at the centre of a drink-driving scandal, sack their captain and be threatened with a severe points deduction.

This final chapter, I confess, could be a book within itself. Had it not been for Richard Keogh's court case, it would have been (Keogh's agent had agreed to his involvement originally before legal matters halted any talks).

So if you're reading this and feel there's a story you want to tell about Derby County and that there are some things that need to be dug deeper into, there's no better place to start than within this season. Hell, even if you're a budding screenwriter, there's more than enough potential for the big screen to snap this one up.

* * *

The bounce was over. Frank Lampard's departure was confirmed deep into the summer. So late was it confirmed that by the time players returned to Moor Farm from their summer breaks, he was still in the job. A club statement on 1 July told supporters the outgoing manager would be excused from training, Darren Wassall instead doing the duties of first-team overseer once more. Only temporarily, because the new man was already lined up.

Phillip Cocu would have liked to get to work as soon as possible. The new incumbent, another footballing legend in his own right, is a gentleman who doesn't see the need for extravagance. In the Camp Nou and the Philips Stadion, he rarely caught the eye. Surrounded by Ronaldinho and Patrick Kluivert, the Eindhoven-born midfielder would do the quieter parts of the game, shunning the limelight. So to have been forced to fly to Florida to meet his squad would not have been his ideal preparation for his first role in English football.

Pre-arranged for Frank Lampard, Cocu would not meet a single member of his playing staff until travelling halfway across the world and arrived in the US in the dead of night.

'We went to America for pre-season and then it was strange for us staff that remained because the first time we actually met the new team, it was me and Stevey Haines, we got to America,' recalls kitman Jon Davidson. 'We had a long flight getting there and found a hotel near the complex where we were training. It was about 11pm and we had this van for all the gear, just leaving to go there to drop the bags off at the complex because we were training at half eight in the morning because of the heat.

'The new manager got out of the taxi with Twan Scheepers and that was the first time we met him. We sat there and just said "I think that's the new gaffer!" so we went and said hello. It was hard for him getting off a plane, getting there in the middle of the night and then having to meet his new players in America. It was difficult all round and it's been very difficult for Phil. From day one he had to travel all the way to America to then meet his squad the next day with no chance to plan how he wanted it. He came in cold to see how things were going there and then we'd lost a lot of players with a few coming in.'

Cocu's pre-season preparations were scandalous and left him completely in the lurch. A friendly against Bristol City was cut short by a storm, he had no time to properly utilise Moor Farm and his early weeks were spent with a squad fully depleted by the losses earlier that summer.

Entering late and without time to delve into where he would look to strengthen his squad, summer business was a disaster. Kieran Dowell, Jamie Patterson and Ben Hamer arrived on loan, the first two departing early after drab spells. Matt Clarke filled the Fikayo Tomori-shaped hole, with £10m being splurged on Krystian Bielik, a leggy defender-turned-midfielder from Arsenal.

Heading into the season away at Huddersfield, the squad looked threadbare. Without Lampard, the focus had gone away from the club and any marketing interest had begun to disappear. That was until news broke that Wayne Rooney would be joining second-tier Derby.

Neither the rumour, nor the signing, came out of the blue. Derby had been in contact with Rooney's representatives after first hearing of his interest in a return to England, with the original plan to pair him with Lampard. The coaching team would consist of Lampard, Rooney and Ashley Cole, three of the finest English players of the past 30 years. Then Lampard upped and left, but the Rooney interest remained.

By this point, journalist Nick Britten had moved closer to the club. He recalls, 'I was in my office minding my own business last August and got a call from Stephen Pearce, the CEO, who said, "I'm in America and nobody knows this but we're signing Wayne

Rooney and we're signing him tomorrow. Will you go and help out managing the comms side?" I had to go to TK Maxx because I was in my shorts and t-shirt and buy a pair of trousers and a shirt, and just hotfoot over to the stadium on the Monday afternoon. We worked late into the evening, Rooney arrived early on the Tuesday morning and signed the contract later that afternoon, before doing a whole load of media on that day.'

An intricate operation was put in place to conceal the story from the waiting press. Britten continued, 'The situation was we were signing him, he'd sign on the Monday, we'd put a teaser out on his social media channels of him at an airport wearing a black and white cap, we wouldn't announce it. And then we were going to drop the big announcement on Sky Sports News at 6am on Tuesday morning when he landed to hit the early morning channels and then run the press through the day; that was their plan. But the *Daily Telegraph* got wind of the story and dropped it at 7pm on Monday night just before we were about to go live on Sky and play Huddersfield, that was the buzz going on around then. But it ruined the plan because the cat was out of the bag.

'The other hitch was that he didn't sign the contract in America. He flew over on the Monday night and arrived with no contract signed. For much of the day until around 2pm, it was all negotiations which helped to build up the buzz really. When he signed, we scrambled a conference for about four and then just did loads of press from then. Before we did the media, we got him down to the stadium, did all of the marketing shots of him with the shirt, happy days. He flew back out to America the next day and we knew we'd see him again come the end of October. But I was fascinated about how it all came about. It turned out it had been some time in the making though I think.'

Rooney's signing would be the biggest story not in English football, but for the sport across the globe. The eyes of the world turned to Derby again. And that night, everything looked like blossoming for the season ahead. Tom Lawrence struck twice in a well-drilled victory at the John Smith's Stadium. Rooney was announced the following day in a player-coach role that would begin upon the reopening of the January window and after his DC United contract had come to a close.

'It's still surreal that it was happening at the time but it's one of those things where nothing totally surprises me here now,' laughs Craig Forsyth. 'I've seen so much but it's still an amazing thing for the club to get somebody like Wayne here.'

The buzz was real, as well as the anger from other clubs. Derby had by now become the financial powerhouse of the division backed by Morris and routinely stayed narrowly within the realms of FFP. Another clever loophole discovered by the club allowed them to bring Rooney in and afford his wages.

* * *

It's worth pointing out at this point that Phillip Cocu may have experienced the worst four months of his footballing career from September to December. He'd had difficulties in Turkey at Fenerbahce, but most of these were footballing.

At Pride Park, his start was so-so. Victory at Huddersfield was the only one in the opening eight games, although he only lost twice. And considering the lack of time he'd had in the summer, things would never click immediately. His problems were most highlighted at Elland Road, where Chris Martin scored a last-minute equaliser (and his first Derby goal in nearly two years) on an afternoon where the Rams were thoroughly outplayed. But at the very least, fight was shown to the death. We all know what happened next, though.

Cocu had a tough ride already, and took the side out for a meal on Tuesday evening to The Joiners Arms in Quarndon. Cocu departed at 8pm alongside most of his squad. With training the next day, he should have had no fears about the rest following suit soon after.

So when he woke up to the news that Tom Lawrence and Mason Bennett had been arrested and his club captain had suffered an ACL injury that would rule him out for the season, he may have been a little pissed off. It took no time for the disturbing full truth of the story to emerge. Keogh, seatbelt-less and perching on the edge of his seat, was travelling to, well, who knows where, in the back of Lawrence's Range Rover. Lawrence was hammered.

Behind him was Mason Bennett. The duo, who turned down transport from the club for the evening, embarked on GTA: Derby, with Lawrence ramming into the back of Bennett's vehicle. That sent the Range Rover into a tree, with Keogh knocked unconscious in the back. Lawrence and Bennett (too drunk to realise the severity) fled the scene. *The Sun* reported that when asked his name by a paramedic at the sight of the crash, Keogh responded 'Alfie'. 'No you're not, you're Richard Keogh,' was the reported reply.

Lawrence and Bennett, both well over the drink driving limit, returned 45 minutes later, to be greeted by police presence. What followed was a national scandal splashed across the front pages of the newspapers and leading TV bulletins. The positive publicity of Wayne Rooney's arrival had been immediately quashed. The chairman spoke out, as did a visibly angry Cocu to the press.

Calls for sackings ensued from all quarters, a difficult ask as Morris later referred to. As the severity of Keogh's injury became clear, so did the truth of the incident. Britten remembers, 'On the Wednesday morning after the incident, we're all trying to manage it and we say to the players, "Look, don't go on social media. But if there's anything that you're worried about, come and talk to us. If there's more to come out, just come and talk to us so we can at least prepare."' Nobody came forward and Tom Huddlestone was installed as the new captain.

Huddlestone didn't mention that he'd already recorded the build-up for his private Snapchat account. Twenty-four hours later, the remnants of those posts were splashed across the tabloids. There was Mason Bennett vomiting into a urinal while claiming 'I've had more than three pints', Scott Malone asleep in the bar.

Tom Lawrence slapping Malone across the face to wake him up. Huddlestone would never captain the side.

Football had to take a back seat but that Saturday's encounter with Birmingham was at the time a pivotal step towards cleansing the club. None of the parties involved would take to the field and the Rams recorded a win that meant more than just three points. The city, at levels of hatred with the squad for what was perceived to be sheer arrogance with a dash of idiocy, reconnected. What had happened was over, with Derby set to move on without those who had dragged the name of the club into dark corners.

That was until Wednesday night, when Cocu elected to put Lawrence back into the starting 11 at Barnsley with Bennett on the bench. 'I kid you not, the shitstorm that came down on us was worse than it was when it first happened, and it set us right back to square one,' says Britten.

'I can totally understand why Phillip picked him and his reasons behind that. But in the PR sense it was really problematic.

'After the initial incident, people could disassociate the players behaving as they did with the club, so they were attacking individuals and could see that we were trying to make it better. But when Phillip picked Tom Lawrence, it was seen as the club's decision, sanctioned by whoever, and therefore we just got it.

'The complaints poured in. Mel and Phillip had done a great job a few days earlier in speaking to supporters ahead of the Birmingham game, and to start building that trust again, but that was quickly forgotten in the eyes of many supporters.

'It was a different kind of comms situation to manage than the original incident, but the anger coming from supporters seemed more intense.'

Cocu saw it as an opportunity, a first step for the two in question to rehabilitate through the sport. But the ferocity of the anger from Rams supporters and the wider footballing world was a PR nightmare. Both men would be victimised by supporters wherever they went, Lawrence spending 90 minutes at the City

Ground where he was told for all of those that 'he should be in jail'.

Both would receive driving bans and community service orders, the threat of prison time passed up by Judge Taaffe. Lawrence would go on to repay the faith shown in him, embarking on his best spell in a Derby shirt after Christmas. Bennett was farmed out to Millwall and uploaded a video to his own Snapchat, screaming at Pride Park to 'fucking burn'. Swings and roundabouts.

For Keogh came dismissal. Offered a pay cut that he saw as insultingly low, the club sacked their skipper for gross misconduct. The Ireland international appealed his sacking, the club rejecting it. And at the time of writing, the court case between the two parties continues.

* * *

Wayne Rooney would inspire Derby. His debut at the beginning of January 2020 saw him operate in a far deeper position than ever seen before, but he was the catalyst for change. Before arriving, the Rams had only a solitary away win to their name for the season and hovered ominously above the bottom three. When Rooney took the armband from Curtis Davies – becoming the fourth captain of the season – Derby sat 17th.

But with Rooney, and a new focus on youth, steadiness arrived. Now, it's a new era for the club. Even as I write this, Derby face further controversy and the threat of a points deduction after EFL action into their financial conduct and the valuation of Pride Park. But it should be the final instalment of seven years of controversy. Moor Farm's academy is proving itself to be one of the best in Europe, evidenced by the Under-18s becoming English champions in 2019 and then reaching the last 16 of the UEFA Youth League. The youth must be the future for this club, because nothing else has worked.

Derby County are at a crossroads. A second-tier football club in the East Midlands should not routinely find themselves in the press the way they have over the 25 years covered in this book.

Yes, if it wasn't for these controversies, this book may be a little quieter, but quiet can be good. Take Sheffield United as an example. In freefall only four years ago, they are proving to be the demonstrator for what Derby and so many more Football League sides should aspire to be. Minimised controversy, a clear ethic as to their footballing mentality, a consistent manager. It's three things Derby have not had for many, many years; if ever over the last quarter of a century.

It begs the question though: would we even be Derby without all of this? Take away the sackings, the courtroom battles, the financial collapses, the wrath of foreign imports, the Wembley capitulations, the car crashes, the prison sentences, and what do you have? Just a standard, normal football club.

Actually yes, I think I'd prefer that please.

ACKNOWLEDGEMENTS

WORKING ON *Pride* has been a wild adventure. Despite a background in sports communications, I had no connections to any players, clubs or anyone at Derby. So to be able to connect with nearly 70 people who gave up their time to contribute towards the product in your hands has been enormously appreciated.

There are a few who particularly stand out for their time and assistance throughout this project, none more so than Jake Buxton. He's not a man who enjoys plaudits, but Jake was a saint. Over four hours of conversation, he let me into his world and was happy to connect me with team-mates, coaches and friends.

Craig Bryson too was fantastic. Over three calls, we got to the bottom of his seven years at the club. As a round-up, I'd like to thank all of those who gave up their time to speak. They were: Adam Pearson, Andreas Weimann, Andy Ellis, Andy Todd, Bradley Johnson, Cameron Jerome, Chris Riggott, Colin Todd, Craig Bryson, Craig Burley, Craig Forsyth, Darren Moore, Deon Burton, Don Amott, Gary Rowett, George Burley, Giles Barnes, Grzegorz Rasiak, Harry Wilson, Ian Taylor, Inigo Idiakez, Jake Buxton, Jamie Ward, Jim Wheeler, John Brayford, John Eustace, Johnny Russell, Jon Davidson, Lee Grant, Lee Morris, Lewin Nyatanga, Mart Poom, Martin Taylor, Matt McGibbon, Matt Oakley, Miles Addison, Morten Bisgaard, Nathan Tyson, Neil

Sullivan, Nick Britten, Pascal Zuberbuhler, Paul Peschisolido, Paul Winstanley, Peter Gadsby, Ross Fletcher, Shaun Barker, Stefano Eranio, Stephen Bywater, Steve McClaren, Terry Westley, Tomasz Cywka, Warren Barton, Will Hughes and Youl Mawene.

Thanks also to Colin Gibson for meeting with me in the early weeks of the project. And sorry to all those players and managers I've bombarded with desperate messages over the years. I promise never to bother you again, unless I think of another book.

A big thank you must go to Jane from Pitch Publishing. It sounds a little foolish, but I didn't consider the publishing side of the book until early 2020. When I did, I really wasn't sure a book about a mid-table Championship side would attract much interest. But it did. When I first got an email from Pitch confirming it might be a good fit, I was at a belated Christmas party. That night, the excitement got the better of me and I took too much of an advantage of the open bar. But a huge thank you to you both for being interested in this book and for allowing me to work with you. I really appreciate it.

I tried to keep this project as under wraps as possible in case it didn't work out, but there were a few people who were exposed to my rambles along the way. So, a special shout to Sian – thank you for being excited about people you have never heard of and for paying such an interest in this. It has really meant a lot. Will, despite being a Red, you're the most closeted Derby fan on the planet. Emma, Cesca and Heidi too, I'm pretty sure you didn't have a clue about any of what I was talking about, but you smiled when I spoke which was a good sign. Then there's the Friday Football lot. When I tweeted out that this book was to be published, the group chat lit up and Jacob said, 'I didn't even know you were working on this.' But I knew that you were just kidding. A bit. *Danke schoen*, see you in Köln.

And finally, two key people. Nick, if it wasn't for you, I'm not sure how my relationship with this club would have developed.

But for all your rants on the goings-on over the years and for your interest in this project, a massive thank you. I'm sorry again that I was ill after Wembley 2019, it was just an emotional day.

And to my mum, thank you for all of your support in everything over the years. I know you know next to nothing about Derby but growing up you put up with my bad moods every Saturday evening. For that, you deserve a medal.